D1269509

CIVIC
EDUCATION
& CULTURE

This book was supported in part by ISI's Center for the Study of American Civic Literacy. For more information, visit www.civicliteracy.org.

CIVIC
EDUCATION
& CULTURE

Edited by
BRADLEY C. S. WATSON

WILMINGTON, DELAWARE

CATALOGING-IN-PUBLICATION DATA:

Civic education & culture / edited with an introduction by Bradley C. S.
Watson. — 1st ed. — Wilmington, Del. : ISI Books, c2005.

    p. ; cm.

    "Based on papers presented at a conference of the same name
held at Saint Vincent College from April 11–12, 2003."—
Acknowledgments.
    Includes index.
    ISBN: 1932236619

    1. Civics—Study and teaching. 2. Political science. 3. Culture. 4. Social
sciences. I. Watson, Bradley C. S., 1961– II. Civic education and culture.

JA76 .C58 2005   2005921728
320—dc22   0506

Published in the United States by:

    ISI Books
    Intercollegiate Studies Institute
    Post Office Box 4431
    Wilmington, DE 19807-0431

Manufactured in the United States of America

*For My Students
Past, Present, and Future*

CONTENTS

ACKNOWLEDGMENTS

THIS VOLUME IS BASED on papers presented at a conference of the same name held at Saint Vincent College from April 11–12, 2003. The conference participants and eventual contributors to this volume met and then exceeded our expectations in every manner, intellectually and socially. The conference was sponsored by the Center for Political and Economic Thought, an interdisciplinary public affairs institute of Saint Vincent's Alex G. McKenna School of Business, Economics, and Government. The Center combines the resources of the College's political science and economics departments. It was founded in 1991 to sponsor research and educational programs in public policy and sociopolitical thought, seeking to advance knowledge of America's political economy, moral-cultural order, and civic traditions.

We at the Center are grateful to Saint Vincent College as a whole for providing a wonderful environment for our biennial Culture and Policy Conferences, as well as our other lectures and conferences—all of which deal with the conditions necessary for a free and decent political, social, economic, and moral order. The Benedictine Order did much to preserve and transmit classical learning and thereby lay the foundations for Western civilization. Saint Vincent today remains open and receptive to the conversation about ideas that is so central to that civilization. Special mention should be made of the Rt. Rev. Douglas R. Nowicki, O.S.B., the archabbot of Saint Vincent Archabbey and chancellor of the seminary and the college; Mr. James F. Will, president of Saint Vincent College; and Dr. Thomas C. Mans, Vice President for Academic Affairs of the college.

As a professor at Saint Vincent, I enjoy the college's bounty in numerous ways, prime among them being the support and friendship of my colleagues in the Center. I would be remiss if I did not mention by name and express personal gratitude to them, who make my academic labors less taxing than they might be. Dr. Andrew R. Herr, the Center's fellow in economics and policy, reminds me that methodological differences do not preclude common goals. T. William Boxx, the Center's senior fellow, is always a source of good conversation and sound ideas. Dr. Gary M. Quinlivan, the executive director of the Center and dean of the McKenna School, never ceases to think of ways to lend energy and aid to our academic projects.

As conference director and editor, I am indebted to many individuals and organizations that made the conference and book possible. Prime among them is Eva Kunkel, the Center's program coordinator, who handled the daunting logistical tasks associated with staging a major academic conference attended by hundreds. She has also helped with the tasks associated with publishing this book. Sandra S. Quinlivan ably indexed the book. The student staff of the Center aided with the conference in ways too numerous to count. I am particularly grateful to my editorial assistant, Mary Beth Mitaly. Her keen proofreading eye, as well as assistance with numerous technical tasks, made production of this volume much easier than it would otherwise have been, and the final product much better.

We also owe special thanks to the foundations and individuals that supported us. The conference would have been impossible without the confidence and generous support of the Sarah Scaife Foundation and its executive vice president, Michael Gleba. Other support was provided by the Philip M. McKenna Foundation, Inc., the Massey Charitable Trust, the late B. Kenneth and Marg Simon, the Intercollegiate Studies Institute, Inc., the Aequus Institute, and an anonymous donor.

We are grateful too to the Intercollegiate Studies Institute and its publishing imprint, ISI Books, for both the beauty and importance of their publishing program. Truly it may be said, if ISI Books did not exist, it would be necessary to invent it. I am personally grateful to ISI for the opportunity to serve as Research Associate at their Center for the Study of American Civic Literacy. In this capacity I am privileged to be part of a dedicated team of scholars developing a scientific survey instrument to test a matter closely related to the theme of the present volume: the state of civic education in the American university. By investigating and reporting the results of its findings, the Center hopes to stimulate positive change in educational standards and practices nationwide, with the aim of ensuring that institutions of higher learning once again teach core American civic principles.

I also owe thanks to my family—Barbara, Victoria, Charles, and James—who always remind me, in the most delightful ways, of the intimate connection between education and civilization.

Then shall we so easily let the children hear just any tales fashioned by just anyone and take into their souls opinions for the most part opposite to those we'll suppose they must have when they are grown up?

—Plato, *Republic*

INTRODUCTION

Just as the Twig is Bent:
Civic Education in an Age of Doubt

BRADLEY C. S. WATSON

"'TIS EDUCATION FORMS the common mind / Just as the twig is bent, the tree's inclined." This, from an epistle of Alexander Pope, reflects an understanding of the influence of education on individual mores and civilization that stretches back in the Western tradition at least as far as Plato. One might claim that before man's educational project was civic, it was individual, following the Delphic admonition to "know thyself." And indeed, some of the greatest works in the Western tradition concern their authors' own education, or the education of the great men on whom the authors dilate. But knowledge of the self cannot help but be a reflection on the self's relation to the outside world, including especially the civic world. Thus does the Roman Stoic Marcus Aurelius reflect on politics and the conditions for decent political life when, in his extremely personal *Meditations*, he admires his brother for introducing him to Thrasea, Cato, Helvidius, Dion, and Brutus, who in turn acquainted him with the twin notions of political equality and freedom. He explicitly admires too his emperor father, for his governing skill and his efforts to suppress pederasty.

Pope, like Plato, knew the youth were mere twigs, particularly susceptible to influence, and that the education they received in this delicate state portended the direction not only of their own lives, but of the civilization they would inherit and remake to suit their understanding of the highest things. This central concern has reasserted itself in the Western tradition time and time again—often in very different forms, but the concern has never been far below the surface. For Plato, as for Rousseau, education in many ways is *the* concern of politics, for through it the passions of the self are tamed and the individual made social. For Aristotle, we are at best deformed, partial beings if we are not educated in the human and non-human phenomena. Further, nothing less than the future of the regime depends on civic education in particular. If the young be not trained by habit and reason in the spirit of the constitution, all is for naught. We can thus say, with Aristotle, that politics is at least one central concern of education insofar as it is the architectonic science of the human good, the highest form of practical reasoning.

In these equivocal times, as we hearken to faith's dull withdrawing roar, we would do well to reflect on the immense resources our civilization offers up to those seriously interested in reinvigorating civic education as a step on the ladder of education itself. It is a critical early step. Without it, we are far less likely, in Michael Oakeshott's turn of phrase, to be aware of the resources of our world, and therefore far more likely to find them inadequate. We are thus more likely to wander off into speculative, revolutionary enterprises that will ultimately prove incompatible with the liberal democratic freedoms we have come to enjoy. In the words of National Endowment for the Humanities chairman Bruce Cole, we in America increasingly suffer from a collective or cultural amnesia. The silent artillery of time plays, as it must, some role in the development of this condition, but the academy offers little in the way of amelioration or reconstruction. Our schools and universities—to name two culprits—have, in Cole's words, robbed American students of the riches of their heritage. Without these riches, they are unlikely to see the manifold benefits their society has conferred on them, and we can consequently expect their civic and political choices to be poor.

The question of civic education is no longer (if it ever was) merely an academic concern. Students who know nothing of the Revolution, the Civil War, or World War II cannot long be expected to remember, or draw intelligent lessons from, September 11, 2001. The lack of seriousness about civic education and civic assimilation has profound consequences, too, when we consider America's openness to immigrants who come—at the deepest level—precisely to share in the riches of our heritage, but are often taught nothing of them. But we must note at the outset that this volume makes clear that civic education is not an uncritical celebration of, or education only in, things American.

Any civic education worthy of the name would begin with our Greek origins, reminding students of what the Greeks bequeathed us, and why. In a word, they gave us philosophy—not today's often dry academic discipline, prone to be as cut off from the rest of the modern university as it is from life itself, but philosophy as the love of wisdom, philosophy as *eros* for the highest things. It is in the ceaseless questioning characteristic of Greek philosophic inquiry that we find the root of Western freedom, so nobly played out today in that form of life and government we know as liberal democracy. (Though it is fair to say that today's students—perhaps especially those at the most elite research universities—are unlikely to see the connection.) Liberal democracy is a form of life and government in which the pursuit of the human good can be made subject to more comprehensive rational reflection and choice than in any other form, or at any other time in the history of human civilization. And this is true whether we conceive that pursuit in terms of divine revelation, politics, aesthetics, scientific advancement, or otherwise.

The Greek Gift

Why and how did the Geeks invent such a precious gift? The answer is complex, but pursuing it—as few American college students are nowadays given the chance to do—is an intellectually exciting and uplifting experience in itself. There is a real story to be told here, which is far from an arid archaeological dig; it is a story that teaches us not merely about a distant past, but about ourselves and the kind of civic order we have created.

If I may permit myself an anecdote, I have for several years now given a synoptic account of this Greek achievement at the beginning of a course I teach entitled Western Political Thought. I have never found intelligent students to be anything but gripped by it, and I have sensed (and often been told) that they too rarely encounter the intellectual gifts of their own civilization without obvious condescension on the part of the instructor. The Greeks, I argue, can be credited with inventing philosophy. In its most obviously civic incarnation, philosophy comes to sight as *political* philosophy, or critical inquiry into the nature of the political things (though its also entails such inquiry into the ontological, epistemological, and ethical realms). Philosophy, this gift of the Greeks, is not instrumental in any immediate sense for it presupposes the necessities of life have been taken care of; it is a search abstracted from necessities. It might, however, be stimulated by some practical problem, or even by some apparent solution to a practical problem. For example, some might claim a materially prosperous society is good because people are comfortable and live a long time. But the philosopher will ask, "live for what end? Are there more important things than material comfort? What does it profit a man if he gain the whole world but lose his own soul?" Philosophy thus does not reduce to economics or health and welfare, though these are important components of civic education and civic literacy.

So, although philosophy might be stimulated by the concerns of the practical world, it does not exist for the sake of them, for *praxis*, as does, for example, technology. Philosophy is not a search for the best method—whether it be a method to hunt bison, grow crops, or travel to Mars. Philosophy is the search for the best, simply; or the true, simply. Further, philosophy is also not merely folk wisdom, or what people in a society customarily or conventionally believe. What we often call a society's "philosophy"—way of life—is not philosophy at all, properly understood. Rather, a society's philosophy, or way of life, is something that is subject to test, to rigorous inquiry, and to criticism by philosophy proper. Received wisdom and traditions are always subject to philosophical critique.

It is interesting to reflect that Confucianism, for example—which arose around 500 BC—doesn't fit this definition of philosophy, to the extent that it was an attempt to reestablish the authority of tradition as an alternative to social chaos. It was an attempt to establish or reestablish a way of life rather than provide a critical framework for inquiry or questioning ways of life, including its own. As children of the West, the philosophic spirit, if not philosophy itself, is something deeply rooted in our civic beings—we are rational, questioning, searching, reasoning people. We are, in short, quite the opposite of what students (particularly college and university students) are often led to believe.

But it is, nonetheless, an understatement to say that the contemporary West offers many hindrances in our quest to be all that we might be, as rational and civically literate beings (a fact noted, with wit, by Josiah Bunting in chapter eight of the present volume). One need only glance at the "philosophy" section in many bookstores to see that they are filled with many things not philosophical, and indeed most unhelpful to any inclination we might have to serve the civic or public world. Books in the "self-help" or pseudo-medicinal vein often crowd the shelves. These books tend to present "philosophies for life," which sometimes amount to little more than one author's assertions of the ten steps one can follow to true self-actualization. In short, such books contain within them recommendations hardly worthy of our nature as political animals, and are hardly philosophical, for they do not question the terms of the debate over what it is to be fully human, or to be citizens of this land, or this civilization.

And indeed more insight can be brought to bear on the nature of our civilization and its inheritance by noting the historical fact that it was the Greeks—not the Gauls, the Saxons, the Africans, the Chinese, or Japanese—to whom we can best attribute our intellectual patrimony. They were the first in history to pursue the fundamental questions and not be content with merely traditional answers to them, or received wisdom. Ancient Greece was the first place in which entire competing schools of philosophy grew and flourished—schools whose goal was to put fundamental questions under searching scrutiny. They—or at least some among them—were the ones who put the terms of the debate into question. It was in ancient Greece that there developed schools of thought that did not take the longevity or "success" of a practice or understanding as the measure of the truth or worthiness of that practice or understanding. The Greeks did this in a rational way that did not rely purely on custom or myth. Indeed, Greek philosophy put into question even its own all-encompassing, largely Homeric, mythic tradition.

But why the Greeks? This is a more difficult question to answer, although an exploration of the most plausible answers gives us, I would claim, as much insight into our civilization and therefore civic inheritance as any inquiry we might undertake. The Greeks possessed unique attributes—some accidental, some chosen—that made them a civilization, and which give us some clue as to what we mean by "Western civilization."[1] Some offer reductionist explanations for the Greek achievement. For example, they say the Greeks invented philosophy because of their favorable climate, or location, though the Greek climate and location were not manifestly more hospitable than others of southern Europe or the Middle East or Asia. Far more plausible than such reductionist or materialist explanations is the nature of the Greek mythic and religious traditions and how they interacted with one another. To spend some time pondering these is, to repeat, not a game of Trivial Pursuit wherein all questions appear in the "history" category. It is a reflection on our own intellectual, cultural, and civic natures.

Characteristic of the Greek mythic tradition (particularly as it is handed down through the Homeric epics) is the principle of what I would call individuation. The human world for the Greeks was a world of individual beings with individual motivations and virtues—rage, jealousy, pride, fear, and the like. There is something deep *inside* the characters of Greek myth that animates them; not everything they do or think is reducible to impersonal, cosmic forces from the outside, or is even in some way referential to such outside forces. The characters might not be *free* in the sense of autonomously choosing their actions or situation, but Greek myth does disclose a deep subject-object distinction.

It is true that the passions and powers of some individuals are greater than those of others. Those whom we know as the heroic characters are the most full of life, passion, and vigor. The *Iliad* famously begins, "sing, o goddess, of the rage of Achilles, son of Peleus." The rage of a hero is, for Homer, characteristically human, and can be noble and justified; it is not something to be shunned, necessarily. When Homeric characters act and either succeed or fail, it is largely because of their virtue, or their lack thereof—for example, their overweening pride. The gods might favor certain people, but those they favor are usually the virtuous ones, where virtue is something of a mean between extremes. For Homer and the Greeks, success or failure was not a consequence of an individual's failure to recognize his divinity, or the unity of the cosmos, as it might be, for example, in the Indian mythic texts such as the Upanishads.

And this raises the unrealized potential of taking our own civilization seriously, particularly in colleges and universities. Such an intellectual seriousness would inexorably lead us to a richer and truer multiculturalism, in the form of inquiry into non-Western cultures. We might again be inclined to take them seriously as objects of study, rather than as necessary and somehow purer alternatives to the West, or mere victim cultures without discernible characteristics, strengths, or weaknesses of their own. In an ideal world that has all but vanished from American campuses, we might, for example, expect that humanists would spend some time contrasting the Greek belief in individuation and the worldly human virtues of action, insight or argument, to other cultural or civilizational understandings.

Consider, for a moment, the Upanishads and the tradition that arose from them—surely another candidate for the origins of philosophic inquiry, being roughly contemporaneous with Homer. The Upanishads are the theoretical parts of the ancient Indian corpus of originally oral literature called the Vedas, and one can certainly find the seeds of critical reflection in them. They attempt to answer some of the large mysteries as to the nature of the cosmos and human life. In particular, they emphasize mythical explanations for basic ontological questions—what is there, and where does it come from? According to the Upanishads, the answers are to be found in *Brahman*—the universal or cosmic soul, the breath, the thing out of which everything is created; and *Atman*—the inner soul of each individual, which shares the eternal cosmic breath, and is therefore a microcosm, of *Brahman*.

Put another way, the individual is in some measure as one with the cosmos, for their animating principle is the same. There is no objectification of the cosmos as something apart from the human condition, as there is in Homer. But this very objectification is arguably a root of Western freedom—and a distinctly Western achievement—even where, as in Homer, the human subject is hardly acting freely in a fully modern sense. Lack of objectification, conversely, results in the lack of a strong sense of the subject, which is ever-present in Homer. Suffice it to say that life's meaning and possibilities in the Upanishads are given more comprehensively by myth, and less by individual insight and action. In this lack of a subject-object distinction, which we in the West take to be fundamental to our philosophical outlook, we see a building block of not one, but two, civilizations.

A yet more obvious example of our civic natures can be discerned by considering that in Homer and among the Greeks generally there is an assumption that human life, and the individual quest for meaning, happens within the context of a *polis*—a city or political community in our parlance. Man, as Aristotle said, is a by nature political animal. The "hearthless, lawless, stateless man" is the least human and most miserable of all figures. When we act, we act individually, but also in a political context, for the sake of the good. What is good for us as individuals points the way toward what is beyond ourselves, what is good simply. Especially in the most compelling matters—those things for which human beings are willing to sacrifice their lives—we act for the sake of others, whether they be our immediate loved ones or our extended family: that is, the political community as a whole.

And we should note that there is a strong subject-object distinction embedded in and reinforced by the very notion of the *polis*. When we consider particular political communities, we realize there is *us*, and there is *them*; we have friends, and enemies. We fight for what is important to us—often what our community thinks are the highest things. In short, what we as individuals value often has little to do with us as individuals, strictly speaking, but us as moral and political actors concerned about people and principles outside of us and apart from our immediate circle.

In turn, the existence of a human community as a natural, intrinsic foundation of the human experience naturally raises the question of justice, which is the question of how one ought to behave toward one's fellow men. When we observe outsiders with different practices in this regard, we naturally ask who's right—us or them? If we are willing to die for our way of life, we must at some very deep level believe that we are right. But how do we know this? Should we be confident of it? All of this—implicit in Homer—prefigures Plato's and Aristotle's detailed and rigorous philosophic examinations of politics, including the good life for man *qua* man.

What the Greek mythic tradition did *not* emphasize is as important as what it did. In particular, the Greeks did not have comprehensive, mythic explanations for all phenomena, human or non-human. Homer gives no comprehensive, cosmic answer to why things happen, whether they be minor happenings, or great tragic events like the Trojan War. Surely the will of the gods accounts for much, but so also do the failings and heroism of men. As well, accident and design each seem to play their part. In Homer and other mythic accounts, there is a genuine mystery to phenomena, and the limitations on our knowing are part of the tragedy of the human condition. Some things simply seem to happen for reasons that are not coherent, and cannot be well accounted for.

Beyond the limitations of these mythic accounts, the gods themselves are limited beings. They are, in fact, men and women—mere mortals—writ large. Oftentimes, they have even fathered mortals. True, the gods are immortal and powerful, but they are not without the full range of human emotions and failings. They are remarkably like us—flawed beings incapable of giving full answers to why *they* are like they are, much less why the cosmos is the way it is in all details. Indeed, they have their own problems to worry about, and are not comprehensively involved in much of what goes on in the human sphere. They are certainly not omnipotent, omniscient, or perfect as is, for example, the Christian God.

More broadly still than the nature of the gods, the entire religious tradition of the Greeks provides little in the way of dogma. The Greeks had no "state religion" that purported to give answers to what the best political practices were. Religious practice in ancient Greece reflected this fact. There were of course religious rituals, temples, and oracles, under the administration of priests. But when the gods spoke through the oracles, their voices were famously in the nature of prediction based on specific questions, rather than comprehensive pronouncements on such matters as the creation, or the rise and fall of man. The priests and oracles of the Greek world simply did not speak in these terms. Greek theology (to the extent "theology"—the *logos* of God—can even be used to describe Greek piety) can be thought of as being indeterminate and non-eschatological. Greeks in short saw themselves as strangers in a strange land, without comprehensive answers to the great questions. Neither the gods nor the religious traditions and practices as a whole provided answers to moral-political, ontological, or epistemological questions.

The lacunas in the Greek mythic tradition, and the essential inability of the gods to "take care" of metaphysics or ethics on behalf of humans, is a situation that simply cried out for philosophy as an independent activity. The result was that, in Greece and in the West, philosophy and religion—Athens and Jerusalem—were never merged to the extent they were, for example, in the Upanishads. There might be philosophical ideas in the Upanishads, but they take symbolic or mythic form and are oriented—as are the religious notions themselves—to practical ends. They seek to free people from illusion, from false pursuits, and from human discontent by pointing them back to the true nature of the cosmos. There is not a strong sense of pursuing knowledge for its own sake, as there is in the unmerged—the bifurcated—Greek context.

Finally, we might say of the Greeks that they were a commercial and military people with wide-ranging contacts with other cultures throughout at least the Mediterranean rim. This led them, naturally, to comparisons—and again to have a strong sense of the subject-object, us-them distinction. It also led them to try to determine why other peoples do things as they do. And, given the diversity of human practices or conventions, it led them to ask which conventions are better, which are right? It even led them to ask, "Is it possible to *answer* this question—is there a standard by which we can make such judgements?"

In the end we must say of the Greeks that they did have a unique "climate" for philosophy, but it was largely a mythical, religious, and political climate rather than an atmospheric or geographic one. Outside of the Greek world then (and outside of the Western world today), there were relatively fewer grounds for skepticism, for intellectual restlessness, for passionate pursuit of intelligible, rational truth about the worldly and otherworldly phenomena. There were fewer grounds for human-centered inquiry into the human and non-human things, and therefore fewer grounds for the eventual development of Western individualistic notions of freedom as autonomy of the rational self. The story of philosphy as a Greek and ultimately Western enterprise still needs to be told for us to understand not simply our intellectual, but our civic nature.

PART I: CIVIC EDUCATION AND THE WESTERN TRADITION

Part I of the present volume deals with these matters and more by concentrating on civic education and the Western tradition. In the opening chapter, Bruce Thornton instructs us on the relationship between civic education and liberal education. He reminds us that, from medicine to politics, Greeks sought to get to the nature of things, independent of superstition or convention. Liberal education ought, today, to provide us the intellectual tools necessary to do the same. Our Greek forebears provided us with words and concepts from philosophy to democracy, but most of all with what Thornton calls "critical consciousness." This critical consciousness "is the impulse and willingness to stand back from humanity and nature, to make them objects of thought and criticism, and to search for their meaning and significance—'to see life steadily, and see it whole,' as Matthew Arnold put it, instead of remaining enslaved to custom, tradition, superstition, nature, or the brute force of political or priestly elites." To be sure, the Greeks uniquely inquired into natural processes, which ensured man would no longer be seen merely as the helpless plaything of the gods. But in addition, of ancient peoples, only the Greeks made the most commonplace civic practices (including slavery and war and their own ways of being) objects of *thought*—thus requiring intellectual defense and thus subject to intellectual attack (and thus allowing sympathetic depiction of what today we might call the "victim classes"[2]). The Greeks were masters at *self*-critique—something the West, and America, remain remarkably good at, despite the often cartoonish depictions emanating from the academic world (particularly from the humanities and social science fields). What, Thornton asks, could be a better critique of Greek misogynistic stereotyping than Aristophanes' *Lysistrata*, in which *men* prove to be more befuddled by sexual desire than the more rational and willful women?

Yet the grotesque caricatures of "the West" (with America as its hideous apotheosis) as a place—*the* place—uniquely hegemonic and cock-sure of itself in the realms of ideas and action, are often the only pictures college students find themselves acquainted with. While Socrates did not claim to have the answers to questions about the true and the beautiful, he did think he knew something of the important questions and therefore something of how to narrow the field of inquiry to direct our attention to the highest things. Today's academics at once profess skepticism not only of "Western answers," but skepticism of the existence of important questions. Along with this two-fold skepticism comes a surprising hubris in proposing alternative political, economic, and moral arrangements for the rest of us. These academics are at once more and less skeptical than Socrates. Perhaps the only thing one may say with confidence of their thought is that they do not know that they do not know.

The rational and democratic Attic Greeks subjected to critical scrutiny even their rationalism and democratic freedom. Plato and Aristotle notably criticized the latter (though one might add they expended considerable energies understanding the limits of the former). In fact, part of the excitement of a broadly-conceived civic education might well come in discovering, for example, the link between Aristotle's doubts about equality in all things and the doubts of America's own most potent critic in this regard—Alexis de Tocqueville. But today's students are unlikely to be directed to such thoughts, much less to how passionately Tocqueville sought to be a friend and supporter of the democratic revolution that America was leading while at the same time a critic of it. One might say Tocqueville possessed critical self-consciousness, not ideological passion. But it is precisely ideological passion that the American academy nowadays so often seeks to inculcate (succeeding, frequently, only in reinforcing the already widespread apathy that college-bound students seem to come equipped with). Students are in effect told that they do not need to think, but only be committed. But true commitment, in materially comfortable societies, does not come easily, and is made less likely by the absence of serious reflection.

In Thornton's view, liberal education might prepare us for a life of democratic freedom by creating free minds—the natural enemies "of what George Orwell called the 'smelly little orthodoxies,' whether these originate on the left or the right." Liberal democracy and the intellectual inheritance of the West—our ways of being and mind—are thus intimately related, and mutually reinforcing. These free minds, borrowing from their Greek ancestors, drove the Enlightenment and Reformation, which was "a return to the human-centered, rational understanding of the world and humanity the Greeks pioneered, a critical consciousness whose ultimate goal was freedom based on a truth humans discovered and validated for themselves." In short, as Christianity leavened the pagan world with its message of universalism and redemption, so the pagan world's great legacy leavened the Christian world's self-understanding and laid the foundation for the fruitful, healthy tension between reason and revelation that is still being worked out today.

But one thing is clear enough for anyone with eyes to see, in the post–9/11 world. The West—the great product of the synthesis of

Judeo-Christian revelation and Greek rationalism—is not today the place of unrestrained fanaticism. But alas, this fact too is likely to go unnoticed by many college graduates thanks to the tendentiousness of American academics (many of whom, as I distinctly recall, were, in the days after 9/11, more righteously indignant over an off-hand and thoughtless comment by the Reverend Jerry Falwell than they were over the opening shot in what might still be a potentially catastrophic war of civilizations). At the very least, one might think this relative lack of fanaticism on the part of the rationalist, humanist West might once again stimulate, in the halls of education higher and lower, a real interest in just what kinds of lessons we teach and have taught our youth. These lessons cannot possibly reduce to the platitudes of tolerance and multiculturalism (themselves the by-products of the very civilization they are now used to attack). One might think, in short, that in these perilous times we would be stimulated, as a culture, once again to study the "great books" of the Western canon—those that survive *because* they display deep critical consciousness. But those familiar with American education at all levels will surely not hold their breath.

Thornton wisely notes that critical consciousness offers challenges to the civic order, as well as benefits. A "critical examination not anchored by some level of moral and epistemic certitude can degenerate into a destructive nihilism," or paralysis in the realm of action (quoting Hamlet, "'thinking too precisely on the event' makes one 'lose the name of action'"). Thus critical consciousness might, in some forms, undermine the very morality and statesmanship essential to the civic life of any regime. Against this, perhaps only the great tidal wave of hope and confidence provided by the continued unfolding of the Judeo-Christian providential order might offer some bulwark.

William Desmond instructs us that the Greeks can not only tell us much about what we teach, but also about who we *are*. In the modern age, our god is freedom, or, in the preferred liberal parlance, autonomy. In this liberal dispensation, freedom is severed from its roots in political community—in, for example, a notion of self-governance. Instead, it emphasizes only governance of the self, or, literally, giving the law to oneself (as the word *autonomy* suggests), though the lawgiver and the one to whom the law is given are one and the same. And so the lawgiver tends necessarily to be lenient and infinitely forgiving. But what of the needs, or the law, of the other?

Desmond argues, in a way markedly suspicious of Kantian liberal universalism, that freedom is pluriform, with certain understandings of freedom particularly appropriate to certain times of life, including the time of youth, in which civic virtues are inculcated. For example, a notion of civic piety, while at a certain level in some tension with autonomy, can in fact *free us* to contribute ethically to a community when we might otherwise not be so inclined. Our jealous god of freedom, if he is to be a just god, must then allow for such piety, or allow us to articulate *pietas* in a way that does not seem idolatrous. Civic education precisely deals with social freedoms, including the familial and local. If we cannot assimilate civic as well as religious pieties into our vocabulary and self-understanding, our god is always in danger of collapsing into will to power.[3] As Desmond notes, patriotism is a centrally important piety, and a recurring one in the life of regimes. Despite the dangers of an unthinking patriotism, there are equally benefits to be had from a reasonable patriotism that cements our gratitude, as individuals, to others for what they have provided us. We need to be open to such civic traditions and practices that allow us to be fully human while not warring with the universals that also demand our piety. Our sense of reverence or gratitude need not be shriveled simply because proper piety itself cannot be determined by a simple rule, or "univocal principle." In order to sort out clashing pieties, each of which might have some claim on our allegiance, there is rather "the need of practical wisdom, *phronesis*, as the Greeks have it. The shaping of human resources in this direction is very important for civic education."

But how can we shape human resources if we are willfully ignorant, or even inconsiderately dismissive, of the resources our regime and civilization have bequeathed us? To the extent we refuse to recognize that we belong to something greater than ourselves, and that it in turn belongs to us—something that defines who we are as a self-critical, rational people—we cannot begin to think of freedom in terms other than self-assertion against an enemy alien. No civic education can be built entirely on rationalist or critical premises. We can love only those things and those people to which and to whom we *belong* in some way. As James Madison notes in *Federalist* 49, decent government, practically speaking, requires "that veneration which time bestows on everything, and without which perhaps the wisest and freest governments would not possess the requisite stability." We need the freedom to be who we are; as Aristotle reminds us in Book 2 of the *Politics*, restless innovation in politics—in the absence of demonstrable gain—prevents the essential habituation necessary for a rule of law. Today's educators often need to be reminded that politics is unlike the arts or natural sciences wherein innovation is generally praiseworthy.

In the absence of piety, there can be no civic education worthy of the name. Anyone who has had the misfortune, in recent years, to spend time in faculty gatherings on American college campuses can attest to this. The great civic exemplars who have gone before us, their ideas and actions—their ways of being—are treated as so much dross to be ridiculed rather than mined. The notion of "civil mimesis" that might serve as a "covenantal binding across generations" is rejected on the grounds that virtually all exemplars of Western and American ideals are themselves corrupt—or certainly indistinguishable from others who manifestly are. The book of their deeds can truly be read no more forever, as our leading academics trip over each other in their rush to distance themselves, and us, from our heritage, both moral and intellectual. Piety dissolves, and, as Desmond notes, "symbolic (or real) patricide becomes the last 'interesting' outrage called art. But of course, these 'interesting' outrages quickly become boring outrages." Our academic culture stands Plato on his head, and introduces an ignoble lie: instead of putting art in the service of reason, reason is made subordinate to outrageous art passing for reason.

The professors' incessant, generally sarcastic attempts at debunking our civic "myths" do not betray Socratic skepticism so much as moral nihilism. Alternatively, theirs is less a serious, full-ranging intellectual critique of the idea of civic piety (which might legitimately be launched, for example, on the grounds of universal reason or revelation), and more a substitution of preferred pieties for traditional ones—largely because they find repulsive the very regime and civilization (and for that matter, the idea of the university) that enables their academic pursuits. They agitate the passions of the youth, often deliberately for the purpose (in Madison's words) of "disturbing the public tranquillity" with respect to established constitutional and cultural forms and formalities, without any consideration of consequences. Such agitation cannot hope to offer what Desmond calls "an enlargement of willingness that is taken into the good of a community with what is beyond our lone selves, be it a family, a place, a nation, or a God."

Such agitation, in its simultaneous rejection of both Athens and Jerusalem along with George Washington, consciously chooses to keep students ignorant of the universal principles or truths which might be in real tension with more particular civic practices, associations, or myths. (Any Western or American civic education worthy of the name would remind students of the universal, else civic piety become hopelessly corrupt.) Students, in short, are given no measure by which to *test* their civic pieties—they are told only to reject them. The very self-criticism the West has made possible is rejected in the name of criticizing the West. But of course, as I have averred, this alleged criticism is really nothing more than the substitution of one set of pieties for another. Concomitantly, the attempt to measure or test the *new* pieties is often considered out of bounds, for the very test is seen to represent "discredited" (by what, or whom?) Western, linear, rationalistic thinking. Because of their enforced ignorance, our students do not even know they have the capacity to be self-critical, or fully engaged in the consideration of the problem of civic piety. Or if they do know it, it is only because they sense it dimly, in spite of the best efforts of their "educators." The opacity and tendentiousness of many denizens of the academy, at all levels, know few bounds in this regard.

In chapter three, Roger Kimball gives us another take on our modern philosophical disposition by examining the thinking of John Stuart Mill. To move from Desmond's Kant to Kimball's Mill is to move from autonomy to affective liberalism. For Kimball, civic education raises the question not simply of what, in a factual sense, we teach our citizens, but what sorts of attitudes or dispositions we stimulate and nurture in them. And in Mill, he argues, we see the move from rational autonomy to the sentimental self. Few books match *On Liberty* in their ability to define the terms of contemporary political discourse. Its emphasis not only on autonomy, but innovation and "experiments in living," and its concomitant attack on custom, prejudice, and tradition, have become the benchmarks of enlightened political argument. "Together with Rousseau, Mill supplied nearly all of the arguments and most of the emotional fuel—the texture of sentiment—that have gone into defining the progressive vision of the world." A good part of the contempt modern intellectuals feel for anything outside the progressive consensus is, according to Kimball, attributable to the language of liberalism that Mill invented. It is a dogmatic language that now stifles all opposition to itself, and stands as barrier to a reinvigoration of a truly broad-spirited civic education.

But in arguing not just for scientific or aesthetic experimentation but "moral, social, and intellectual" experiments more broadly, Mill and his intellectual heirs break sharply with Aristotle, for whom each science has its own standards and methodologies. Innovation in the moral-political realm is not to be prized in itself, for decent politics always relies on custom, prejudice, and habitual ways of doing and being. (In fact, as Kimball notes, Mill "was instrumental in getting the public to associate 'prejudice' indelibly with 'bigotry.'") Laws and social arrangements are always precarious because of people's passions, and without the force of habit they are destined for extinction. The spirit of the innovator or experimenter is thus the spirit of the dangerous revolutionary. In this, Aristotle is at the beginning of a tradition of political analysis that stretches through Aquinas to *The Federalist*. Kimball's point is that, under the influence of Mill, we have come almost to embrace change as a good in itself ("do we have the courage to change?" as if courage is always required). And have come reflexively to celebrate the spirit of the innovator and to dismiss as hopelessly reactionary the political conservative. "Granted that every change for the better has depended on someone embarking on a new departure: well, so too has every change for the worse."

When Kimball points to our worship of innovation, he reminds us that such worship will annihilate any remaining civic pieties. We will have no moral principles on which to educate, and no regime icons to preserve or love. For example, one hardly needs to be a teacher of political science to intuit that, in the contemporary university, the American Founders (to the extent they are mentioned) are more likely to be objects of derision rather than serious study or emulation. In fact, the implicit or explicit assumptions of the humanities and social sciences today are that we have transcended our rather more corrupt forebears and are in all important respects morally and politically superior to them. The very fact that they're "old" seems, in the minds of some students and many faculty, to point to their defectiveness and our need to trade them in, preferably for some far less intelligent but more fashionable contemporary political analyst or theorist who specializes in idiosyncrasies and trifles. Students are thus guided to the new, the flashy, or the eccentric, and discouraged from allowing the greatest minds to help them think for themselves. Kimball quotes a critic of Mill who might well be speaking directly to our contemporary academic culture's fascination with the newfangled and tendentious, and its concomitant denigration of our civilization's rich inheritance: "Eccentricity is far more often a mark of weakness than a mark of strength. Weakness wishes, as a rule, to attract attention by trifling distinctions, strength wishes to avoid it. Originality consists in thinking for yourself, not in thinking differently from other people."

Of course, not only are the Founders old (and dead and white and male), but they were foolish enough to argue that certain moral/political principles were not time-bound, but fixed in their meaning. They argued for natural rights, among other things. And such moral fixity is contrary to, and indeed antithetical to, the spirit of innovation in politics and morals, and therefore contemptible. In such an environment, civic education is undertaken more in the spirit of tearing down than building up, and can best be understood as civic re-education.

PART II: CIVIC EDUCATION AND THE AMERICAN REGIME

And this brings us directly to Part II of the book, dealing with civic education and the American regime. In chapter four, Colleen Sheehan looks at America through the eyes of two of its shapers and dreamers: James Madison and Robert Frost. Each had something to say about who we are and what we might become, and therefore what we must know about ourselves. "The Gift Outright," Frost's poem of the American Revolution, reminds us of Madison's and the founding generation's sacrifices—their gift to us, who inherit it undeserved. Frost saw in Madison something beyond the superficial history-book account, wherein Madison is the brilliant creator of mechanistic institutions that do away with the need for civic virtue, character formation, or even communication among citizens engaged in a common moral-political enterprise.

If the argument of *Federalist* 10 calls for barriers to citizens acting collectively, *Federalist* 14 calls for the spread of ideas and interactions across the large republic. Majority faction can be tamed, as popular government and robust citizenship can be encouraged—the latter depending on "the cultivation of American mind and character." According to *Federalist* 14, Americans are—and must be—"knit together . . . by so many cords of affection . . . mutual guardians of their mutual happiness . . . fellow-citizens of one great, respectable, and flourishing empire." To preserve this happy state, a commerce of ideas must be maintained. As Sheehan writes, "Having demonstrated the negative effects of the extensive territory on communication in the tenth *Federalist*, Madison can then show in the fourteenth essay how representation in a large territory encourages communicative activity in the nation."

As Madison remarks elsewhere in the *Federalist*, the primary control on government is dependence on the people—who therefore must express a sound public opinion. The print media, among others, "are charged with the role of civic educators in Madison's republic," by effectively contracting its size. In essence, the thoughtful and virtuous would keep the people well-schooled in politics and mores, thereby making public opinion respectable. For Frost, Madison is the best "dreamer" of this American dream, a dream of measured ascent into freedom—a freedom to form ideas rather than mere opinions, a freedom to create a public mind that reflects the cool and deliberate sense of the community, "to occupy a new land with character."

But what can we know of this estimable dream, of this land or its founders, when we are confronted by an educational system that makes it its mission to transform rather than transmit the American regime? This is precisely the question addressed by John Fonte in chapter five, which serves as a sweeping summary of the traditional and modern approaches to citizenship education in America and also as an insightful analysis of the nature of the civic re-education project currently under way in American schools. Fonte exposes the single-mindedness of the modern re-educators who would destroy rather than build. For several decades, he claims, there has been a conflict between those who wish to transmit American citizenship versus those who wish to transform it. Inculcating good citizenship in any traditional sense is not the aim of the transformers—rather, it is the creation of nothing less than a counter-regime.

The Founders sought to create republican citizens, i.e., to cultivate such qualities of character as would be conducive to self-government. Education (including especially public education) was to be directed toward this end. Their goal was a proper patriotism—or "patriotic assimilation"—oriented toward the timeless principles and salutary personal and civic habits on which the American constitutional order is based. This required students to understand, first, their own political system. Today, of course, under the influence of various related ideologies that often go under the name "multiculturalism," both patriotism and education in Western or American ways is distinctly unfashionable.

In fact, our contemporary educational orthodoxies are far removed from Sidney Hook's sensible advice that American students should study the heroes and achievements of their admittedly imperfect democratic society. Hook, according to Fonte,

> thoroughly rejected the core multicultural argument that demographic changes require drastically revising and diluting our nation's story in order to make the curriculum 'relevant' to new (non-Western and non-Anglo) immigrants and native-born minorities. Instead (like the Founders, Lincoln, and early twentieth-century American leaders . . .) Hook called for the patriotic assimilation of all young Americans into the mainstream of our civic culture.

Unfortunately, Hook's advice is likely to continue falling on the deaf ears of the American professoriate who are training our future educators, both higher and lower. Their all too common preference for incessant deconstructionist self-flagellation is unlikely to be halted by any forces within the contemporary university (a topic dealt with more fully in section three of the book). For many years to come, well-positioned members of our intellectual classes are likely to continue using the language of "regime transformation" rather than "regime transmission." In these dangerous times, it might, as I have intimated, be reasonable to expect reasonable people to see that a new fascism threatens free peoples everywhere. Yet we still cannot count on an intelligentsia or educational establishment that is ready, willing, or able to explicate what it is that makes us different from, and superior to, our enemies.

The extent and implications of our failure to acculturate America's youth properly is brought into further relief by considering America's perennial "racial gap." Abigail Thernstrom paints a stark picture of the failure of our public schools—by painting a glowing picture of the success of a few outstanding ones. Thernstrom points to what should be clear to all: that moral principles, character, and technical skills—the culture—of the young can be changed by their social environment, including particularly the schools they attend. Further, not all schools are equal, for reasons that have little to do with state or federal educational budgets. Put simply, "culture matters," and culture is something that dedicated educators can profoundly affect. For example, Asian-American students, as a group, tend to perform better in school that whites, and far better than Hispanics or blacks, because they have fully embraced the American work ethic. But there is no reason why this ethic—and the rewards it offers—cannot be embraced by all. By contrast, according to Thernstrom, blacks tend to be academically under-prepared when they start school, and far less ready than Asians or some other groups to conform to behavioral demands. Good schools can change this: "Their unstated goal, it might be said, is to replicate the culture that has served Asian families so well—within the schoolhouse walls."

Thernstrom can best be described as an optimist when it comes to the power of our society to mend its educational ways and change for the better (she is perhaps more optimistic than some of the other contributors to this volume). She offers up examples of institutions that can move cultural mountains. They offer students serious academic content, discipline, long hours, and habituation in each of these things—the academic equivalent of blood, toil, tears, and sweat. The best schools teach human virtues, and American ones, including the "rules of the American game" such as competition, hard work, and personal responsibility for one's actions, successes, and failures. They offer up the best that the human mind and soul have produced, in writing, music, and statesmanship, without excessive regard to multicultural sensibilities. They are the builders of a mainstream culture whose riches they prepare all to share. They try to create students who "come to think of themselves as unique, free to choose their identity, to emphasize their racial and ethnic group ties as much or little as they wish." They want to create citizens who "come to understand that they belong in the country in which they live" and who understand that they "will have an excellent chance of going far if they acquire solid skills." These schools are, in short, civic-minded in a comprehensive sense.

Finally in part two, Thomas Pangle moves us away from consideration of philosophies, exemplars, or institutions of civic education to more indirect, but no less important, ways in which society implicitly teaches civic lessons.[4] In asking whether felons should vote, Pangle induces us to "grapple with puzzles that deepen our awareness of the conflicting dimensions and goals of civic responsibility." In contemporary court cases and academic writings in the United States and Canada, we see arguments maintaining that felons should not lose their right to vote, and therefore to participate in the political system in a concrete way. According to Pangle, these arguments clarify a great debate in democratic political theory between liberal individualists and civic republicans.

Disenfranchisement can be seen as part of the punishment for a crime, or as a moral disqualification of the criminal. The argument against disenfranchisement is made primarily on the basis of liberal individualist principles. If disenfranchisement is seen as a punishment, the argument for it fails because it is reflective of outmoded English common-law notions of "civil death," *i.e.*, that a person convicted of a serious crime can no longer be considered a member of civil society. But, it also fails on other premises more acceptable to liberal modernity: deterrence and rehabilitation among them. If seen as a disqualification, disenfranchisement parallels the universally accepted disenfranchisement of the young, albeit on different bases. But they are bases that adherents of liberal principles find unacceptable—we have, so the argument goes, systematically extended the franchise to hitherto marginalized groups on the basis of universal liberal principles, so we should now extend it to felons.

The arguments in favor of disenfranchisement are inspired more by civic republican ideas: that civil society has a legitimate interest in educative activities, implicit as well as explicit, that are designed to form citizens. Understanding that the right to vote is always restricted (by age or mental ability, for example), civic republicans argue that there is a compelling argument for restriction in the case of those who have not met minimum standards of civic virtue. This is not because such people could realistically corrupt the outcome of an election, but because it is the job of society to teach civic lessons—to criminals, but also to the citizenry as a whole. As Plato argues in his *Laws,* law has an "expressive" function. It defines to all who study it or see it in action what a society is, and what its expectations are. According to Pangle's presentation of the civic republican side to the debate, law "needs to become self-conscious about its educative purpose and potential function." In democratic societies in particular, individuals need to be shaped into citizens, with a measure of concern for, and participation in, the creation and maintenance of the common good. Felons are disqualified because of the lack of concern they have shown for the good of their fellow citizens as individuals, but also for the laws created by those citizens, and, finally, for the social compact by which they are mutually bound. Voting, along with war, is perhaps the only endeavor in a liberal democratic society involving the mind and soul of the community as a whole. In precluding adults from voting, electoral laws provide us one of the few great opportunities to teach comprehensive civic lessons by reminding us all of the "minimal standards of civic responsibility below which voting citizens in a free and democratic society ought not to fall."

PART III: CIVIC EDUCATION AND THE UNIVERSITY

As we move to the third and final part of the book, we deal squarely with what might serve as one of the great institutions for the molding of citizens: the college or university. Alas, it is perhaps too much to expect the college or university to form, or re-form, the character of the already poorly turned-out young people who arrive at its doorstep each fall.

In chapter eight, former college president Josiah Bunting makes a sobering argument: the civic character of America's college-bound students is not what it once was, and by college age it is probably too late to make students virtuous, civically or otherwise (would that there were more schools of Thernstrom's choosing). Liberal education can only leaven what already exists—it can illuminate, soften, ennoble, or inspire, but it must work on a rightly oriented soul. Liberal education emphasizes the intellectual virtues, but it depends on the moral virtues to take hold. If teaching be the greatest act of charity, it requires a love that moves in two directions—from master to student, and from student to master. But the student in particular must discipline his love for learning with a firmness of character and a quietude and receptiveness that are best understood as stemming from moral training.

For Bunting, "character" and "civic character" flourish together—"'We say a man with no business in the state is a man with no business at all,' Pericles said to the Athenians." Bunting, as superintendent of the Virginia Military Institute, enjoyed something perhaps few college presidents can lay claim to: incoming freshmen whose parents emphasized the students' lifelong character, including their civic patriotic character. His students, and their parents, seemed to stand apart from what appears increasingly to be the mainstream of a culture of dependence, in which blame can be shifted because an individual's actions are allegedly conditioned by something over which he is said to have no control. It is a culture in which moral and medicinal fads become the enemies of character. They imply that those character traits we most admire—including perseverance and doing what we ought to do regardless of discomfort or worse—can be purchased for a price, without moral effort or personal sacrifice:

> Our full diagnosis—our identification of the enemies of character—would go far, far beyond the funny epiphenomena we mention, such as botox and grief counselors and devices to help us sculpt the abs of our dreams. It would comprise the whole family of activities, props, prizes, rewards, luxuries, and palliatives prepared to make those things which should be hard, and challenging, easier; those decisions over which we should agonize, seemingly simpler. In short, those things and habits designed not only to remove us from the consequences of our acts, but to explain away those acts as being the consequences of forces beyond our control.

But students who stand outside this culture are increasingly rare gems, a fact evinced by certain manifestations of the civic character of students at America's most elite institutions of higher learning. How many such students were in, are in, or ever will be in, "the service?" Bunting's answer: almost none. Military service is not required of those whom many consider our best and brightest, and they in turn do not freely choose it. There has been a dramatic change in this regard over the last few generations, and Bunting urges us to ponder the civic implications of this shift.

For Bunting, liberal education cannot in itself fill the gaps in the civic-mindedness and character of America's youth. That indeed is not its purpose. The liberation of true liberal education does not unequivocally point to civic virtue; the philosopher is not necessarily a good citizen. How then to inculcate the uniquely civic virtues necessary to support a decent regime? For Bunting, this is admittedly a difficult question to answer. But much rests on the spirit of emulation—of seeing, and understanding, and having empathy for—the lives of those who have embodied civic virtue. Fortunately, America has been blessed with many exemplars in this regard. And so the university, to the extent it actually, rather than nominally, cares about its civic mission, might be expected to enable students to see, and understand, and feel for these individuals. And these individuals, in turn, themselves grew up in a particular civic culture. A Washington, an Adams, a Franklin, and others of this generation were

> trained and bred to self-reliance and duty . . . schooled to be ashamed to fall short of . . . duty . . . soaked in the Bible, in history, in the political philosophy of seventeenth- and eighteenth-century England and Europe . . . [knowing] the histories of Attic Greece and its Hellenistic culture, and of Rome. . . . They appear not to have had a concept of what our generation calls 'stress.' They did their work and then retired for the evening—without complaining very much. They tended to be men of broad talents broadly cultivated. . . . They wielded fluent pens as they directed accurate artillery fire.

It is too much to ask of the modern university—or any institution or set of institutions within modern America—to produce citizens comparable to those of that greatest generation. But it is not, according to Bunting, too much to ask those concerned with civic education to try, as best they might, to replicate the conditions and educational influences under which that generation was raised, and to offer its members as examples to the youth of today.

Any hope we might have that the contemporary American university will step up to this plate is dashed by Stephen H. Balch. In chapter nine, he examines what might be called the crisis of confidence in the university—confidence in the civilization that produced it, and therefore in itself as the transmitter of the best that has been said and thought—and done—in the world. For him (and I think for all in this volume), civic education does not reduce to civics. It is that part of liberal education that allows us to understand the life of mankind, and therefore allows us a glimpse of the highest things by reflecting on man's place in the cosmos. And arguably, from a slightly different perspective, civic education cannot help but be at the core of all liberal education. In the words of the political philosopher Leo Strauss, "The philosopher who, transcending the sphere of moral or political things, engages in the quest for the essence of all beings, has to give an account of his doings by answering the question 'why philosophy?' That question cannot be answered but with a view to the natural aim of man which is happiness, and in so far as man is by nature a political being, it cannot be answered but within a political framework."

According to Balch, the university has lost its sense of mission when it comes to identifying and explicating the great people, events, and ideas that have animated civilization (and particularly Western civilization). If there remains within the university any passion, it is often to undermine, denigrate, or even deny the signal achievements of the West. This sad state of affairs is driven by a number of factors. Prime among them is faculty self-interest in specialization and the consequent disintegration of anything approaching a core curriculum. The resulting smorgasbord of courses in humanities and social sciences is offered up for consumption to unsuspecting students, and when they do partake, they taste of a relativistic and egalitarian "adversarial mentality" among a professoriate intent on "persistently jiggering the moral accounts to accentuate the debits."

Balch of course does not argue that no debits exist, but he does claim that in earlier times "teaching about high civilization and free institutions had usually been conducted with a certain sympathy for their content . . . even its strongest critics generally acknowledged civilization's formidable achievements, regarding themselves as inheritors."

But no more. Modern American higher education is a child of the "research university" created in the nineteenth century, which emphasized progress and change in the humanistic spheres as much as the scientific or economic. Emphasizing practical service to society, rather than transmission of moral and civic foundations and purposes, the university became, in fact if not in rhetoric, civically subversive. Faculties of business and professional education grew as the university drifted away from concern with traditional disciplines that could not prove their immediate social utility.

Thus, both faculty and institutional imperatives increasingly served to undermine what might be called the general educational mission of the university. The institutions themselves were freed to hustle for enrollments, and, as the institutional gaze turned to the utilitarian, professors were freed (particularly in the humanistic disciplines), to pursue esotericism and outright nihilism.

The very idea of greatness, or a minimal level civic unity, are casualties. According to Balch, the ethos of contemporary educators generates "a gush of leveling enthusiasm that 'celebrates diversity' instead of simply acknowledging it, and transforms 'the affirmation of difference' into the kind of absolute it purports to overthrow." Great works become mere "texts," each on a rough par with any other. Great men and their acts of statesmanship exemplify nothing but an ever-shifting dynamic of hegemony, oppression, and victimization.

Even those old-fashioned liberals within the academy who might be sympathetic to their civilization tend to be feckless in the face of the new postmodern multicultural sensibility, which is political in a strong sense. For those who continue to speak up for it at all, liberal education becomes, in Balch's apt words, "critical thought without much to think about." Under the influence of the ever-changing, experimental sciences, and assaulted by the new wave of humanists, the old liberal tends to content himself with the questionable, if not absurd, assertion that "facts" no longer matter; that encouraging "thought processes" is at the heart of liberal education.[5] Lectures are out; discussion groups and student opining are in. Such intellectual emptiness—preached and put into practice in the form of watered-down, content-and-value-free curricula—is unlikely to excite the passion or command the following enjoyed by liberal education's most rabid enemies.

In Balch's estimation, a civic-minded liberal education could once again be reinvigorated—and students motivated—by an educational system that asks them to consider why the modern civilization of the West—so desirable to so many, producing everything they take for granted—is what it is. Such a demanding task would require students to study, in a substantive, content-filled manner, "history, politics, philosophy, culture, economics, technology, and science." And, yes, it would require that they engage seriously and critically the prospects and problems of other, non-Western cultures.

Rounding out the volume, Timothy Fuller in chapter ten claims that university classrooms have, in their politicization, done nothing less than obscure "the encounter with transcendence." Politicization takes several forms. Ideologies come and go, but the passion for them—particularly in the university—does not. The university ought to be a place apart from passionate conviction calling for action. It should rather be a place for dispassionate dialogue with others, which, if it be serious, requires a genuine discipline—it does not allow us to be prisoners of our own feelings and partial interpretations. It requires an openness that the politicized university rarely allows.

Politicization also aggressively seeks to undermine traditional practices, including the engagement in a liberal learning that might at least partly transcend time and place. The attributes of politicization include lust for change, boredom with conversation, a preference for activism over reflection, a taste for melodramatic tension and "creative problem-solving," quests for the authentic life through policy formation, rejection of tradition for fear of the influence of the past, demand for diversity as a function of a desire for ultimate homogeneity, the belief that there is an ideal pattern of historical existence of which actual historical conditions are a mere distortion and caricature. . . .

How different is Fuller's claim—"the purpose of the university is to understand the world, not to change it"—from the self-understanding of so many of today's teachers and higher educrats. For the professor, the university, ideally, "is the place that provides a modest existence with no other calling but to think, and the peace, which this requires." The academic freedom the university holds dear has as its *raison d'être* inquiry as an end in itself that incidentally furthers the human quest for self-realization and self-knowledge when we encounter that which transcends learning for its own sake. For Fuller, the "essential experience" of liberal learning that guides us, broadly speaking, in our choice of subjects is a question prior to the also important question of the content of liberal learning. In a manner reminiscent of Balch, Fuller argues that "contemporary preoccupations" cause the university to become a mere responder to temporal events, and to turn away from the transcendent.

Recovery of the university is difficult because, to the current emancipators, "traditionalists" seem defensive, if not irrelevant to the pressing problems of the day—they are proponents of "useless studies." Traditionalists are more inclined to experience change as loss; to wish to build bridges to prior rather than future centuries. They are not policy wonks, and they do not believe the business of America is business. Contrary to the spirit of the social engineer criticized by Edward C. Banfield, they are not driven by the impulse, always and everywhere, to "do something!" each time a social problem is identified. This gives them a posture—in the eyes of the dominant, socially conscious progressive forces within the university—somewhere between quaint and vaguely threatening to the brave new world of learning.

But the engagement in restoration must be undertaken, nonetheless—for the sake of the present rather than an antiquarian past; for the sake of the university as a place of learning rather than a place of politics. By this account, academic traditionalism appropriates the past for our present use and enjoyment in the pursuit of learning for its own sake.

When we study the great books of our civilization, it is not to go back to an earlier time; it is, rather, to make vivid to ourselves the presentness of thought about, and response to, the human condition, eliciting our own thought and response. These works evoke dialogue, both inviting and constraining our subjectivity, rescuing us from easy opinions, imposing upon us the hard distinction between opinion and knowledge, between advocacy and explanation.

In the end, Fuller suggests that the truest university approaches the philosophical ideal: the truth beyond each time or all time; with Plato, never forgetting the tragedy inherent in the opposition between philosophy and politics.

And so we return where we began: liberal education, and its civic component, require the disposition to philosophize. But this disposition must be grounded in the civic things: the intellectual and moral virtues, and their exemplars, which together have defined us as a particular civilization and nation. It is a grounding that requires us to keep one eye on what might be termed tradition and piety, but the other unflinchingly on philosophic reason, for philosophy itself is a decidedly Western intellectual virtue or activity. To philosophize is, for us, to be engaged at some level in what we might legitimately call a civic activity. But, with Socrates, we cannot, if we are to be serious about civic education, ignore the concerns of the city in the course of exercising our intellectual virtue. Prudence and moderation—respectively intellectual and moral virtues *par excellence*—demand that philosophy be political, and politics philosophical.

The glaring shortcomings or worse—chronicled in this book—in our efforts to educate citizens stem from many sources, and will require many remediations. Among them are our understandings of the Western philosophic tradition, and our own regime. Fortunately, each of these offer remarkably rich resources for civic education, if only we might again develop the vision to see them. The university in so many ways affects our ability to see—from what it teaches its students and citizens to what it teaches the future teachers. Thus, the remediation or restoration of the university is as good a place as any to begin to restore our vision.

NOTES

1. And we need not say this term with the derisive intonation of a humanities or social sciences professor at many an American college or university. But perhaps even the word "derisive" implies a thoughtfulness that is often not to be found there. I distinctly recall being on a job search committee

for a tenure-track social sciences position at a college at which I taught. One of the candidates was asked by one or two concerned committee members what the candidate thought of "Western civilization" (a question broad and interesting enough, one might think, to elicit a variety of broad and interesting responses). Instead, the candidate replied, incredulously, with a simple "what's that?"—with the emphasis on *that*. The question seemed, to this young Ph.D.-bearing citizen, arrogant, irrelevant, or unanswerable—and perhaps all three. It was as if, as it were, the committee members were speaking Greek. But one can hardly blame the current crop of young academics. We do after all live in an era of academic specialization conjoined with condescension or ignorance (and often both—the ultimate form of arrogance) on the part of the senior faculty members who produce the new humanists and social scientists—those who are to become the teachers and scholars of tomorrow. Ignorance and condescension have produced—*mirabile dictu*—amnesia, perhaps the ultimate weapon of mass destruction aimed at our country, culture, and civilization.

2. It is interesting to reflect on the extent to which Greek thought is often casually reduced to Greek practice on questions such as slavery. This reductionism is symptomatic of the contemporary academy's collapsing of thought into action, or perhaps ignorance of the existence of thought as a realm independent of action. We see this in practice—and see also the disappearance of the very possibility of civic education—when professors, in Max Weber's phrase, begin to substitute speeches for lectures. Working for one or another contemporary version of "social justice" is hardly synonymous with, and in many cases antithetical to, being civically or otherwise educated.

3. For an extended discussion of some of the political implications of this danger, see my *Civil Rights and the Paradox of Liberal Democracy* (Lanham, MD: Lexington Books, 1999).

4. Implicit civic instruction is everywhere, though its power often seems more fully recognized by the cultural left than the right. One of the great domestic controversies besetting contemporary America is the status of marriage—whether such a term can be applied to the union of same-sex couples. Since identical material benefits can be conferred on homosexual couples through so-called "civil union" statutes, one suspects same-sex marriage proponents really wish to teach a civic lesson. It is a lesson stemming from, and reinforcing, the desire for equal recognition via appropriation of the most powerful teaching tool: language itself. *We are the same as you—for there is no natural order—and you will see and accept us as such.* To say that claiming a right to a noun is a novel legal argument is an understatement (has there been an unequal pattern of "noun distribution" in American history?). It is an argument that might well have been dreamt up in a cutting-edge college English department rather than by lawyers, for it

is an argument not so much with the laws or the Constitution as with the Oxford English Dictionary.

5. In fairness to the natural sciences, we should note that even they do not go so far. Being on the whole more serious and intellectually disciplined than the humanities and social sciences, they do not pooh pooh the facts, or empirical reality—neither of which terms appear in quotation marks in respectable scientific journals. Can one, for example, consider oneself a student of political philosophy without really knowing Plato—without having an intimate sense of the warp and woof of the *Republic*? Is it enough, from the professor's standpoint, simply to encourage student interpretations of such a seminal work?

Part I
Civic Education and the Western Tradition

1

Critical Consciousness and Liberal Education
BRUCE S. THORNTON

THE DEBATE OVER THE content of a liberal education and the so-called "canon" of books with which students should be familiar frequently resembles a Swiftian "Battle of the Books." On one side we have the "dead white European males," those aged shock-troops of cultural and racial hegemony; on the other the riotous variety of the multicultural "oppressed," the "relevant" writers who allegedly represent those constituencies long excluded on the basis of race, sex, and sexual orientation. But pitting one "canon" against the other obscures the genuine good a liberal education should deliver to its students: not merely exposure to one set of names and works rather than another, but a particular way of looking at the world. I'd like to talk about this habit of thought by focussing on the originators of the West, those whom Bernard Knox has called "the oldest dead white European males," the ancient Greeks.

When asked to define the achievement of the Greeks we usually list the intellectual, artistic, and political equipment we have inherited from them: philosophy, history, logic, physics, criticism, rhetoric, dialectic, dialogue, tragedy, comedy, epic, lyric, aesthetics, analysis, democracy—these are all Greek words. Taken together they constitute the cultural and mental framework of Western civilization, and the works embodying these "categories and concepts" once formed the content of a liberal education. Yet such a list perhaps obscures a more interesting question: What is it in Greek culture that provides the common denominator of all these words?

The answer is that they are all the formalized expressions of the essence of the Greek achievement: critical consciousness. This is the impulse and willingness to stand back from humanity and nature, to make them objects of thought and criticism, and to search for their meaning and significance—"to see life steadily, and see it whole," as Matthew Arnold put it, instead of remaining enslaved to custom, tradition, superstition, nature, or the brute force of political or priestly elites.

The impulse to critical consciousness has long been recognized as setting the Greeks apart from the other civilizations of the ancient Mediterranean. The Greeks, the nineteenth-century historian Jacob Burckhardt said, "seem original, spontaneous and conscious, in circumstances in which all others were ruled by a more or less mindless necessity."[1] What distinguished the Greeks from their Mediterranean neighbors, then, was not so much how they lived, but how they *thought* about how they lived, and how they gave formal expression to this thinking.

Thus while all ancient societies kept slaves and viewed slavery as a natural, unexceptional practice, only the Greeks made slavery an object of thought. This thinking could lead to a theoretical justification of slavery, as in Aristotle's view of the "natural" slave, the person who by a deficiency of rational self-control could be justly controlled by another.[2] But thinking critically about slavery could also lead to questioning the justice of such an institution, as the early fourth century BC rhetorician Alcidamas did when he said, "The god gave freedom to all men, and nature created no one a slave."[3]

Or consider war. All ancient peoples made war on their neighbors, competing violently for territory and wealth and honor. So too the Greeks. But to an extent unthinkable for any other ancient people, they thought and wrote about war analytically, so to speak, pondering its meaning and consequences, its complexities and horrors. Nowhere else in the ancient world can one find a work of literature like Aeschylus's *Persians*, about the Battle of Salamis in 480 BC, when the mighty Persian invading armada was destroyed by the coalition of Greek city-states. Performed a mere eight years later in the very city, Athens, burned by the invaders, before an audience of veterans and those who had lost friends and family, the play sympathetically depicts the effects of the defeat on the Persians.

Not only could the Greeks be generous to an enemy, but they could examine critically their own behavior during wartime. During the Peloponnesian War between Athens and Sparta, Euripides produced plays that sympathetically portrayed the disastrous effects of Athenian policies, and laid bare the suffering, moral corruption, and dehumanizing passions unleashed by war. A mere nine months after the Athenians massacred the males of the Greek island Melos, once their ally, and enslaved the women and children, Euripides staged *The Trojan Women* (415 BC). In that play he used the brutal aftermath of the mythic Trojan War and the suffering of the surviving women to comment on recent Athenian behavior. The princess Cassandra movingly describes the price of war—the sons never returning home, the children left orphaned, the wives bereft of protection and support—and with bitter irony finishes, "For such success as this congratulate the Greeks."[4] How could any Athenian in the audience not think of the Melian wives and children they had sold into slavery less than a year earlier?

These generous and self-critical attitudes are a dividend of critical consciousness, the ability to step back from the passions and prejudices of the moment and look at events from a larger perspective that illuminates the common human condition, the way even an enemy suffers and grieves just as we do.

As the Greek examination of war and slavery shows, critical consciousness can lead to the improvement and reform of human institutions and behavior, for once the mind is liberated from the authority of tradition or the supernatural, it can criticize the ways things are done and consider alternatives. In addition, the evidence of experience can then take on a greater importance, trumping the petrified dogmas sanctioned by mere authority or even sheer mental inertia, and so foster a scientific rather than a supernatural view of nature.

Indeed, the Greeks were conscious of this clash between superstition and experience, and recognized that two very different ways of understanding the world were in conflict. Plutarch in his biography of Pericles, the fifth century BC Athenian statesman, reports an incident that illustrates this struggle between traditional superstition and empirical reasoning. When a one-horned ram was born on Pericles's estate, the soothsayer interpreted the unusual phenomenon as a sign from the gods that signified future events in Pericles' life. But the philosopher Anaxagoras dissected the skull and showed how the deformation had been caused naturally.[5]

This conflict between traditional religious explanations and the rationalism of the new philosophy turns up everywhere in the literature of the later fifth century, and the Greeks' recognition of this struggle is itself an example of their critical self-consciousness. Consider, for example, Euripides' *Bacchae* (405 BC). In the play the young ruler Pentheus resents the social disorder caused by the ecstatic worship of the god of the irrational, Dionysus. The god ultimately destroys Pentheus after the king's futile attempts at controlling Dionysus and his worshipers fail miserably. Early in the play the conflict of traditional religious wisdom and the "new philosophy" is expressed by the old priest Teiresias: "We are the heirs of customs and traditions / hallowed by age and handed down to us / by our fathers. No quibbling logic can topple *them*, / whatever subtleties this clever age invents."[6] This same resentment of the new rationalism's tendency to erode the wisdom of custom and religion partly accounts for the execution of Socrates, who was unfairly tarred with the brush of a destructive sophistic cleverness.

This new way of looking at the world, however, was creative as well as being destructive of the old ways. The most obvious example of the improving power of critical consciousness when systematized into an empirical science can be found in ancient Greek medicine. Numerous medical writings from ancient Egypt and Mesopotamia survive, but their detailed empirical observations are subordinated to superstition: they are, as historian of medicine Roy Porter puts it, "sorcery systematized."[7] The Greek medical writers, on the other hand, for the most part ignored supernatural explanations and focused instead on their own observations and the consistent patterns of nature. That's why our word "physician" derives from the Greek word for nature, *phusis*. The following statement, from a Hippocratic work called *On the Sacred Disease*, a treatise on epilepsy, is unique in the ancient world outside Greece. "It [epilepsy] is not," the author says, "in my opinion, any more divine or more sacred than other diseases, but has a natural cause, and its supposed divine origin is due to men's inexperience, and to their wonder at its peculiar character."[8]

Critical consciousness defines the Greek achievement, and its most obvious manifestation is that uniquely Greek invention, philosophy, which can be characterized as critical consciousness systematized. Of all the Greek philosophers, the spirit of critical consciousness is best embodied in the late fifth century BC philosopher Socrates, Plato's mentor, who was executed by Athens in 399 BC.

Socrates's famous method was the "dialectic," from the Greek word that suggests both "discussion" and "analytical sorting." The purpose of dialectic was to strip away the false knowledge and incoherent opinion that most people inherit from their societies and unthinkingly depend on to manage their lives. Although Socrates claimed to doubt that he or anyone else could acquire true knowledge about the good and the beautiful, he nonetheless believed that what he called "examination," critical consciousness applied to questions of virtue and the good, could eliminate false knowledge and opinion. Most important,

Socrates saw this activity of rational examination and pursuit of truth and virtue as the essence of what a human being is and the highest expression of human nature. That is why he chose to die rather than to give it up: "The unexamined life," he said in his defense speech, "is no life worth living for a human being."[9]

The invention of philosophy formalized the Greek penchant for critical consciousness. Such an achievement is remarkable enough. Yet true to their drive to question and criticize everything, the Greeks turned critical consciousness not just on nature and other peoples, but, as we've already seen in their willingness to scrutinize their own beliefs about slavery or their behavior in war, they criticized their own culture and even rationalism itself.

This impulse to self-criticism is implicit in Greek literature from the very start. The first work of literature in the West, Homer's *Iliad* (ca. 750 BC) is at once a celebration of aristocratic heroic values and a powerful critique of them, a recognition of their destructiveness to the larger community. Homer captures this ambiguity in the figure of Achilles, whom the poet compares to the star Sirius, "whose conspicuous brightness / far outshines the stars that are numbered in the night's darkening / . . . Orion's dog, which is brightest / among the stars, and yet is wrought as a sign of evil."[10] Tragedy itself was a genre that dramatized the fundamental limits of human aspiration and achievement, and the weaknesses of Athenian political and cultural values. And comedy explicitly held the politicians of Athens up to critical scrutiny and moral condemnation, naming names and employing a vocabulary of invective and obscene abuse that makes our own political discourse sound like an afternoon tea in a Jane Austen novel. And Greek comedy, remember, was organized and presented by the very state whose politicians were mercilessly attacked on the public stage.

One of the best examples of ancient comedy's willingness to examine publicly the received wisdom and orthodoxy of the audience is Aristophanes' *Lysistrata* (411 BC), about the Greek women going on a sex-strike to force their men to end the Peloponnesian War, in its twentieth year when Aristophanes produced his play. In the Greek male repertoire of misogynistic stereotypes, two of the most common were the charges that women are less capable than men at controlling themselves sexually, and that they are incapable of the sort of rational deliberation and cooperation necessary for political action. Yet by play's end, it is the *men*, not the women, who cannot control themselves sexually, and it is the organizational and executive skills of Lysistrata that prevail over the men befuddled by desire. The stereotypes have been turned on their heads—not in a private performance, but in a production that was part of a civic ritual financed and sanctioned by the male-dominated city.

This impulse to self-examination, however, can perhaps best be illustrated by the critical questions raised about two of the Greeks' most important inventions, rationalism and democratic freedom.

At the moment in the mid-fifth century BC when philosophy was being born and formalizing the rational pursuit of knowledge, the tragic poets were questioning the power of reason to acquire significant or even useful knowledge about the human condition. In the *Oedipus Turannos* (431 BC), for example, Sophocles explored the limits of rationalism and its ability to know anything significant or valuable about human identity. Oedipus is a hero of the intellect who liberates Thebes from the Sphinx by solving her famous riddle about the creature that walks on four feet in the morning, two at noon, and three in the evening. The answer, of course, is a human being, a natural creature defined by a body subject to time, dependence, unforeseen change, its own passions, and ultimately death.

Yet at the same time Oedipus knows what a human being is abstractly, he does not even know his own real name or parents. He is abstractly wise and concretely ignorant. His destructive pursuit of self-knowledge horrifies us, for *we* know the answer to the riddle of Oedipus: for all his excellence and intelligence, he is at the same time a creature guilty of parricide and incest, the worst crimes that can be incited by the passions of sex and violence.

Oedipus and his fate suggest that reason is at best only half the story of human identity: humans are also creatures of the body and its appetites, time and change, chance and death. We live in a realm of intricate possibility and consequences no mind can ever fully know or predict. The point is not so much that reason is powerless—Oedipus, after all, does figure out the answer to the mystery of King Laius' death, and he does save the city from the plague. Rather, the larger point is that the knowledge reason discovers ultimately can not liberate us from the irrational destructiveness both in ourselves and in a world of chance and change. Sophocles seems to suggest that in the end, critical self-awareness can only reveal to us the brutal truth about the tragic and nonnegotiable limits to our aspirations and achievements.

Sophocles's younger contemporary Euripides likewise details in his tragedies the limits of reason and the destructive power of passion. Euripides was particularly skeptical of Socrates's famous contention that virtue is knowledge, that if we know the good, we will do the good. This long-lived idea, still powerful today, implied that reason properly developed and trained can resist the forces of appetite and passion and mitigate their disorder.

In his plays Euripides created characters who are driven to violence or consumed by sexual passion, all while they are fully conscious that what they are doing is wrong. Medea, whose husband Jason plans to bring a new, younger bride into their home, plots the murder of her rival and her own children. As she agonizes over this decision, she cries, "Passion is mightier than my counsels, and this is the greatest cause of evil for mortals."[11] So too Phaedra, suffering from the disease of lust for her stepson Hippolytus, directly refutes Socrates when she says, "We know the good and recognize it, but we cannot accomplish it."[12] Tragic critical consciousness did not allow the claims of reason to pass unchallenged, and initiated the dialectic of philosophy and tragedy still with us today.

Like rationalism, democratic freedom is one of the signature achievements of the Greeks, a potent ideal also still vital today. Yet in Athens, the city of its birth, searching questions were raised about the ideals of freedom and egalitarianism. Critics of Athenian democracy noted that its assumption of equality codified in the equal access Athenian citizens enjoyed to the institutions and offices of the state would lead to a radical egalitarianism in which the very real differences in talent, ability, and achievement among people would be ignored. As Aristotle put it, radical egalitarianism arises "out of the notion that those who are equal in any respect are equal in all respects; because men are equally free, they claim to be absolutely equal."[13] Plato agreed, claiming that democratic egalitarianism destroyed all distinctions based on talent, worth, and achievement, dragging everybody down to the same level until even "the horses and asses have a way of marching along with all the rights and dignities of freemen; and they will run at any body who comes in their way if he does not leave the road clear for them."[14]

Plato detailed further the consequences of what to him was a false claim of absolute equality, particularly the tendency for absolute freedom to deteriorate into mere licentiousness, as it must, for only in the kingdom of appetite are all truly equal. In the *Republic* Socrates asks rhetorically of democratic citizens, "Are they not free, and is not the city full of freedom and frankness—a man may say and do what he likes . . . [and] the individual is clearly able to order for himself his own life as he pleases?"[15] The problem with this freedom is that not all people are virtuous or even intelligent enough to use it responsibly. Thus the city will be full of "variety and disorder," its citizens fickle and shallow, dominated by appetite and pleasure. Chafing at any limits to pursuing his whims and desires, Democratic Man will ignore self-control and temperance and be given over to "the freedom and libertinism of useless and unnecessary pleasures."[16]

Critical consciousness is the precious inheritance the West received from the Greeks. Even during the dominance of Christian intellectual and cultural unity, this impulse to challenge and question and criticize persisted, as can be seen in the numerous theological debates and heresies throughout the Christian period, culminating in that great movement of Christian self-criticism, the Reformation. Both the Renaissance and the Enlightenment were to some degree expressions of the liberation of this critical self-consciousness from the traditional restraints of Christian dogma and fossilized custom. The Enlightenment particularly took place in what Peter Gay calls a "climate of criticism" in which philosophy was defined as "the organized habit of criticism."[17] This "climate" was, of course, a return to the human-centered, rational understanding of the world and humanity the Greeks pioneered, a critical consciousness whose ultimate goal was freedom based on a truth humans discovered and validated for themselves rather than blindly accepting from traditional superstitions and prejudices.

Since then, Western culture has been defined by critical consciousness, the willingness to examine and challenge traditional wisdom and answers in the pursuit of truth, and to stand in opposition to the political and social powers whose authority and legitimacy rest on the unexamined acceptance of received dogma. Science obviously has progressed in this fashion, but even in literature we find an impatience with tradition and a restless searching for ever greater and more finely nuanced explorations of the human condition. A whole genre, the aptly named novel, was invented partly as a vehicle for examining the fluid complexities of human psychology and social relations, a complexity ignored in the stock characters and plots of traditional romance. In this sense Western literature has been the creation of what Lionel Trilling called "opposing sel[ves]," all those dissidents who, like Socrates, are driven to examine the human condition and probe beyond the traditional answers.

If we turn to liberal education, we can see that its fundamental purpose should not be the force-feeding of ideas or values codified in some exclusionary list of Great Books. Rather, liberal education should aim for the inculcation of critical consciousness as this impulse is expressed in the best works of history, philosophy, and literature, no matter whose ideological ox is gored. Needless to say, any list of those works we care to make would resemble closely the traditional canon of Great Works, for over time the literature that survives in most cases comprises the poems and novels and plays that at some level display critical consciousness. An education centered on such works, then, will foster in students the curiosity to know what Matthew Arnold called "the best that is known and thought in the world, irrespectively of practice, politics, and everything of the kind; and to value knowledge and thought as they approach this best, without the intrusion of any other considerations whatever."[18]

The spirit of liberal education thus should be, as Allan Bloom suggested, "Socratic," a process of raising important questions and examining critically the tradition of answers, as this examination is embodied in works of enduring excellence.[19] The ultimate goal will be the freedom of the mind, a freedom underwritten by a habit of critical thinking that is not satisfied with the easy or emotionally gratifying answers and the received wisdom promulgated by the various economic or political interests of society. The alternative to a liberal education of this sort will necessarily be some form of indoctrination that imprisons the mind in the shackles of ideology, race, gender, or ethnicity.

The role of liberal education in training citizens for democratic freedom is what is under siege today from many sides, for a free mind is the greatest enemy of what George Orwell called the "smelly little orthodoxies," whether these originate on the left or the right. For us today, however, it is a tendentious multiculturalism that represents the greater threat, for it demands a reading list that validates and flatters the student's ethnic or gender esteem and preconceived notions rather than one that challenges and compels an examination of these received ideas. Thus a multicultural education is diametrically opposed to traditional liberal education, and will not deliver to its students education's most important goal, as defined by Cardinal Newman: "The force, the steadiness, the comprehensiveness and the versatility of intellect, the command over our own powers, the instinctive just estimate of things as they pass before us."[20]

I would not be true to the spirit of the Greeks, however, if I neglected to emphasize that critical consciousness has its dangers as well as boons. As Euripides recognized, not all the wisdom of tradition is necessarily false, nor is it always amenable to rational justification or accounting. Moreover, a critical examination not anchored by some level of moral and epistemic certitude can degenerate into a destructive nihilism or an intellectual paralysis. In *Hamlet* Shakespeare made clear this connection between moral relativism and a paralyzing ratio-cination, for the same Hamlet who recognizes that "thinking too pre-cisely on the event" makes one "lose the name of action," also asserts that "nothing's good or bad, but thinking makes it so." These days we see the same unholy alliance—between an aggressively critical intellec-tual inquisition and an epistemic and moral nihilism—in the antics of the postmoderns, who tear down not to rebuild, but merely to revel in the act of destruction.

Yet even with these reservations, one still must opt for a liberal education centered on critical consciousness, on a habit of thinking that resists unreflective acceptance of received wisdom and popular dogma. After all, most of the horrors of this century have resulted not from individual acts but from vast collectives enslaved to unexamined doctrines and ideologies that privilege the group, sect, or clan over free and independent minds. Creating such minds should be the task of liberal education, and that education itself should expose students to the great exemplars of Western critical consciousness.

NOTES

1. *The Greeks and Greek Civilization*, trans. Sheila Stern, ed. Oswyn Murray (New York, 1998), 11–12.

2. *Politics* 1254a–1260a.

3. Quoted in Peter Garnsey, *Ideas of Slavery from Aristotle to Augustine* (Cambridge, 1996), 75.

4. *The Trojan Women*, 383, in Euripides III, trans. Richmond Lattimore (Chicago, 1958), 141.

5. Plutarch, *Life of Pericles*, in *The Rise and Fall of Athens*, trans. Ian Scott-Kilvert (Harmondsworth, Eng., 1960), 1706.

6. *Bacchae*, 200–203, in *Euripides V*, trans. William Arrowsmith (Chicago, 1959), 163.

7. In *The Greatest Benefit to Mankind: A Medical History of Humanity* (New York, 1997), 46–47.

8. *On The Sacred Disease*, I, trans. W. H. S. Jones, in *Hippocrates* (Cambridge, MA and London, 1923).

9. Plato, *Apology* 38a, my translation.

10. *Iliad* 22.27–30, in *The Iliad*, trans. Richmond Lattimore (Chicago, 1962).

11. *Medea* 1079–80, my translation.

12. *Hippolytus* 380–81, my translation.

13. *Politics* 1301a, trans. by Benjamin Jowett, in *The Complete Works of Aristotle, vol. 2* (Princeton, 1984), 2066.

14. *Republic* 5632c, trans. by Benjamin Jowett, in *The Dialogues of Plato, vol. 1* (New York, 1937), 822.

15. *Republic* 557b–558c, trans. by Benjamin Jowett, 815.

16. *Republic* 560e–561c, trans. by Benjamin Jowett, 819.

17. In *The Enlightenment: An Interpretation. The Rise of Modern Paganism* (New York, 1966), 130.

18. In "The Function of Criticism at the Present Time," in *Selected Prose*, ed. P. J. Keating (Harmondsworth, England, 1970), 141.

19. In *The Closing of the American Mind* (New York, 1987), 267.

20. *The Idea of a University*, xxiii.

2

Autonomy, Loyalty, and Civic Piety
WILLIAM DESMOND

I. PRIVATIZED AUTONOMY AS "GOD"

MODERNITY MIGHT WELL BE characterized as an epoch in which the only god seems to be freedom. You might ask, why should we not have a polytheism of freedom? Surely there are many freedoms? Yet this god turns out to be also a jealous god, and drives us more and more, it seems, towards a kind of monotheism of freedom. There is a name this god goes by almost exclusively, and this name is "autonomy." I think that freedom is pluriform: what freedom is for the child is not the same as what it is for the adolescent; then again there are freedoms more suitable to the middle years of human maturity; and further again what it means to be free in older age is not exactly the same as with these other freedoms. The will ages, as does freedom itself; and there are forms of freedom where it is less that we insist on being free as that we hope to be freed, and indeed freed from false forms of freedom, or illusory freedoms that are really dungeons. What is fitting for ethical civility will be differently fitting for different freedoms, or phases in the unfolding of freedom. The plurality of different freedoms, appropriate to different times of life, is very relevant to the task of civic education. Most importantly, one must ask what is freedom appropriate to the learning time of youth, and its civic education. (Of course, one must not also forget the time of *those older*, those who are to serve as educators, teachers, exemplars.) I want to focus overall on what I see are important tensions between different understandings of freedom and the idea of civic piety. It is important to be clear about these tensions, if we are to be truly civic in our pedagogy.

If I am not mistaken there is a general trend in our time to let the name autonomy usurp the meaning of freedom. The words "autonomy" and "freedom" are often used as if they were identical, without much reflective thought, and indeed often without a lot of meaning. More particularly again, one might say that autonomy is more and more understood in an entirely individualized sense, perhaps even in a privatized sense: my autonomy. This is ironical in that initially autonomy referred directly to the political arena, and bore upon the notion of self-governance, of a people, or a region, or an aspiring nation. But in line with one of the major trends in modernity, it has migrated in a more individualized, even privatized direction. And of course, this is a part of the difficulty. There is a gain in that there is something right about a certain singular absoluteness of value invested in the unique individual. But there is difficulty in that freedom as autonomy becomes more and more literally what the word itself betokens: *nomos* of *to auto*: law of the same or the self. Law only of self, only of the same?

While freedom is inseparable from the singularity of the human person, the question does arise about the other: one's relation to others, and the law of the other. Of course, those familiar with modern discussions will immediately realize that this issue of the other brings in the questionable *heteronomy*, over against which autonomy insists upon its own power of self-determination. Heteronomy is to be under the law of another, and at the extreme to be under a tyrannical other, such as a repressive father, or a domineering king. We are well rid of that, we say. Indeed we can go to the extreme of the famous Kant, perhaps the high point of a certain rational autonomy: to allow morality to be contaminated with any trace of heteronomy is to risk the entire corruption of the purity of our moral being.

Again the question comes back: What then of others and our relation to these others? Kantians have some resources here in the following guise. They might claim that true autonomy is defined by the categorical imperative, and this entails that the individual take all other rational agents into account: these must be included in the demand for universalizability. Hence autonomy points to a principle of universality, understood as testing its consistency or self-coherence against all other possible rational others. There is some truth to this, and it is concretized in Kant's notion of the kingdom of ends. Is this the faceless universalism of a rationalistic cosmopolitanism that loves humanity as such but no human being in particular?

Leaving that aside for now, I would say this at most only goes half way, even if that. For the basic form of freedom is still one defined by autonomy, and hence by self-law, self-legislation, and hence the risk is always there that the other and our relation to others is put in a recessive, or ambiguous position. It is defined relative to the primacy of autonomy, understood as *self*-determination.

But what if this self-determination were itself embedded in, and in some measure derived from, *communal* relations to others that are more primary? Then a kind of "heteronomy" would have to come back into serious consideration. Certainly our being for ourselves would have to be revised or qualified. The trend towards the jealous monotheism of autonomy would have to be softened, and perhaps other freedoms, and even rival gods, such as social freedoms, familial and local freedoms, would have to be given holier names. I take civic education to deal with such social freedoms, though it often takes shape between individual autonomies and larger commitments, responsibilities, and loyalties.

I do not want to rehearse debates between communitarians and liberals that, obviously, have some relevance here. But I deliberately set out by situating autonomy in an ethos of religious value, and I do it just to state something of the difficulty that attends the notion of piety, civic and religious in a stronger sense. I now want to give some attention to these bonds of loyalty to something other than oneself, other than one's own self-determination, involved in the notion of piety. Without these bonds of loyalty there are no human communities, and hence also no matrices of enabling value that allow individual autonomy itself to be freed. Autonomies are freed to be themselves in the ethos of the enabling matrices of loyalty.

I will come to this more, but I cannot forbear one last remark on autonomy in the line of descent from Kant, and again with regard to the issue of the one god. I mean something like this: Kant is famous for inaugurating the project of an autonomous morality, precisely by insisting that to build morality on a religious basis would be to corrupt morality just in terms of a heteronomous ground: nothing other than autonomous morality can supply the ground for itself; nothing other than itself will do, and not the will of God or the gods as traditional views held. Morality might lead to a kind of rational religion in Kant, but religion does not lead to morality. You might see this as the jealous monotheism of autonomy—a monotheism without God, in the sense that autonomy is the one absolute that through itself is rationally self-justifying. The old God fails, perhaps even corrupts. There are many who are the heirs of Kant in this secularization of morality. It often seems in modernity that no substantive goods are recognized as ultimate, with the exception of freedom. But what kind of freedom? What kind of ultimate?

This secularization, I want to claim, mimics some of the features of religious piety, in so far as it claims this as the one end in itself and hence the one secular god, if you like, and this even among secular thinkers from whom there is no god at all. I would say they have not fully attended to what they have set up as worthy to be loved as absolute. But is it absolute?

I find an interesting ally in one for whom the traditions of Biblical religion are to be overcome: Nietzsche. He too insists on a radical autonomy, but his god ceases to be rational as with Kant: it dips down into more rhapsodic sources and Dionysian origins. Instead of rational autonomy, we need this frenzied autonomy, for only in this is the augur of our released creativity fulfilled. Nietzsche gives us a polytheistic atheism of autonomy, an autonomy more primitive, and also, he holds, higher than the rational moral autonomy of Kant. Nietzsche thinks that he explodes the piety of Judaism and Christianity, and also the rational "piety" of Kantian autonomy. In the name of autonomy? Or by exploding autonomy? Many post-modern thinkers are heirs to that explosion. One might see it as an outcome of the divinization of a certain kind of autonomy, though this divinization is now polytheistic, not monotheistic. But in this polytheistic divinization, the truth of the god becomes plain, for even autonomy is a mask of the more ultimate god, and this god is now more nakedly revealed as will to power. The divinity of this autonomy reveals itself as will to power, for whom all things are nothing. And so the night of nihilism is deepened rather than illuminated by all this. But then if this be so, to what is the ultimate loyalty of this postmodern autonomy given? Where is its piety, be it familial, or local, or civic, or religious? Do we seem to be left with nothing? Or has autonomy mutated into a tyranny of will to power? What could civic education now possibly mean?

In sum then: a certain understanding of autonomy seems to undermine the bonds of more local loyalties that bind us to others, or at least render them equivocal, if our catch cry is always "my autonomy"; or a radicalization of that autonomy, even its deconstruction. Are we led, at an extreme, to will to power, and nihilism, and hence also to the weakening, if not destruction of the same bonds of loyalty? And leaving us, again at an extreme, at the mercy of the tyrannical self-insistence of a particular social, or national will to power, such as we found with Nazi Germany? But can there be a loyalty to nothing? Do we not again have to bring back some notion of piety, in so far as piety has a bearing on our ultimate loyalties?

II. COMMUNAL LOYALTIES AND PIETY

But let me say something about *piety*—an idea that sounds either strange, or quaint, or outmoded to many modern or contemporary ears. Sounding so, I suppose, because of the legacy of forms of individual autonomy that have shaped our perceptions of value. And yet, how it astounds some advanced commentators that old-fashioned habits like patriotism seem not to go away, sleeping perhaps for extended periods, and then astonishingly to wake up, or be awoken, in situations of threat or crisis or war. But this awakening has to do with our ultimate loyalties, or pieties, most of the time simply taken for granted, but no less effective for all that.

What more to say about piety? Some today have an essentially shriveled sense of piety, as they do of reverence, or gratitude, and other related ways of being in relation to what is other to our own autonomous self-determination. Piety is pluriform, like freedom. Sometimes different pieties clash; sometimes they are nested together more harmoniously; sometimes they require of us a finesse to determine what is fitting, with reference to patriotism, or local allegiances, for instance. There is no one simple rule, no univocal principle. There is the need of practical wisdom, *phronesis*, as the Greeks have it. The shaping of human resources in this direction is very important for civic education.

Piety has to do with a reverence towards that to which we belong in a special way. It need not be exclusively accented in a more recognizable religious direction, since we talk about familial piety, as well as civic piety, indeed of a local piety, and I will come to these. I think the accent has to fall on the specialness of the belonging, and what it evokes from us in terms of loyalties—loyalties to what we love, and of which we might have great difficulties in giving a neutral and homogeneous rational justification. We love those to whom we belong—not that which belongs to us—and why we do, we cannot always articulate with full measure of rational self-consciousness. We live this belonging and loyalty, live out of it. In it we first and elementally participate, and our efforts to account rationally for it, or justify it, more often than not fall short of the living event of participation itself. Obviously the loyalties that bind us here cannot be to some faceless, anonymous universal which, though it be said to free us, frees us into nothing—nothing in particular. I do not think there is an absolute contradiction between loyalties as particular and a more universal openness. I do wonder if this can be separated from an ultimate belonging in which the religious universal must be acknowledged, even though being religious need not be identified with this or that institutional or sectarian form. I will return to this below.

Pietas was certainly one of the major manifestations of distinctive human honor and nobility in the pre-modern world. Perhaps with the Enlightenment and after there is the view among intellectuals that identifies piety with a kind of superstition, or abjectness, incompatible with our upright autonomy—a toothless crone or a Crazy Jane jabbering away in an empty church. I think of Kant saying to the effect that to be caught in a position of prayer was perhaps the most humiliating; and then there is his indignant outburst about groveling, even in the presence of the most high.

But put aside issues connected with religion for now. We speak also of filial and civic and local piety, and these reveal some of the more positive sense. Filial or familial piety signifies the special bond of loyalty and respect between parents and children, a spiritual bond based on the physical kinship of blood (see, for instance, ancestor worship). Local piety signifies the special loyalty for one's own place, one's home—a spiritual kinship again closely tied to a physical reality (cf. sacred kingship as wedded to place). Think of the homely example of how people are loyal to their *home team*.[1] Civic piety in the past was closely allied with local piety, in so far as people were more sedentary in a particular place, as well as the fact that communities were more circumscribed in demographical dimensions. As an example here, think of the *pietas* of some of the great Italian cities—such as Florence and Venice. Of course, one could further back to Rome, Athens, Jerusalem, and other places.

The horror we feel at crimes like *patricide* and *treason* shows how deep these pieties still go. A like sense of a kinship or bond or community of loyalty can be found in religious piety. As has been pointed out, by Augustine among others, the roots of "*religio*" imply a binding together, a bond of connectedness. Religious piety, in this sense, acknowledges our link with divine powers more ultimate than ourselves, signifies our intimacy with the sacred, even though we may also feel our difference from it. Such piety need not be tied to metaphysical abjectness but may be born in an (ontological) reverence, open to praise of the powers that vitalize and beautify and perfect creation.

I will just make one point. Such piety, as a bond with what is beyond us, or other, need not be an affront to our autonomy, a deprivation of our freedom. Rather it indicates a rich embeddedness of that freedom in the bonds of belonging somewhere and with someone. It also indicates our embeddedness in often *incognito* loyalties that give the individual a commitment to values more ample than self-regarding self-insistence. Piety has nothing to do with an enforced abdication of our wills by our being made supine but with an enlargement of willingness that is taken into the good of a community with what is beyond our lone selves, be it a family, a place, a nation, or a God.

Think of the piety that, in such a sense, is enlarged by its love of a specific and special *place*: one loves *this* town, or this range of hills, or these green fields. Think of the power of certain songs that celebrate place: I left my heart in San Francisco. Piety would hardly be the word on the lips of those thinking about this song; and yet a love of a place can steal into one's soul, and it is not that the place then belongs to one, but something intimate in oneself belongs to that place. One's heart is there, one leaves one's heart there, even if one leaves. People who emigrate know this, and there was so much of immigration in the history of the United States. One thinks too of students who study abroad: on leaving home, they learn something of what they took for granted at home, it being so intimate to their lives they could not see it there; and maybe they come to know it in distance, and perhaps even to love it more.

III. Autonomy and Loyalty in Tension

One could argue that there is an inherent tension between freedom understood as individual autonomy, and that loyalty of belonging that is of the essence of civic piety. My point is not an argument against freedom or liberty, but a question put to an understanding of freedom that cannot see the reality of the pieties of life, cannot see that, without those loyalties, human life can quickly become a threadbare thing.[2] If we insist on our own autonomy as freedom in its absolute form, then we must relativize this loyalty, indeed we may not be able to see it, appreciate its call, and less and less we may come to participate in it.

I think that there are intellectual currents that have always had difficulties acknowledging the deep power of these loyalties, and that are amazed, shocked, stunned when they emerge for manifestation— more often than not as now, in times of stress or attack or a threat to a way of life, or war. A claim to autonomy is not coincident with the claim to *perpetuation* that a way of life makes on us. And the roots of the latter go deeper than what can be determined through oneself alone. The roots of these loyalties resist a completely rationalized account.

They bear on what we love most intimately, and most ultimately.

To think one can lay them bare in a univocally rationalized way might be to kill them, or at least to weaken or mutilate them, since their work must be done out of sight, at least to a degree. The roots are in the ground but they are what enables all growing (up), granting that the conditions above ground are also properly favorable to growth.[3] To insist that what is below ground or on the ground, or home ground itself, should be exactly the same as what grows above ground is disastrous for growing (up) overall. It should be clear that the manner of the upsurgence of patriotism in circumstances of danger testifies to sources of energy that are mostly hidden in the unexceptional conditions of everyday life but which flare up into self-expression when a serious threat is experienced to a way of life. The flare is as much expressive of what is ongoing in a way of life, mostly unnoticed and unnamed, as it is defensive of a commitment that is willed to continue to be.

In such circumstances, the tension between freedom and loyalty also becomes more stressed, and stressed in particular ways when that freedom is identified with my autonomy. If freedom is primarily my autonomy, then it must subordinate the loyalty of civic piety to itself: the first is first, the second secondary, if even essential at all. As I already suggested, there is in Western societies a huge trend to all but identify freedom with autonomy understood as mine, with consequences for those bonds of loyalty that constitute the tissue of civic piety. Pushed in certain directions those bonds are weakened, or dissolved. Is there then a freedom that is more than autonomy as mine?

Of course, in Western society the *pietas* we have inherited, even if it is often masked, or seemingly non-existent in secularized forms of life, is rooted in a religious tradition that is potentially universal in range. I mean primarily the tradition of Biblical personalism, whether Christian or Jewish. (Islam is also a child of this Abrahamic tradition, but I am not competent to comment more.) The places of the Western dialogue, Athens and Jerusalem, are cities of the universal, be it of reason or of revelation. That very germ of universality is itself in tension with the particularity of some more local pieties and commitments, as much as with a too contracted individual notion of freedom as autonomy. And the freedom that comes from that more ecumenical piety, if I can call it that, relativizes many of the more local and particularized pieties. The question: Would this more ecumenical piety be a friend of the local pieties, or merely an alien power imposed on them or extirpating them? It seems to me that this tension of universal and particular springs up, whether we take a more secular or religious view of the universal. That it is *piety* that is at stake in our fundamental loyalties indicates for me that a purely secular understanding of the difficulty is not enough to articulate the difficulty itself, much less address it with a persuasive response.

Hence again, the stunned amazement and rationalized irritation that not a few secular intellectuals exhibit when religious movements, or movements religiously inspired, show an extraordinary power of shifting attitudes on a large social scale—be this the civil rights movement, or more intransigently, the rise of a variety of fundamentalisms. No doubt, these surges of astonishing energy are as often full of danger, as they are sometimes full of promise. Granted there may be formations of these surges of energy that are potentially destructive, and against them it may be necessary to fight: Nazism is an example. But these surges of energy have also to be understood, not just denounced. But do we have the terms to understand them?

On the whole, since the religious wars of early modernity, we have tried to dampen down the dangerous aspects of these energies. And yet these energies also migrate into secular form, and instead of religious wars, we are fighting even more destructive wars against the idols of totalitarian regimes. But idolatry is a religious category, even when we claim to have superseded religion. With idols we are dealing with what I would call the counterfeit doubles of God. These counterfeit doubles seem to release our more dangerous energies, and yet energies with sometimes massive power to effect all of life—and not necessarily for the good always.

We need to give more thought than we have to the religious universal. I would call this the intimate universal. As with all things universal, we deal with our relation to what is more encompassing than our lone selves. But as with all things intimate, we deal with our *great loves*, what we love greatly, but also with our dangerous loves, what is greatly dangerous.

For there are dangers here. One's inarticulate loyalties, more often than not dark to themselves, can be given over to forms of life that raise serious ethical questions. Consider the Nazi language, for instance, of *Blut und Boden*—blood and soil. In this one sees the danger of a people's celebration of the passion of their belonging together, a passion that intoxicates the people with their power to affirm themselves, and to the humiliation, if not destruction, of those who are said to be other to one's own. One could say that the power of Nazism was a form of civic piety, in racist form; indeed the place, or space of Germania/Deutschland itself was sacralized as the space of singular destiny itself. This is an example in which a people's loves, dark to themselves, can also be dark loves. One might want to argue that this is a situation where the power of freedom as autonomy comes into its own. It might seem so, in that the individual seems called to stand for himself or herself over against the powers of the social whole.

This standing fast is crucial, I agree. But is the concept of freedom as autonomy up to it? I have my doubts. Is it just enough to stand for oneself? If one is standing against a false piety, must it not be in the name of a truer piety, and hence in terms of a loyalty and belonging to what is beyond oneself? In some currents of thought, of course, it is not the individual autonomy that is the final autonomy: the last autonomy is that of the *social whole*. But how then guard against the mutation of this autonomy into a kind of tyranny? The unconstrained autonomy of the social whole becomes hard to disentangle from a *people's* will to power. Think of the Jacobinism of a kind of rationalism for which the human community is a faceless universal.[4] Where then the ethical relation to what is other? And what form does civic piety, or any piety, occupy in such a tyrannous social holism? Is autonomy revealed in a will capable of terrorizing the other? (The human community is not faceless; hence the importance of religion as revealing the *intimate* universal.)

I would argue that many conceptions of autonomy are provisional masks in which a secret will to power bides its time. Oddly to some, I again see Nietzsche as in a line of inheritance from Kant: the rational will of Kant becomes the darker Dionysian will to power of Nietzsche, and in so far as both claim to be self-legislating, there is a line of familial continuity between them. In each I would say that the issue is not of a heteronomous submission versus an autonomous self-legislation; the issue concerns, paradoxically it might seem, what freedom *obeys*.[5]

IV. Loyalty, Civic Education, and Obedience

What does civic education have to do with obedience? Obedience is not necessarily some forced submission, or craven abjectness. It can be a free giving over to what is worthy to be followed, a disciplined commitment to what is of value. No doubt, often at the beginning we are not self-conscious about this, or capable of fully comprehending what is at stake. So is it with children and younger people in terms of their being committed to fundamental values of a way of life: our being committed by another is prior to our more self-conscious commitment of ourselves. An other, or others, who has or have us in their care, has or have already passed along a way to which we are being committed by growing up into, and being educated to, a way of life. But nothing worthy, much less great, is possible in human life without disciplined obedience.[6] Think of the discipline of obedience involved in learning to play the violin. But there you see the virtuoso twenty years later who plays with effortless verve, and the history of obedience to the discipline has made itself invisible in the astonishing mastery. And yet it is there. Can you educate citizens like that?

The notion of obedience is hard to handle in terms of my autonomy. Once again, obedience entails a being given over, of giving oneself over, to something more than and other than oneself. One is not simply obeying oneself. And so obedience looks all too like the dreaded "heteronomy" that lovers of autonomy denounce and shun. Kant may claim we obey the moral law, and he is not wrong; but then if we submit to the law, where is the *self-legislation? How can we give ourselves the law, if the law is already given to us, and we must submit to it?* Nietzsche is perhaps less disingenuous when he says in effect: no God above me, and no man either. In essence: I am the law. But this is a self-assertive claim to a higher autonomy for which there is nothing higher than itself. And what then could one obey? *Amor fati!* Let Nietzsche say fate, but why obey *that*? I say nothing of the fact that free obedience to fate seems like a peculiar self-canceling notion. But this seems a response that hides the equivocation between freedom and obedience by repeating it, rather than answering it.

In any case, the equivocal relation to what is other and beyond me is just what the self-legislation of my autonomy cannot fully address. For it is the relation to what is beyond me that is at issue. And this is so, whether we think of the positive sense of loyalties and pieties that free us into creative contributions to an ethical community, or of the tyrannous sense in which we are submerged in social intoxications and bewitchments that seem to release us from the burden of self-responsibility.

I do not think there is any simple and univocal answer to the tensions and stresses here. If there is an answer, it would be less a matter of having a theory and more a matter of having the right religious and ethical orientation to life. This orientation bears on what we are and what we are to be. But this we learn first by *imitation*, not self-determination, or self-creation. Imitation is more basic than creation in (civic) education. A child or young person can only learn in this matter by example and by witness. Civic knowledge may be diverse, but crucial is knowledge by imitation of an exemplary other, not by study of a theory, or by insisting on creativity or autonomy. There is a civil mimesis that is a covenantal binding across generations, learnt more like learning a native language. We listen to others before we speak for ourselves. Thus too an inheritance of civilizing form, a civic heritage, is communicated from one generation to the next.

Civic education is bound up with what one might call an *ancestral knowing*. Ancestral knowing involves a covenant with human generations, both the predecessors and the descendants, those now gone, those yet to come (Burke knew this deeply). This has regard for a *long* time, not just the long ago. You might define a true conservative as one concerned with the future: not lost in the past, since his or her care is with what is worthy to be passed on in life (tradition as a handing on: *tradere*). The seeds of the new must be planted in the ground of the old, else there is no growing.[7] This must involve the study of the history of the becoming of a people. This will include ancestral knowing of those exemplars of its way of life, both those confirming what is inherently good in it, as well as those who have heroically challenged its deficiencies, and kept a people truer to its more authentic religious and ethical values.

Such an ancestral knowing is something that is becoming well-nigh incomprehensible in a culture where the values of *youth* are considered absolute. But this incomprehension tells us something about ourselves: tells against us. If we have no comprehension of this covanental bond, no gratitude, no reverence, no piety, will be found. And symbolic (or real) patricide becomes the last "interesting" outrage called art. But of course, these "interesting" outrages quickly become boring outrages.

There is, of course, always the tension between more particular, local pieties, and the call of some more universal responsibility, such as comes to us, certainly in the West, from the great monotheistic traditions, and perhaps their secular doubles. In a certain sense, we are always in between the more local and the more universal, diversely stressed by different calls on our ethical, civic, and religious responsibilities. Civic education happens more in the moderate middle; this last piety comes from the extremes. But in times of great disturbance, such as war, the extremes invade the middle, and test our ultimate pieties. Our local pieties are not immune from a more radical accounting, which they may not always answer in their own terms alone. They too are not autonomous, but under a higher measure of justice.

This, I think, is again a religious-ethical matter, in which, yes, there is a singular responsibility on the singular individual, but that responsibility is not completely of its own self-legislation, or self-determination, and even though only the singular self can choose for itself. In such situations, perhaps what we most need are those singular *witnesses* who have the spiritual courage to stand against the social self-intoxications which threaten freedom and sometimes perhaps even in the name of freedom. We need prophetic witnesses. A prophetic witness is one who places himself or herself at risk under the responsibility of an ultimate value that is even more ultimate than the immanent values here and now of prospering or not, of surviving or not surviving. Prophetic witnessing means living in obedience to the light of ultimate good that is not of one's own autonomous self-determination but which defines the very inherent good of one's own being at all. This is a piety that requires of us a courage for transcendence beyond ourselves.[8] This witness may not be what is asked of us in civic education, but if civic education is not open to its possibility, it is a question if civic piety can sustain, on its own, its own health. At its best it can intimate the loyalty of this other reverence.

This last universalism is not quite civic religion nor quite the rational cosmopolitanism of a Kant or a Nussbaum. But because it is religious, it knows something of the kink in the soul and will. It knows our temptation to hubris, and pride and tyranny. Its piety is inseparable from a humility that knows we cannot plan and construct our own absolute salvation. If this intimate universal chastens hubris and tyranny, it is not *per se* hostile to more particular pieties. Nevertheless, it is tempered enough to allow, so to say, the becoming glory that is fitting to the immanent pieties of family and place and people.

NOTES

1. An example from a time when I lived in Baltimore back in the 1980s: the local perception was that the Baltimore Colts were "stolen" by their then new "owner," Bob Irsay. In the middle of the night, a winter night, the new owner sneaked away with the team to a new location, stealing away. There were pictures on the television of older men weeping when they woke up to the betrayal. One might say: the team belonged to such supporters because they belonged to the team. Though the team belonged to the owner, he did not know that loyalty, that belonging.

2. Civic education is sometimes seen as the prerogative of civil society, or of the state. But if familial and locale pieties are not rich in their own terms, it is hard to know if civic piety can be dictated from the state down. It may well be that there will be dictated from above down something smack-

ing more of totalitarian impiety, matched from below up by the empty souls of otherwise atomized human units. Facelessness from above meets facelessness from below, but genuine loyalty and reverence is not what is engendered when they meet in the middle. The state becomes in Hobbes's phrase, a "mortal god," where rather than piety we find forced submission, and enforced obeisance.

3. Of course some roots can grow weeds. We see something of the root in the effect: *poisoned fruit*. It is a question of judgment what to do about such fruits. But an *a priori* attitude or abstract theory that roots must be uprooted could mean destroying the wheat along with the tares. Sometimes the time is not ripe for a harvest of sweeter fruits and it is wiser to be patient (Christ's counsel).

4. Robespierre's "Republic of Virtue"—imposing a "despotism of liberty" to purify the people by terror: "Without virtue, terror is useless; without terror, virtue is powerless."

5. One might remark here on the tension between autonomy and the idea of service. There can be a tendency to reduce service to *servility*. What then of public service? Surely civic education has much to do with preparing individuals to see themselves as not always being served, but as being placed in service to their society and fellows. The civil servants are not the only ones for whom the role of service is important. On autonomy and service, see my *Ethics and the Between* (Albany, NY: State University of New York Press, 2001), chapters 11 and 16.

6. [In]discipline in the class: before for indiscipline a student would get into trouble with the parents; now it is, or can be, the teacher who gets into trouble!

7. A civic culture is a matter of tending and growing: thus the relation of *colere, cultus* and culture. See Josef Pieper, *Leisure: The Basis of Culture*, trans. Alexander Dru (New York: New American Library, 1963) on the relation of culture and religious cultus. Being religious can keep open the space of porosity between the universal and the particular: reminding one of more ultimate exigencies and values, and keeping true our necessary duties, responsibilities, pleasures, and trials of the daily middle. It too is a *memorial* knowing: ancestral, and *more* than ancestral. This includes being critical of idolatrous pieties. Pieties may require their purification of idolatry.

8. See my "The Secret Sources of Strengthening: Philosophical Reflections on Courage," in *Courage*, ed. Barbara Darling-Smith (Notre Dame, IN: University of Notre Dame Press, 2002), chapter 1.

3

On Liberty, Or, How John Stuart Mill Went Wrong

ROGER KIMBALL

WHEN WE PONDER the question "What do we teach our citizens?" it behooves us to consider not only the facts and doctrines we inculcate, but also the attitudes—moral, intellectual, and affective—that we nurture. As many commentators have noted, the terrorist attacks of September 11 seem to have inaugurated a change in the emotional weather of American culture: the frivolous anti-Americanism that seemed de rigueur on September 10 seemed embarrassing or worse on September 12. The run-up to the war with Iraq saw a reversion to the status quo ante in many segments of elite culture, but the extraordinary success of the coalition forces has, at least for the moment (I write in mid-April 2003), rather taken the wind out of the sails of the liberal, anti-Bush consensus represented by the so-called mainstream media and most academic intellectuals.

Nevertheless, there are certain important elements of the liberal consensus that have survived the frost of reality and continue, I believe, to pose a threat to civic education. I would like to discuss one element in this mosaic: the idea, the assumption—perhaps I should say the *presumption*—that the liberal consensus represents the sole source of intelligence, sensitivity, and humane understanding. As the English historian Maurice Cowling noted in his book *Mill and Liberalism*, for many years now "to use liberal language has been taken to be *intelligent*: to reject it evidence of *stupidity*." That conviction has long since been elevated into a fundamental *donnée* of intellectual life: an unspoken assumption that colors every aspect of political and moral deliberation.

No one was more important in bringing about this state of affairs than Cowling's subject, John Stuart Mill. Mill would not have been surprised that to speak as he taught one to speak—to speak in Mill, as it were—was to be thought intelligent, while to speak otherwise was to be thought stupid. He believed it himself; and he did everything in his very considerable powers to encourage the belief in others. "The stupid party" was Mill's own summary description of the Conservative Party. For anyone interested in understanding the nature of the modern liberal consensus—what John Fonte has dubbed the consensus of "transnational progressivism"—the extraordinary success of Mill's rhetoric and the doctrines it advances afford a number of lessons. Above all, it provides an object lesson in the immense seductiveness inherent in a certain type of skeptical moralizing. Together with Rousseau, Mill supplied nearly all of the arguments and most of the emotional fuel— the texture of sentiment—that have gone into defining the progressive vision of the world. His peculiar brand of utilitarianism—a cake of Benthamite hedonism glazed with Wordsworthian sentimentality—has proven to be irresistible for the multitudes susceptible to that sort of confection.

I should begin by noting that I am going to give a very one-sided picture of Mill, who was an exceedingly complex and multifacted figure. As the historian Gertrude Himmelfarb has shown in her book *On Liberty and Liberalism: The Case of John Stuart Mill* (New York, 1974), Mill the apostle of radical liberalism was matched by a more circumspect figure, an "other Mill" whose ideas about the limits of freedom are often at odds with those of his alter ego. But the Mill who matters for my subject is the radical Mill, the Mill of *On Liberty*. More than any other work, this brief manifesto provides the intellectual and affective keys to understanding the success of Mill's doctrine. *On Liberty* was published in 1859, coincidentally the same year as *On the Origin of Species*. Darwin's book has been credited—and blamed— for all manner of moral and religious mischief. But in the long run *On Liberty* may have abetted an even greater revolution in sentiment. It did an immense amount to codify the way we think, not about the world, exactly—Mill was not a scientist—but about what matters in the way we comport ourselves in the world.

The first thing to be said about *On Liberty* is that it is a masterpiece of liberal polemic. Its core ideas are as the air we breathe: unnoticed because ubiquitous. Mill's arguments and pronouncements about man as a "progressive being," what he says about the extent of individual autonomy, the limits of acceptable moral and legal censure, the importance of innovation and (perhaps his most famous phrase) "experiments in living" are all familiar to the point of invisibility. Likewise his corollary insistence on the poverty of custom, prejudice, and tradition. Mill's contentions on these subjects are nowadays less objects of debate than of reverence: moral principles that discussion is expected to presuppose, not challenge. As Professor Himmelfarb put it, "What Mill proposed as a bold new doctrine has come down to us as an obvious, axiomatic truth."

But the success of Mill's teaching in the estimate of public sentiment says nothing about the cogency of his arguments. In fact, Mill's central arguments are open to—and have from the beginning been subjected to—serious criticism. Yet they have raged like wildfire through the Western world, consuming everything that stands in their path. Which means, among other things, that they exert an appeal quite distinct from any intellectual merit they may possess.

As for the nature of Mill's arguments, consider, for example, his famous plea on behalf of moral, social, and intellectual "experiments." Throughout history, Mill argues, the authors of such innovations have been objects of ridicule, persecution, and oppression; they have been ignored, silenced, exiled, imprisoned, even killed. But (Mill continues) we owe every step of progress, intellectual as well as moral, to the daring of innovators. "Without them," he writes, "human life would become a stagnant pool. Not only is it they who introduce good things which did not before exist; it is they who keep the life in those which already exist." Ergo, innovators—"developed human beings" is one phrase Mill uses for such paragons—should not merely be tolerated but positively be encouraged as beacons of future improvement.

The philosopher David Stove had a good name for this gambit. He called it the "They All Laughed at Christopher Columbus" argument. Stove noted that "the Columbus argument" (as he called it for short) "has swept the world."[1]

> With every day that has passed since Mill published it, it has been more influential than it was the day before. In the intellectual and moral dissolution of the West in the twentieth century, every step has depended on conservatives being disarmed, at some critical point, by the Columbus argument; by revolutionaries claiming that any resistance made to them is only another instance of that undeserved hostility which beneficial innovators have so regularly met with in the past.

The amazing thing about the success of the Columbus argument is that it depends on premises that are so obviously faulty. Granted that every change for the better has depended on someone embarking on a new departure: well, so too has every change for the worse. And surely, as Stove notes, there have been at least as many proposed innovations which "were or would have been for the worse as ones which were or would have been for the better." Which means that we have at least as much reason to discourage innovators as to encourage them, especially when their innovations bear on things as immensely complex as the organization of society.

Let me pause here to stress that this caveat does not mean that innovation is *always* a bad thing, that it should *never* be encouraged. My argument is directed, rather, against what we might call the *worship* of innovation: against the widespread tendency to grant a blanket exemption from criticism to anything that can be regarded as "innovative."

The triumph of Millian liberalism shows that such concerns have fallen on deaf ears. But why? Why have "innovation," "originality," etc., become mesmerizing charms that neutralize criticism before it even gets started when so much that is produced in the name of innovation is obviously a change for the worse? An inventory of the fearsome social, political, and moral innovations made in the last century alone should have made every thinking person wary of unchaperoned innovation. One reason that innovation has survived with its reputation intact is that Mill and his heirs have been careful to supply what Stove calls a "one-sided diet of examples." It is a technique as simple as it is effective:

> Mention no past innovators except those who were innovators-for-the-better. Harp away endlessly on the examples of Columbus and Copernicus, Galileo and Bruno, Socrates and (if you think the traffic will bear it) Jesus. Conceal the fact that there must have been at least one innovator-for-the-worse for every one of these (very overworked) good guys. Never mention Lenin or Pol Pot, Marx or Hegel, Robespierre or the Marquis de Sade.

Mill never missed an opportunity to expatiate on the value of "originality," "eccentricity," and the like. "The amount of eccentricity in a society," he wrote, "has generally been proportional to the amount of genius, mental vigor, and moral courage it contained." But you never caught Mill dilating on the "improvement on established practice" inaugurated by Robespierre and St. Just, or the "experiments in living" conducted by the Marquis de Sade. (It is hardly surprising that, today, the phrase "experiments in living" is redolent of the fatuous lifestyle "experiments" of the 1960s; whatever else can be said about the phrase, Stove is surely right that it represented "a sickeningly dishonest attempt to capture some of the deserved prestige of science for things that had not the remotest connection with science"—principally "certain sexual and domestic arrangements of a then-novel kind.")

David Stove offers some telling insights into the weaknesses of Mill's liberalism. But in order to understand its world-conquering success, one has to go beyond simple credulity and an abundance of one-sided examples. Flattery comes into it. Mill was exceptionally adroit at appealing to his readers' moral vanity. When he spoke (as he was always speaking) of "persons of decided mental superiority" he made it seem as though he might actually be speaking about *them*.

Mill's blandishments went even deeper. In *On Liberty*, Mill presented himself as a prophet of individual freedom. He has often been regarded as such, especially by liberal academics, who of course have been instrumental in propagating the gospel according to Mill. And "gospel" is the *mot juste*. Like many radical reformers, Mill promised almost boundless freedom, but he arrived bearing an exacting new system of belief. In this sense, as Maurice Cowling argues, *On Liberty* has been "one of the most influential of modern political tracts," chiefly because "its purpose has been misunderstood." Contrary to common opinion, Cowling wrote, Mill's book was

> not so much a plea for individual freedom, as a means of ensuring that Christianity would be superseded by that form of liberal, rationalising utilitarianism which went by the name of the Religion of Humanity. Mill's liberalism was a dogmatic, religious one, not the soothing night-comforter for which it is sometimes mistaken. Mill's object was not to free men, but to convert them, and convert them to a peculiarly exclusive, peculiarly insinuating moral doctrine. Mill wished to moralize all social activity. . . . Mill, no less than Marx, Nietzsche, or Comte, claimed to replace Christianity by "something better." Atheists and agnostics, humanists and freethinkers may properly give thanks to Mill.

This tension in Mill's work—between Mill the libertarian and Mill the moralistic utilitarian—helps to account for the vertiginous quality that suffuses the liberalism for which *On Liberty* was a kind of founding scripture. Mill's announced enemy can be summed up in words like "custom," "prejudice," "established morality." All his work goes to undermine these qualities—not because the positions they articulate are necessarily in error but simply because, being customary, accepted on trust, established by tradition, they have not been subjected to the acid-test of his version of the utilitarian calculus. The tradition that Mill opposed celebrated custom, prejudice, and established morality precisely because they had prevailed and given good service through the vicissitudes of time and change; their longevity was an important token of their worthiness. It was in this sense, for example, that Edmund Burke extolled prejudice, writing that "prejudice renders a man's virtue his habit. . . .

Through just prejudice, his duty becomes a part of his nature."

Mill overturned this traditional view. Indeed, he was instrumental in getting the public to associate "prejudice" indelibly with "bigotry." For Mill, established morality is suspect first of all *because* it is established. His liberalism is essentially corrosive of existing societal arrangements, institutions, and morality. He constantly castigated such things as the "magical influence of custom" ("magical" being a negative epithet for Mill), the "despotism of custom [that] is everywhere the standing hindrance to human advancement" and the "tyranny of opinion" that makes it so difficult for "the progressive principle" to flourish. According to Mill, the "greater part of the world has, properly speaking, no history because the sway of custom has been complete." Such passages reveal the core of moral arrogance inhabiting Mill's liberalism. They also suggest to what extent he remained—despite the various criticisms he made of the master—a faithful heir of Jeremy Bentham's utilitarianism. And I do not mean only the Bentham who propounded the principle of "the greatest happiness for the greatest number," but also the Bentham who applauded the proceedings of the Star Chamber, advocated the imprisonment of beggars, defended torture, and devised the "Panopticon"—a machine, he said, for "grinding rogues honest"—to keep miscreants under constant surveillance.[2] Liberty was always on Mill's lips; a new orthodoxy was ever in his heart. There is an important sense in which the libertarian streak in *On Liberty* is little more than a prophylactic against the coerciveness that its assumption of virtuous rationality presupposes.

Such "paradoxes" show themselves wherever the constructive part of Mill's doctrine is glimpsed through his cheerleading for freedom and eccentricity. Mill's doctrine of liberty begins with a promise of emancipation. The individual, in order to construct a "life plan" worthy of his nature, must shed the carapace of inherited opinion. He must learn to subject all his former beliefs to rational scrutiny. He must dare to be "eccentric," "novel," "original." At the same time, Mill notes, not without misgiving, that

> As mankind improve, the number of doctrines which are no longer disputed or doubted will be constantly on the increase; the well-being of mankind may almost be measured by the number and gravity of the truths which have reached the point of being uncontested. The cessation, on one question after another, of serious controversy is one of the necessary incidents of the consolidation of opinion—a consolidation as salutary in the case of true opinions as it is dangerous and noxious when the opinions are erroneous.

In other words, the partisan of Millian liberalism undertakes the destruction of inherited custom and belief in order to construct a bulwark of custom and belief that can be inherited and form what he called a new "unanimity of sentiment." As Mill put it in his *Autobiography* (posthumously published in 1873),

> I looked forward, through the present age of loud disputes but generally weak convictions, to a future . . . [in which] convictions as to what is right and wrong, useful and pernicious, [will be] deeply engraven on the feelings by early education and general unanimity of sentiment, and so firmly grounded in reason and in the true exigencies of life, that they shall not, like all former and present creeds, religious, ethical, and political, require to be periodically thrown off and replaced by others.

So: a "unanimity of sentiment" (a.k.a. custom) is all well and good as long as it is grounded in the "true exigencies of life"—as defined, of course, by J. S. Mill.

One measure of Mill's triumph is that the "unanimity" of sentiment that he looked forward to has long since been achieved. Not that Mill has lacked critics. On the contrary, from the very beginning both his utilitarianism and his doctrine of liberty have been subjected to searching, indeed devastating, criticism. That they not only survived but also thrived is a testament to—among other things—the beguiling power of Mill's rhetoric and the seductive spell of his core doctrines.

By far the most concentrated and damaging attack on Mill's liberalism is a book called *Liberty, Equality, Fraternity*, published serially in the *Pall Mall Gazette* in 1872–1873, and then in book form in March 1873, the last year of Mill's life. It was written by the lawyer, judge, and journalist Sir James Fitzjames Stephen, Leslie Stephen's older brother and hence—such is the irony of history—Virginia Woolf's uncle. Mill himself never responded to Stephen's book beyond observing, as Leslie Stephen reports in his excellent biography of his brother, that he thought the book "more likely to repel than attract." But several of Mill's disciples responded—the most famous of whom was the liberal politician and journalist John Morley (1838–1923). Stephen brought out a second edition of his book the following year, 1874, in which he reproduces and replies to many criticisms raised by Morley and others. Leslie Stephen described *Liberty, Equality, Fraternity* as "mainly controversial and negative." *Pugnacious* and *devastating* would be equally appropriate adjectives. As one commentator put it, Stephen made "mincemeat" of Mill. And when it appeared, the book sparked a lively controversy, rousing, as Leslie Stephen noted, "the anger of some, the sympathy of others, and the admiration of all who liked to see hard hitting on any side of a great question." And yet for nearly one hundred years *Liberty, Equality, Fraternity* disappeared almost without a trace. After 1874, it was not republished until Cambridge University Press brought out a new edition in 1967.[3]

Writing in the introduction to the Chicago edition of *Liberty, Equality, Fraternity*, Richard Posner described the book as "a magnificent period piece: as vivid and revealing a document of British imperialism in its heyday as John Buchan's novel *Prester John* and Kipling's verse would be a generation later." Judge Posner was at least partly right. Written directly after Stephen completed a stint as Chief Justice of Calcutta, the book is full of the justified confidence of flourishing empire. Stephen saw the great good that the English had brought to India in health and education, in maintaining civic order, in putting down barbaric customs like suttee. He recognized clearly that following Mill's liberal principles would make carrying out that civilizing mandate difficult if not impossible. And he decided forthrightly that the fault lay with Mill's liberalism, not with civilization.

It would be a mistake, however, to regard *Liberty, Equality, Fraternity* merely as a "period piece." As Judge Posner acknowledges, it is also "an audacious and radical challenge to classical liberalism." The challenge is all the more audacious because it emerged from ground very close to Mill. Stephen was himself a Liberal (though one of conservative temperament) and a utilitarian of decidedly undoctrinaire persuasion. He comments at one point that "Bentham's whole conception of happiness as something which could, as it were, be served out in rations, is open to great objection." Stephen was too moral to be a strict utilitarian, too pragmatic to abandon that philosophy altogether. Stephen was also an ardent admirer of many aspects of Mill's philosophy; early on in *Liberty, Equality, Fraternity* he called Mill "a great man to whom I am in every way indebted." He had even reviewed *On Liberty* warmly in the *Saturday Review* when it first appeared. But in time he came to regard Mill's doctrine of liberty—and the apotheosis of an abstract equality and fraternity that flows from it—as an unmitigated disaster. *Liberty, Equality, Fraternity* explains why.

Richard Posner described as "naughty" Stephen's decision to adopt the revolutionary motto "Liberty, Equality, Fraternity" as the title of a book about Millian liberalism. But that is perhaps because Posner's sympathies on many issues are closer to Mill's than to Stephen's. In fact, the title is perfect. As Stephen explains in his opening pages, the book is an effort to examine "the doctrines which are rather hinted at than expressed by the phrase 'Liberty, Equality, Fraternity.'" Although that phrase had its origin in the French Revolution, Stephen noted, it nonetheless had come to express "the creed of a religion"—one "less definite than most forms of Christianity, but not on that account the less powerful." Indeed, the motto "Liberty, Equality, Fraternity" epitomized "one of the most penetrating influences of the day," namely the "Religion of Humanity"—the secular, socialistic *alternative* to Christianity put forward in different ways by thinkers like Auguste Comte, Jeremy Bentham, and John Stuart Mill. "It is one of the commonest beliefs of the day," Stephen wrote, "that the human race collectively has before it splendid destinies of various kinds, and that the road to them is to be found in the removal of all restraints on human conduct, in the recognition of a substantial equality between all human creatures, and in fraternity in general." Stephen shows in tonic detail why these beliefs are mistaken and why, should they be put into practice, they are bound to result in moral chaos and widespread personal unhappiness.

The phrase "liberty, equality, fraternity" suggests the immense rhetorical advantage that liberalism begins with. One can hardly criticize the slogan without arousing the suspicion that one must be a partisan of oppression, servitude, and dissension. "Liberty," Stephen notes, "is a eulogistic word." Therein lies its magic. Substitute a neutral synonym—"permission," for example, or "leave" (as in "I give you leave to go")—and the spell is broken: the troops will not rally. It is the same with *equality* and *fraternity*.

Stephen begins by pointing out that Mill and other advocates of the Religion of Humanity have exaggerated the advantages and minimized the disadvantages that these qualities involve. For one thing, taken without further specification "liberty, equality, fraternity" are far too abstract to form the basis of anything like a religion. They are also inherently *dis*establishing with regard to existing social arrangements; that indeed is one reason they exert so great an appeal for the radical sensibility. Take Mill's doctrine of liberty, which boils down to the exhortation: Let everyone please himself in any way he likes so long as he does not hurt his neighbor. According to Mill, any moral system that aimed at more—that aimed, for example, at improving the moral character of society at large or the individuals in it—would be wrong in principle.[4] But this view, Stephen notes, would "condemn every existing system of morals."

> Strenuously preach and rigorously practise the doctrine that our neighbor's private character is nothing to us, and the number of unfavorable judgments formed, and therefore the number of inconveniences inflicted by them

can be reduced as much as we please, and the province of liberty can be enlarged in corresponding ratio. Does any reasonable man wish for this? Could anyone desire gross licentiousness, monstrous extravagance, ridiculous vanity, or the like, to be unnoticed, or, being known, to inflict no inconveniences which can possibly be avoided?

As Stephen dryly observes, pace Mill, "the custom of looking upon certain courses of conduct with aversion is the essence of morality."

The great pragmatic lesson to be drawn from *Liberty, Equality, Fraternity* concerns the relation between freedom and power. "Power," Stephen insists, "precedes liberty"—that is, "liberty, from the very nature of things, is dependent upon power; and . . . it is only under the protection of a powerful, well-organized, and intelligent government that any liberty can exist at all." It is for this reason that it makes no sense to ask whether liberty *tout court* is a good thing. The question whether liberty is a good or bad thing, Stephen writes, "is as irrational as the question whether fire is a good or bad thing. It is both good and bad according to time, place, and circumstance." Mill's failure to recognize these truths endows his doctrine of liberty with extraordinary malleability. It also infuses that doctrine with an air of unreality whenever it approaches the problem of freedom in everyday life. It is axiomatic with Mill that "society has no business *as* society to decide anything to be wrong which concerns only the individual." It follows, Mill writes, that "fornication, for example, must be tolerated and so must gambling." But should a person be free to be a pimp? Or to keep a gambling house? Mill thinks these are exceptionally difficult questions and engages in some inadvertently comical hand-wringing about them.

> Although the public, or the State are not warranted in authoritatively deciding, for purposes of repression or punishment, that such or such conduct affecting only the interests of the individual is good or bad, they are fully justified in assuming, if they regard it as bad, that its being so or not is at least a disputable question: That, this being supposed, they cannot be acting wrongly in endeavoring to exclude the influence of solicitations which are not disinterested, of instigators who cannot possibly be impartial— who have a direct personal interest on one side, and that side the one which the State believes to be wrong, and who confessedly promote it for personal objects only.

For his part, Stephen notes that "There is a kind of ingenuity which carries its own refutation on its face. How can the State or the public be competent to determine any question whatever if it is not competent to decide that gross vice is a bad thing? I do not," Stephen continues, "think the State ought to stand bandying compliments with pimps."

"Without offence to your better judgment, dear sir, and without presuming to set up my opinion against yours, I beg to observe that I am entitled for certain purposes to treat the question whether your views of life are right as one which admits of two opinions. I am far from expressing absolute condemnation of an experiment in living from which I dissent, . . . but still I am compelled to observe that you are not altogether unbiased by personal considerations. . . ." My feeling is that if society gets its grip on the collar of such a fellow it should say to him, "You dirty rascal, it may be a question whether you should be suffered to remain in your native filth untouched, or whether my opinion about you should be printed by the lash on your bare back. That question will be determined without the smallest reference to your wishes or feelings; but as to the nature of my opinion about you, there can be no question at all."

The contrast of tone between Mill and Stephen could not be more graphic. And here we approach a subject that has become almost undiscussable. As Stephen noted in his letters, there was a peculiar "want of virility" about Mill. In part it was a matter of abstractedness: Mill seemed to him "comparable to a superlatively crammed senior wrangler, whose body has been stunted by his brains." He was "too much a calculating machine and too little of a human being." There was an element of what Leslie Stephen called "feminine tenderness" about Mill: his character, his prose, his doctrines. It is not, I think, coincidental that one senses something similar in Rousseau: a smothering fussiness, grown rancorous and paranoid in Rousseau's case, merely querulous and impertinent in Mill's. The "feminization of society" we occasionally read about is in this sense a coefficient of the triumph of liberalism. Its distrust of masculine directness is the other side of its inveterate impulse to moralize all social activity.

This stereoscopic quality in Mill's doctrine of liberty shows itself in other ways as well. One moment it seems to license unrestrained liberty; the next moment, it seems to sanction the most sweeping coercion. When Stephen says that "the great defect" of Mill's doctrine of liberty is that it implies "too favorable an estimate of human nature," we know exactly what he means. Mill writes as if people, finally awakened to their rational interests, would put aside all petty concerns and devote themselves to "lofty minded" relationships and the happiness of mankind in general. "He appears to believe," Stephen writes with barely concealed incredulity, "that if men are all freed from restraints and put, as far as possible, on an equal footing, they will naturally treat each other as brothers, and work together harmoniously for their common good." At the same time, Mill's estimation of actually existing men and women is very unfavorable. "Ninety-nine in a hundred," he tells us, act in ignorance of their real motives. In this respect, too, he resembles Rousseau, who late in life confessed that "I think I know man, but as for men, I know them not."

In fact, when it comes to his view of mankind, Mill vacillates between the two caricatures: a flattering one and a repulsive one (actually, they are both repulsive, though in different ways). The friction between the two produces an illusion of benevolence; that illusion is at the heart of liberalism's appeal. Yet what Mill describes is an ideal that, in proportion as it is realized, tends to grow into its opposite. In his book *Utilitarianism*, Mill writes that "as between his own happiness and that of others, justice requires [everyone] to be as strictly impartial as a disinterested and benevolent spectator." Stephen comments: "If this be so, I can only say that nearly the whole of nearly every human creature is one continued course of injustice, for nearly everyone passes his life in providing the means of happiness for himself and those who are closely connected with him, leaving others all but entirely out of account." And this, Stephen argues, is as it should be, not merely for prudential but for moral reasons.

> The man who works from himself outwards, whose conduct is governed by ordinary motives, and who acts with a view to his own advantage and the advantage of those who are connected with himself in definite, assignable ways, produces in the ordinary course of things much more happiness to others . . . than a moral Don Quixote who is always liable to sacrifice himself and his neighbors. On the other hand, a man who has a disinterested love of the human race—that is to say, who has got a fixed idea about some way of providing for the management of the concerns of mankind—is an unaccountable person . . . who is capable of making his love for men in general the ground of all sorts of violence against men in particular.

"The real truth is that the human race is so big, so various, so little known, that no one can really love it."

Mill's refusal to recognize this is a standing invitation to irony. Truth in advertising should have required *On Liberty* to begin with the words, "Once upon a time . . ." Although written by a learned man and talented philosopher, there is a sense in which it really belongs more to the genre of fantasy than moral philosophy. It says a number of emollient things about human capabilities, but outlines a moral-political system more or less guaranteed to stymie those capabilities.

Consider Mill's paeans to the value of eccentricity, diversity, and originality as solvents of "the tyranny of opinion." Doubtless he is sincere in his eulogies. But as we can see from looking around at our own society, the growth of Mill's equalizing liberty always tends to

homogenize society and hence to reduce the expression of genuine originality and individuality. Mill's philosophy declares originality desirable even as it works to make it impossible. Uniformity becomes the
order of the day. In a memorable analogy, Stephen says that Mill's notion of liberty as a politically "progressive" imperative in combination
with his demand for originality is "like plucking a bird's feathers in
order to put it on a level with beasts, and then telling it to fly."

Furthermore, by confounding, as Stephen puts it, the proposition
that "variety is good with the proposition that goodness is various,"
Mill's teaching tends to encourage a shallow worship of mere variety,
diversity for its own sake with no regard for value of the specific "di-
versities" being celebrated. This is obviously a lesson we still have not
learned. Notwithstanding the slogans of our cultural commissars, "diversity" itself is neither good nor bad. Signs announcing a "commitment to diversity" that one sees at college campuses and businesses
across the country are so nauseating precisely because they are little
more than badges declaring the owner's virtue. The odor of political
correctness surrounding them is the odor of unearned self-satisfaction.

In *On Liberty*, Mill says that "exceptional individuals . . . should
be encouraged in acting differently from the mass" in order that they
might "point the way" for the rest of us. But Stephen is right that

> if this advice were followed, we should have as many little oddities in man-
> ner and behaviour as we have people who wish to pass for men of genius.
> Eccentricity is far more often a mark of weakness than a mark of strength.
> Weakness wishes, as a rule, to attract attention by trifling distinctions,
> strength wishes to avoid it. Originality consists in thinking for yourself,
> not in thinking differently from other people.

It is part of Mill's polemical purpose to claim that society hitherto
had persecuted eccentricity out of fear and small-mindedness. But again
Stephen is surely right that

> it would be hard to show that the great reformers of the world have been
> persecuted for "eccentricity." They were persecuted because their doctrines
> were disliked, rightly or wrongly as the case may be. The difference be-
> tween Mr. Mill's views and mine is that he instinctively assumes that what-
> ever is is wrong. I say, try each case on its merits.

Stephen's recourse to the particular—he would have cited his allegiance to utilitarian principles of expediency—infuses his discussion
of the relation between liberty and power with robust common sense.
It also sets it sharply at odds with Mill's treatment. In one of the most
famous passages in *On Liberty*, Mill outlines what he thinks are the
limits of acceptable interference in an individual's "liberty of action."

The object of this essay is to assert one very simple principle, as entitled to govern absolutely the dealings of society with the individual in the way of compulsion and control, whether the means used be physical force in the form of legal penalties or the moral coercion of public opinion. That principle is that the sole end for which mankind are warranted, individually or collectively, in interfering with the liberty of action of any of their number is self-protection. That the only purpose for which power can be rightfully exercised over any member of a civilized community, against his will, is to prevent harm to others. His own good, either physical or moral, is not a sufficient warrant.

Mill adds various qualifications. He notes, for example, that this license applies only to "human beings in the maturity of their faculties," not to "children or young persons below the age which the law may fix as that of manhood or womanhood." He further notes, in a passage that has caused great hand-wringing among his disciples, that "despotism is a legitimate form of government in dealing with barbarians, provided the end be their improvement." But—and here is the nub of his argument restated—"as soon as mankind have attained the capacity of being guided to their own improvement by conviction or persuasion (a period long since reached in all nations with whom we need here concern ourselves), compulsion is no longer admissible as a means to their own good, and is justifiable only for the security of others." Consequently, for Mill "the appropriate region of human freedom [demands] absolute freedom of opinion and sentiment on all subjects, practical or speculative, scientific, moral, or theological."

Mill's description of his "one very simple principle" shows the extent to which his liberalism rests, as the philosopher Roger Scruton put it in *The Meaning of Conservatism*, on a "generalization of the first-person point of view." His apotheosis of the "I" is also a movement of abstraction. One of the first things one notices about Mill's "individuals" is how little air there is around them. They exist as flat, abstract cut-outs. Arguing for the relativity of moral values, Mill notes that "the same causes which make [someone] a churchman in London would have made him a Buddhist or a Confucian in Peking." But this is to take an entirely disembodied view of the relevant "causes." Part of what makes (or once made) someone a churchgoer in London is living in London; that is not an "accidental" datum that can be subtracted without cost from an individual's identity. Our culture and history are essential ingredients: remove them and you remove the individual. Individuality is not fungible.

Mill's assumptions about the nature of individuality stand at the heart of his liberalism. They also highlight what is most problematic about it. In the first place, it is by no means clear that we have knowledge (in Stephen's paraphrase) of any "very simple principles as entitled to govern absolutely the dealings of society with the individual in the way of compulsion and control." Mill's bland language conceals an extraordinary, and completely unjustified, presumption. In the second place, Stephen notes, Mill's famous distinction between "self-regarding" and "other-regarding" acts is "radically vicious. It assumes that some acts regard the agent only, and that some regard other people. In fact, by far the most important part of our conduct regards both ourselves and others." As Stephen observes, "men are so closely connected together that it is quite impossible to say how far the influence of acts apparently of the most personal character may extend." The splendid isolation that Mill's imperative requires is a chimera. Individuals exist not in autonomous segregation but in a network of relationships. Thus it is, as Stephen argues, that

> every human creature is deeply interested not only in the conduct, but in the thoughts, feelings, and opinions of millions of persons who stand in no other assignable relation to him than that of being his fellow-creatures. A great writer who makes a mistake in his speculations may mislead multitudes whom he has never seen. The strong metaphor that we are all members one of another is little more than the expression of a fact. A man would be no more a man if he was alone in the world than a hand would be a hand without the rest of the body.

When it comes to education, Mill admits that society must exert a moral influence on the young. But he then argues that, because society enjoys moral authority over the young, it must not presume to dictate the behavior or shape the manners of adults. But how can this be? How, Stephen asks, "is it possible for society to accept the position of an educator unless it has moral principles on which to educate? How, having accepted that position and having educated people up to a certain point, can it draw a line at which education ends and perfect moral indifference begins?"

Some of Mill's qualifications concede something to common sense; but they do so at the cost of turning his "one very simple principle" into a vacuous cliché. "Either," Stephen observes, Mill means that "superior wisdom is not in every case a reason why one man should control another—which is a mere commonplace—or else [he] means that in all the countries which we are accustomed to call civilised the mass of adults are so well acquainted with their own interests and so much disposed to pursue them that no compulsion or restraint" is ever justified, which is incredible. It is precisely this oscillation between the commonplace and the fantastic that has made Mill's liberalism such a durable commodity. Its radical promise is hedged by common-sense qualifications that can be wheeled out when objections are raised and then promptly retired when the work of remaking society is meant to proceed.

Stephen is quick to admit that "if Mr. Mill had limited himself to the proposition that in our own time and country it is highly important that the great questions of morals and theology should be discussed openly and with complete freedom from all legal restraints, I should agree with him." He agrees, too, that "neither legislation nor public opinion ought to be meddlesome," and that "those who have due regard to the incurable weaknesses of human nature will be very careful how they inflict penalties upon mere vice, or even upon those who make a trade of promoting it, unless special circumstances call for their infliction." But he goes on to note that it is "one thing . . . to tolerate vice so long as it is inoffensive, and quite another to give it a legal right not only to exist, but to assert itself in the face of the world as an 'experiment in living' as good as another, and entitled to the same protection from the law." No doubt "the busybody and world-betterer who will never let things alone" is a "contemptible character." But, Stephen continues, "to try to put [him] down by denying the connection between law and morality is like shutting all light and air out of a house in order to keep out gnats and blue-bottle flies."

Mill's "one very simple principle" depends on a variety of questionable assumptions about human nature and the way moral life ought to be conducted. Above all, it depends on a notably anemic view of moral life: one in which the sociocultural fabric that gives body to freedom is redefined as the enemy of freedom and the actual process of moral choice is turned into a process of frigid ratiocination. Mill's view of liberty is at once far too simplistic and far too rigorous. It is simplistic in its demonization of the customary and conventional; it is overly rigorous in its demand that moral choices be arrived at through "the collision of adverse opinions." "On no other terms," Mill says, "can a being with human faculties have any rational assurance of being right."

Mill argues that to deny this—to hold that sanctions, even the sanctions of negative public opinion, ought to be otherwise enjoined—"is to assume our own infallibility." But this is surely not the case. As Stephen points out, "the incalculable majority of mankind form their opinions" not by a process of ratiocination but out of a network of transmitted custom, prejudice, and conventional practice. "Doctrines come home to most people in general, not if and in so far as they are free to discuss all their applications, but if and in so far as they happen to interest them and appear to illustrate and interpret their own experience." Furthermore, on the issue of infallibility, Stephen points out that there are innumerable propositions about which we have rational assurance, even though we may not claim infallibility. The fact that we *might* be wrong says nothing against this, as Mill's own work in logic and probability ought to have reminded him. (Abstract possibility is always a cheap commodity.) Rational assurance is not the same thing as perfect certitude. "There are plenty of reasons," Stephen observes, "for not forbidding people to deny the existence of London Bridge and the river Thames, but the fear that the proof of those propositions would be weakened or that the person making the law would claim infallibility is not among the number." Mill argued that programmatic support for "the collision of adverse opinions" ultimately helps to secure "rational assurance." Its real results, however, have been intellectual and moral anomie. As Gertrude Himmelfarb noted with respect to this side of Mill's teaching, "by making truth so dependent upon error as to require not only the freest circulation of error but its deliberate cultivation, [Mill] reenforced the relativism of later generations."

Mill hoped that his regime of liberty would replace the reign of prejudice with the reign of reason. In fact, it has had the effect of camouflaging prejudices with rational-sounding rhetoric. The effort to unseat customary practice and belief has resulted not, as Mill predicted, in encouraging a drift toward unanimity but in increasing chaos.

Today, we are living with the institutionalization of Mill's paradoxes—above all, perhaps, the institutionalization of the paradox that in aiming to achieve a society that is maximally tolerant we at the same time give (in David Stove's words) "maximum scope to the activities of those who have set themselves to achieve the maximally-intolerant society." The activities of the American Civil Liberties Union, for example, daily bear witness to the hopeless muddle of this anchorless liberalism. Maximum tolerance, it turns out, leads to maximum impotence. The refusal to criticize results in a moral paralysis. That paralysis is the secret poison at the heart of Mill's liberalism. Among other things, it saps the springs of civic education by weakening our allegiance to tradition and customary modes of feeling and behavior, the rich network of inherited moral judgment.

Stephen noted that Mill's "very simple principle"—the principle that coercive public opinion ought to be exercised only for self-protective purposes—was "a paradox so startling that it is almost impossible to argue against." He was right. As Maurice Cowling observed, to argue with Mill, in Mill's terms, is to concede defeat. *Rational* does not *have* to mean conclusions reached by critical self-examination. *Prejudice* may reasonably be used to mean commitments about which argument has been declined, but to decline argument is not in itself *irrational*. *Bigotry* and *prejudice* are not necessarily the best descriptions of opinions which Comtean determinism has stigmatized as historically outdated.

Mill claimed a monopoly on the word "rational." So long as that monopoly remains unchallenged our paralysis will be complete. The antidote to the moral helplessness that Mill's liberalism generates is not to be found by digging deeper in the trench of liberal rationalization. On the contrary, it begins with the forthright recognition that no "one very simple principle" can relieve us of the duties we owe to the inhabited world that we, for this brief while, share with many others.

NOTES

1. See "The Columbus Argument" in *On Enlightenment* by David Stove, edited by Andrew Irvine and with a preface by Roger Kimball (New Brunswick, NJ: Transaction Publishers, 2003), pages 149–154.

2. See Richard A. Posner's *The Economics of Justice* (Cambridge, MA: Harvard, 1981), pages 33–35, on this aspect of Bentham's teaching.

3. The Cambridge edition, with notes by R. J. White, has since gone out of print. But that text, edited and with a new introduction by the legal philosopher Richard A. Posner, was reprinted by the University of Chicago in 1991. Another edition, edited and with an introduction by Stuart D. Warner, was published by Liberty Fund in 1993.

4. Not that Mill held to this radical doctrine consistently. In a letter of 1829, for example, Mill writes, in direct contradiction to the position he put forward in *On Liberty*, that "government exists for all purposes whatever that are for man's good: and the highest and most important of these purposes is the improvement of man himself as a moral and intelligent being."

Part II
Civic Education and the American Regime

4

The Commerce of Ideas and the Cultivation of Character in Madison's Republic

Colleen A. Sheehan

ROBERT FROST IS deservedly considered "America's Poet." In unadorned phrases he captures what it means to be an American. At the same time that he tells us who we are, he is at work shaping our minds and characters and making us into something more. At President Kennedy's inauguration in 1961, the capital blanketed with freshly fallen snow and capped by a glaring winter's sun, Frost was scheduled to read his newly composed poem "Dedication." The conditions made it impossible for him to see the pages, so instead he delivered from memory an older verse, a poem about the American Revolution—"about what Madison may have thought." "The land was ours before we were the land's," he recited. Later, in discovering within ourselves what had been withheld, we became the possession of the land. Frost's lines remind us of the ultimate sacrifice made by men whose bodies rest in soldiers' graves across the original thirteen states. They also evoke the cause to which our founding generation gave themselves wholly. In surrender to the land we became "her people." The gift made us true proprietors, owned by the land which called us to own ourselves. Madison's vision of a land populated by a self-governing people was perfectly expressed by Tocqueville a generation later: "I saw in America more than America." Madison's dream for America, like the soldiers' sacrifice, was a gift to us that could never be, and never was intended to be, repaid. It was "the gift outright."

How is it that Frost's understanding of Madison can be so at odds with much of the scholarship on Madison? Why is Madison so often understood to have envisioned a system of clever mechanistic political arrangements that make it possible to dispense with civic participation and the need for forming an American character? What is it that the poet saw that others may have missed? I think that it was the democratic soul of Madison. However politically cautious and non-sentimental Madison may have been, he was as alive to the prose of freedom and the poetry of the human drama as any man who ever lived. Frost had the ability to read a man's character by the way he thrust his hoe into the earth, "blade-end up and five feet tall," at the call of his neighbor for a friendly chat; to understand how the old woman at the black cottage would have felt—though she did not say so—if the Creed were changed: "the bare thought of her tremulous bonnet in the pew" was enough to know. It has been said about Frost that he was "a philosopher, but [that] his ideas are behind his poems, not in them."[1] I think that something similar could be said of Madison and that Frost saw this about him, and admired him for it.

Genuine democracy, whether of the pure or representative type, is grounded in the active participation of the citizenry in the affairs of the political community. Democracy is a reflection of the real character and concerns of real people. I remember a few years ago when I was running for political office, a perceptive friend of mine saying: Most of the pollsters and pundits don't get it. It's not purely an abstract calculation. One can measure the niceties of voting behavior, but at bottom, it's about real people with real issues. If you remember that, you will know more than most folks in politics.

For many scholars the problem with Madison is that he conceived of the sovereignty of the people in abstract terms and undermined the democratic principles of the founding. By dispensing with the need for civic participation and thwarting communicative activity among the citizenry, he created a "ghostly body politic."[2] His remedy for the problem of majority faction in the tenth *Federalist,* they say, was intended to make it virtually impossible for the people to act in a collective capacity. An extensive territory composed of a multiplicity of interests and parties not only deters the formation of majority faction, but it makes it difficult for the people to communicate effectively and to discover a common opinion. The doctrine of separation of powers increases the difficulty of forming a majority consensus on any given issue. Madison's paean to popular sovereignty and self-government was in reality a death knell for popular government, these critics claim. Some of them argue that his aim was to deadlock democracy;[3] others that his object was an end-run around democracy. Though couched in democratic language, the Federalists disingenuously used democratic rhetoric to establish and justify an aristocratic system.[4]

What is not generally attended to in scholarly analysis, however, is that the tenth *Federalist* is not Madison's last word on communicative activity among the citizenry. In his very next contribution to *The Federalist Papers,* in fact, he reverses his tack. In *Federalist* 14 he explicitly discusses how to *encourage* the communication of ideas throughout the large republic. Madison is both pro and con the activity of political communication, or at least for some kinds of communication and against others. Madison's theory of republicanism involves five major component parts, each of which is designed to minimize the factious effects of communicative activity and draw forth its didactic potential. These are: the extent of territory, the principle of representation, separation of powers and checks and balances, the influence of the enlightened men of letters on public opinion, and the influence of public opinion on government. In a new approach to the problem of political communication and public opinion Madison believed he had discovered the way to solve the evils of majority faction and at the same time preserve the spirit and form of popular government. The latter depended, as Robert Frost so well understood, on the cultivation of the American mind and character.

THE PROBLEM OF COMMUNICATION

Madison identifies human nature, with its composite of opinion, passion, and interest, as the latent source of faction. When men freely and coolly exercise their reason on various questions, they naturally form different opinions on some of them. When they are actuated by a common passion, he argues, their opinions, if they are to be so called, will be the same.[5] The problem with opinion, then, is of a specific nature: it is not opinion that results from the independent operation of the opining faculty that constitutes the source of danger. Rather, it is opinions which are actuated by the "impulse of passion, or of interest" that pose a threat to individual rights and the common good.

When this type of opinion is easily transmitted and spread, the activity of political communication exacerbates the baneful effects of faction. This is what tends to happen in a pure democracy or small republic. Given the ease of communication in a relatively small area with a limited populace and a limited number of interests and parties, there are few obstacles in the path of a factious majority. If a majority of citizens happen to hold a particular interest or passion, which given the probable lack of geographical, occupational, and other forms of differentiation would not be unlikely, it is relatively easy for them to discover the others who share their view and to act together to obtain their common object. This is the case of impulse coinciding with opportunity.[6] The impulse is passion or interest; opportunity is provided by the ease of communication and recognition of a shared purpose. Once impulse and opportunity have intersected and a majority faction has formed, it is futile to rely on other, better motives such as religion, morality, or respect for character.[7] In proportion to the number of people who are known to share the same viewpoint, the greater the confidence a member of the majority has in his opinion, further increasing the danger of an interested majority. "The reason of man, like man himself," Madison writes in *Federalist* 49, "is timid and cautious when left alone, and acquires firmness and confidence in proportion to the number with which it is associated."[8] Madison's analysis of majoritarian politics is grounded in a psychological analysis of the power of opinion, or what is today called "group dynamics" or "group think." The larger the group which shares the same opinion, the more it inspires confidence in others, stymies independent thought and private judgment, discourages checks upon the majority, and removes obstacles in the path toward tyranny. This is the problem that so disturbed Tocqueville about democracy; Madison saw it forty years earlier.

In a civilized nation constituted by an extensive territory and large population, the multiplicity of interests and parties which naturally arises in it makes it less likely that a majority will hold the same interest or passion at the same time. In the case that it did, however, Madison claims that the size of the territory and number of inhabitants will impede political communication. In essence, he wrote a prescription that would prevent the contagion of majority tyranny by a kind of quarantine of factious opinions. If a majority of citizens were to share a common passion or interest at any given time, the challenge of communicating across the extensive territory would make it difficult for them to discover their common motive. The size of the nation has the effect of isolating factions and rendering them unable to spread their communicable disease. In general, effective communication is harder in a large than in a small republic or pure democracy, whether the opinions communicated are factious ones or not. But the size of the territory presents a tougher challenge to those who are knowingly seeking an unjust or dishonorable objective. "Where there is a consciousness of unjust or dishonorable purposes, communication is always checked by distrust in proportion to the number whose concurrence is necessary,"[9] Madison writes. In other words, there is no honor among thieves—and they know it. Madison's insight into the psychology of shame is particularly interesting when juxtaposed against his idea that men acquire confidence and firmness in their own opinions in proportion to the number of other people who are known to concur. Confidence in an opinion is increased in proportion to the number of people who are believed to hold it, but *only when the motivation seems honorable, or at least not dishonorable.* Shame undermines the infectious quality of popular opinion. When a man's own motives are surreptitious, he tends to be distrustful of the motives of others.

While Madison's proffered solution of the extended territory diminishes the odds that a majority faction will form or unite, it does not forestall the possibility. If Americans lack a consciousness about what constitutes unjust or dishonorable purposes, that is, if there is a lack of enlightened understanding about the principles of justice and honor, then all bets are off.[10] Under these circumstances a majority faction would find it less difficult to communicate a common purpose and activate the contagious effect of opinion. Madison discusses a possible counter to this problem of a united, unjust majority in *Federalist* 63, arguing that it is the duty of the Senate in particular to check the overbearing majority's "misguided career." But this is at best a temporary solution, which can only be effective in the long term if "reason, justice, and truth . . . regain their authority over the public mind."[11]

Madison seeks to check the communication of this type of opinion via the enlargement of the orbit. It is not his design, however, to stymie the communication of "ideas" among the citizenry, between them and their representatives, or within the legislative body itself. At each of these levels, communication is a double-edged sword. It is both part of the political problem Madison identifies and an integral part of the republican solution he presents. Communication is the means by which a majority faction forms and unites, but it is also the vehicle necessary to collect, form and refine the will of the society. Attention to the dynamics of communicative activity makes possible both a public check on majority tyranny and the formation of a positive agency that directs governmental measures.

COMMUNICATION AND THE EXTENT OF TERRITORY

Though Madison criticizes theoretic politicians who disregard the nature of man and attempt to give all citizens the same opinions, passions, and interests (e.g., Rousseau), this does not mean that he rejects the idea of forming "a people" united by common principles and a common purpose. In fact, he believed that such a task requires the leg-islator to recognize and confront the concrete realities of the causes of human differences and distinctions. Given the nature of man, citizens who possess the free exercise of their faculties will naturally form dif-ferent opinions, be led by different passions, and assume diverse inter-ests—either real or supposed. These differences unavoidably lead to the formation of distinct groups or parties in political societies. The art of politics, Madison argues, is to make the different parties and interests checks and balances to each other.[12] However, he emphati-cally declares that this should not be construed to mean that artificial parties should be created or even that natural parties should be en-couraged. Artificial parties are presumably those based on personal attachments, while natural parties occur as a result of the diverse fac-ulties of mankind. As far as possible and consistent with free govern-ment, the republican legislator will prevent the existence of parties or accommodate their views.[13] The object is to diminish prejudices and artificial distinctions and to isolate the real but partial interests that prevent or disturb a general coalition of opinion.[14] The diminution of prejudice and supposed interest is contrary to a society constructed on the British model, wherein two major parties are encouraged in their incessant contest for political power. Such a system fails to isolate par-tial interests; instead it promotes attachment to one party or the other through patronage, bribery and corruption. Isolation of the local and partial interests of society can be accomplished only in a polity that encompasses a "multiplicity of interests," as distinct from a party sys-tem grounded in two major conflicting economic and social interests. The contribution that a multiplicity of interests and sects makes to republican government is the establishment of the circumstance neces-sary to achieve "equilibrium in the interests & passions of the Soci-ety."[15] Madison does not conceive of this multiplicity of interests and parties as an end in itself. Its purpose is to place obstacles in the path of those groups which are actuated merely by interest and passion, and thus themselves are impediments to the discovery of the "comprehen-sive interests"[16] of the society.

In *Federalist* 14 Madison continues his discussion of the benefits of the extensive republic. Here he focuses not on the divisive effects of a large territory, but on the chords of blood and affection that unite Americans across the broad swath of republican land. They have mingled and shed their blood in defense of freedom and the sacred rights of humanity. They are "knit together . . . by so many cords of affection," forming one family that has built and inhabits a great and respectable empire. They have a shared past and triumph in governing themselves: they are "mutual guardians of their mutual happiness." They have, in a word, consecrated their union.

Madison's critique in the tenth *Federalist* was aimed at direct democracies and small republics because they make it too easy for majority factions to form. In the forteenth essay he doubles back and adds another concern: that the republic is not too large. The proper sphere of the union, he argues, must be "practicable."[17] In other words, it must not be so *large* that it cannot practically accomplish its ends by republican means. If the society is too large, communication across the territory is stymied and the public voice is silenced. Madison favors neither the facile formation of majorities nor the silencing of the public voice. Instead, his aim is to establish a territory of "a mean extent," in which there are checks on communication as well as the development of a rational and effectual public voice. Contrary to the predominant interpretation of his theory of the extended republic, Madison's preoccupation with the issue of territorial size is not for the sole purpose of preventing the formation of a factious majority. *It is also to establish the conditions in which a certain kind of majority can feasibly form.* This is a theme he suggests in *The Federalist* and then underscores in the "Party Press Essays" and the "Notes on Government" a few years later.

When public opinion is formed and fixed, Madison argues, "it must be obeyed by the government;" when it is not fixed, "it may be influenced by the government."[18] The challenge, as Madison conceptualized it, was to establish representation in a territory large enough to make it difficult to "counterfeit" the real opinion of the society, but sufficiently limited in its sphere to allow for its "real" opinion to be ascertained and acted upon. The formation of the "real" or nonfactious opinion of the public is encouraged by "contracting" the territorial limits in order to promote communication among the citizenry. In the Party Press Essay "Public Opinion" Madison states: "Whatever facilitates a general intercourse of sentiments, as good roads, domestic commerce, a free press, and particularly a *circulation of newspapers through the entire body of the people,* and *Representatives going from, and returning among every part of them,* is equivalent to a contraction of territorial limits, and is favorable to liberty, where these may be too extensive."[19]

COMMUNICATION AND REPRESENTATION

Madison rejects the Rousseauian view that the will of the society is best formed by isolating each citizen in the formation of his opinions, thereby protecting him against the contagion that results from a communication with others. He rejects the notion that public opinion draws its moral force from the judgments of the conscience made in splendid isolation. Rather, his aim is to encourage the kind of communicative activity that results in the exchange of ideas and the deliberation about means to republican ends. His object is to encourage a commerce of ideas at the level of government and throughout "the entire body of the people."[20] Unlike Rousseau, who rejected the principle of representation, Madison envisioned using a scheme of representation to facilitate a general intercommunication of sentiments and views throughout the land. Representatives traveling to and from the capital facilitate the exchange of ideas at the seat of government, between the representative and his constituents, and between his constituents and those from other parts of the country. This multifaceted and dynamic process of communication fosters the formation of a real, enlarged, and fixed opinion within the society.[21]

However, Madison also recognized certain potential problems associated with the principle of representation. "The advantage enjoyed by the public bodies in the light struck out by the collision of arguments," he said,

> is but too often overbalanced by the heat of the proceeding from the same source. Many other sources of involuntary error might be added. It is no reflection on Congs. to admit for one, the united voice of the place, where they may happen to deliberate. Nothing is more contagious than opinion, especially on questions, which being susceptible of very different glosses, beget in the mind a distrust of itself. It is extremely difficult also to avoid confounding the local with the public opinion, and to withhold the respect due to the latter, from the fallacious specimens exhibited by the former.[22]

Madison's political realism is reflected in his assessment of what we would today in the United States call "Beltway Politics." The heat of capital politics too often engulfs the members of the national legislature and skews their judgment. This danger is especially acute in members whose mental abilities and/or confidence in themselves are of a weaker nature. The tendency for human beings to distrust their own judgment when they are surrounded by a united opinion results from the contagious force of opinion. In numerous assemblies the danger is particularly great, Madison argues, since they are marked by the confusion and immoderation that accompanies the gathering of a multitude. Under such conditions, it is impossible "to secure the benefits of free consultation and discussion . . . [for] in all very numerous assemblies, of whatever characters composed, passion never fails to wrest the scepter from reason."[23]

Although Madison is acutely aware of the aggravating effects of seductive rhetoric within legislative chambers, he also claims that there is an "advantage enjoyed by public bodies struck out by the collision of arguments." We know from the tenth *Federalist* that Madison considers the principle of representation part of the republican solution to the problem of majority faction. We also know that politicians cannot be depended on to exercise reason and restraint. In order to derive the benefit of the "full effect" of representation, Madison tells us in *Federalist* 63, it must be combined with an extensive territory.[24] Those who argue that the ancients were unaware or did not incorporate the idea of representation in classical polities (Rousseau again) are mistaken, according to Madison. In *Federalist* 63 Madison offers a number of examples of the institution of popularly elected representative assemblies and councils in classical Greece and Rome.[25] What the ancients failed to do was exclude the people from direct participation in government, and they did not combine the principle of representation with territorial extension. The establishment of representation in a small polity does not sufficiently distance the representatives from popular passions and partial interests; even with the existence of a senate to check the representative assemblies of the people, the will of the latter tends ultimately to be irresistible.[26] Conversely, the extension of the territory considered by itself achieves the inclusion of a multiplicity of interests and sects within the society, thereby making factious combinations of the majority improbable, but lacks a vehicle for the political formation and expression of the will of the society. The purpose of "the great principle of representation" is not simply to exclude the direct participation of the people; it also functions as the "great mechanical power in government, by the simple agency of which the will of the largest political body may be concentered and its force directed to any object which the public good requires."[27] Representation is the political vehicle for the collection and expression of the will of the society. Having demonstrated the negative effects of the extensive territory on communication in the tenth *Federalist,* Madison can then show in the fourteenth essay how representation in a large territory encourages communicative activity in the nation. Improvements in transportation and communication under the new government will facilitate intercourse throughout the society,[28] thereby adding to the extent of territory that may be considered practicable for the formation of a majority whose actuating purpose is neither unjust nor dishonorable.

The purpose of combining the principle of representation and an extensive territory is to distance the representatives from the influence of the passions and interests within the society; the purpose of limiting the territory to a practicable sphere is to keep the representatives dependent on the will of the society. This may seem paradoxical. However, if the society is broken into a plethora of isolated interests and parties, it is unlikely that a majority of the representatives will be influenced or pressured by any one particular faction. Simultaneously, through frequent elections, separation of powers, and the force of public opinion, the representatives are kept dependent on the will of the people.

SEPARATION OF POWERS AND RESPONSIBILITY

In ancient democracies, Madison notes, popular assemblies were often unduly influenced by a single orator.[29] Despite the various "Checks devised in Democracies marking self-distrust,"[30] such as age requirements and moral examinations prior to being permitted to take part in public affairs, and ostracism, petalism, and death for orators who unsuccessfully advance proposed changes in the law, these attempts to instill in politicians a due responsibility to the public were often no match for the cunning and sophistry of a particularly skilled orator. Rejecting the direct checks on individuals in government that the ancients utilized (with the exception of the direct check of impeachment), Madison proposes instead the modern conception of separation of powers devised by Montesquieu. Separation of powers is intended as a guard against government tyrannizing over the people as well as a check on a majority faction working its wiles via the legislative representatives.

While Madison agreed with Montesquieu that the separation of powers is an effective device to prevent tyranny, he did not place the same high degree of dependence on the doctrine that Montesquieu did. For Madison, separation of powers and checks and balances are not the chief means of security and liberty for a free people; they are but "auxiliary precautions." The primary control on government is a dependence on the will and reason of the society.[31] In the Party Press Essay "British Government" Madison argues that, contrary to what is often believed, the chief cause of stability and liberty (to the extent it exists) in the British system of government is not separation of powers but the force of public opinion. Separation of powers assists in the promotion of a due "responsibility" of government officials to the constitution and the community, i.e., to public opinion. The "great principle of responsibility" is jeopardized when the powers of government are not effectively divided, and it is sacrificed when the powers are mixed.[32] The purpose of the separation of powers in Madisonian theory is both a defensive invention to prevent government tyranny and a prudential contrivance to promote a "chain of dependence" on the public.[33] In the first Congress of the United States Madison spent considerable time on the floor of the House of Representatives arguing against the proposal to combine the Senate with the Executive in the power of removal of officials from the executive branch. Such a mixture of the powers of government violates the principle of separation of powers, he said, for it invites influence and corruption and negates the intended effect of providing for responsibility to the community.

In Madison's scheme representatives are responsible to public opinion when it is a settled opinion throughout the community. We are reminded, however, that the extensive size of the territory and large population has made it difficult for the citizens to communicate and discover a common opinion that might become a settled view. The formation of public opinion must have an impetus outside of government if Madison's scheme is not to depend solely on the good works of enlightened statesmen. In addition to the role of commuting representatives, Madison identifies and emphasizes the role of the print media in providing an equivalent to the contraction of the territorial boundaries. The "peculiar distance" of the federal capital from the great body of the people, and the "peculiar difficulty" in circulating knowledge of the proceedings of the federal government to the people, makes the freedom of the press of particular importance in the extended republic of America. In our situation, he argues, the press "alone can give efficacy to [the federal government's] responsibility to its constituents."[34]

THE COMMERCE OF IDEAS AND CULTIVATION OF MIND AND CHARACTER

The critical importance Madison attaches to the role of a free press is indicative of the singular place he envisions for the natural aristocracy in a free society—a role at least as significant, perhaps even more so, as that of the people's official representatives. "If we are to take for the criterion of truth the majority of suffrages," Madison wrote in early 1790, "they ought to be gathered from those philosophic and patriotic citizens who cultivate their reason, apart from the scenes which distract its operations, and expose it to the influence of the passions."[35] Indeed, "it is the duty. . . of intelligent and faithful citizens to discuss and promulgate [political information and ideas] freely" in order to control government by the "censorship of public opinion" and "according to the rules of the Constitution."[36] A circulating print media serves as the vehicle for the communication of the ideas of the educated and patriotic members of society to the people at large. They are charged with the role of civic educators in Madison's republic, and their contribution to the common benefit of the community is no less necessary than that of the husbandman or the manufacturer. The "literati," Madison declares,

> are the cultivators of the human mind—the manufacturers of useful knowledge—the agents of the commerce of ideas—the censors of public manners—the teachers of the arts of life and the means of happiness.[37]

The indispensable role Madison assigns the enlightened members of society clearly demonstrates that he was no adherent of the notion that private ambition is an effective substitute for better minds in a republican society. In fact, he looks to the most thoughtful and virtuous citizens to keep the people informed about political activity at the seat of government, to prompt them, when necessary, to censure governmental measures, and in general to instruct the citizenry in the morals and manners of republicanism.

THE REIGN OF PUBLIC OPINION

The rise of circulating newspapers in the eighteenth century and the concomitant ability of the intelligentsia to communicate their ideas to a large audience led a number of political thinkers, particularly in France, to declare the advent of a new politics grounded in the authority of public opinion.[38] Public opinion, they proclaimed, is a force that even kings must bow before and is ignored by government only at great peril. In a word, public opinion is "Queen of the World." According to this eighteenth century conception, public opinion is not a mere aggregate of popular sentiments or interests. Rather, it is the result of a process of educational refinement that, "by reason, time, and an universal conformity of sentiments" renders it respectable and sacred.[39] Public opinion results over time from the influence of the enlightened men on the views of the people. It is the settled view of the community on which government depends for its direction. Accordingly, public opinion is both acted upon as well as itself an active political agent. This eighteenth century conception of public opinion must be distinguished from the current one, which conceives of public opinion as a numerical snapshot of public views, capable of being captured in political polling data on any given day.

Madison was well versed in the French literature on the politics of public opinion, and he agreed with its basic tenets. He also added to it. Unlike the French authors who claimed that public opinion was a modern invention, Madison argued that it was in fact a phenomenon known to the ancient philosopher Aristotle.[40] Nonetheless, in the absence of the invention of the printing press and the circulation of the printed word, the transmission of opinion in ancient times was essentially restricted to oral communication and thus to a small area. In the eighteenth century, the rise of the circulation press made communication over a large territory possible. This changed the face of politics in modern times. On the one hand, an extensive territory serves as an obstacle to the communication of opinions, particularly those motivated by passion or interest and which beget distrust. On the other hand, other factors can be encouraged which foster a genuine "commerce of ideas" throughout the citizenry of a large nation. In particular, Madison envisioned newspapers serving as vehicles for the circulation of the ideas of the literati to the people, effecting a refinement and enlargement of the public views and the emergence of an enlightened public opinion. Madison's analysis of political communication in a large republic was his unique and momentous insight into the age-old problem of popular government. It was a discovery that he alone made, though in characteristic fashion, he understated his personal claim. Instead, he claimed for America the glory to have invented "the government for which philosophy has been searching, and humanity been sighing, from the most remote ages."[41] The discovery of the means to make self-government a political reality was the accomplishment of America and her people.

"Public Opinion sets bounds to every government, and is the real sovereign in every free one," Madison proclaimed in 1791.[42] All political power is grounded in public opinion; it is the source of stability in every government and the primary basis for the security of all rights.[43] The central role that public opinion plays in Madison's political theory of republicanism can be seen from the period of *The Federalist* throughout his post-presidential years. In *Federalist* 49 he remarks that "all governments rest on opinion." He returned to this theme many times throughout the 1790s, and in 1822 he summarized his reasons for the prominent place he had long given public opinion: "In a Government of opinion, like ours, the only effectual guard must be found in the soundness and stability of the general opinion."[44]

Madison's solution to the control of factions does involve political ballasts and balances, but his political theory is nonetheless chiefly concerned with achieving a sound public opinion that will serve republican ends. This is all through his writings. Madison's pronouncement in *Federalist* 51 that "a dependence on the people" is the "primary control on government" is not empty political rhetoric, though it has often been treated as such. Dependence on the people is, for Madison, dependence on public opinion, which, when properly formed, is tantamount to "the reason of the public" that controls government and ought to sit in judgment on its measures.[45] He believed that the dependence of the government on the will and reason of the public was essential if the American polity was to be considered not merely in form but also in "aspect" and character "strictly republican." No other kind of government, he said, is reconcilable with the principles of the American Revolution or "with that honorable determination which animates every votary of freedom to rest all our political experiments on the capacity of mankind for self-government."[46]

The fundamental disagreement between the Republicans and the Federalists of the 1790s stemmed from their divergent conceptions of republican government and the authority of public opinion. Madison led the Republican charge to preserve for public opinion its sovereign and rightful place in the constitutional and the ordinary operations of free government. The Federalist Party, he claimed, had "debauched themselves into a persuasion that mankind are incapable of governing themselves," and so appealed "less to the reason of the many than to their weaknesses." The Republicans, on the other hand, took offense "at every public measure that does not appeal to the understanding and to the general interest of the community, or that is not strictly conformable to the principles, and conducive to the preservation of republican government."[47] Believing that the people cannot be trusted, the Federalists preached confidence in and obedience to an enlightened government. By contrast, Madison said, Republicans believe that "the people ought to be enlightened, to be awakened, to be united, [and] that after establishing a government they should watch over it as well as obey it."

Madison conceived of public opinion as the result of a dynamic educative process of refinement and enlargement of the views of the citizenry. This process involves civic education by the literati and the representatives. It also includes the expression of opinion and the practice of self-government at the local level, the citizens' dedication to the principles of the Constitution and the Bill of Rights, and the influence of moral principles on the sense of duty to one's fellow citizens.

The federal character of the union, Madison argues, is an essential component of the formation and collection of the public voice. Without a due degree of power at the state and local levels of governments, the extent of the territory would make it impossible for the people to communicate effectively and convey a united voice by which to control and direct the measures of government.[48] Conversely, "the most arbitrary government is controuled where the public opinion is fixed."[49] Thus, when Madison perceived a Federalist threat to the rightful authority of the states, he exhorted citizens to support the federal nature of the union and to maintain power within its proper boundaries.[50] In 1792 he called upon Americans to dedicate themselves, "with a holy zeal," to their constitutional "scriptures." As social compacts, constitutions are superior to all other forms of political obligations. They are in fact, "sacred" trusts, "bound on the conscience by the religious sanctions of an oath."[51] Deriving their moral force from "the only earthly source of authority," they represent the most fundamental expression of the sovereignty of the people and of public opinion. "As metes and bounds of government, they transcend all other landmarks, because every public usurpation is an encroachment on the private right, not of one, but of all."

It is commonly known that when Madison introduced the Bill of Rights in the first Congress under the new Constitution, he did so with some reluctance. His concern was that the amendments specifying civil liberties might be construed as a limitation on freedom, that they might be erroneously understood to mean that anything not listed was therefore to be considered within the province of government. He insisted many times over that the United States Constitution was one in which the people gave to government certain enumerated powers, not vice versa. Still, the opponents of the new Constitution had expressed serious reservations about whether the proposed plan would effectually limit the powers of government. In 1788 Madison pledged his support for a Bill of Rights. His support was a tactical move to win ratification of the Constitution without calling a second convention. But he also had another motive: a bill of rights would contribute to establishing the principles of free government not merely on paper, but in the minds and hearts of the American citizens. "In proportion as government is influenced by opinion," he wrote, "it must be so, by whatever influences opinion. This decides the question concerning a *Constitutional Declaration of Rights*, which requires an influence on government, by becoming part of the public opinion."[52]

Among a republican people, a bill of rights has the effect of educating public opinion on the fundamental principles of free government. As respect for these rights becomes incorporated in public opinion, public opinion defines and limits the demands of the majority. Over time, a bill of rights acts as a kind of republican schoolmaster, serving as a civic lexicon by which the people teach themselves the grammar and meaning of freedom. A bill of rights serves to enlist the prejudices of the society on the side of republican reason; the more ancient the lineage of the constitutional declaration, the more influence it exerts on the minds and hearts of the populace. As an expression of the political principles and moral sentiments of the society, a bill of rights is a manifestation of how ethical motives can and do influence the formation of majority opinion. Majority opinion does not form in a vacuum; it is constantly in the process of taking shape within a sphere of settled public opinion that is older and greater than itself. As Madison, and later Tocqueville, so well understood, public opinion is an all-encompassing moral atmosphere that permeates the very souls of the people over whom it reigns. The formative processes of public opinion are the means by which the mind and manners of the citizenry can be educated and their views transformed into a united opinion consistent with the requirements of republican justice.

Madison believed that the great experiment in constitutional government originated in the United States and was a "revolution" no less great than that for which Americans fought and died at Lexington and Saratoga. Marking a new and triumphant epoch in the political practice of the world, it established "the legitimate authority of the people" as the only just basis of government. In a genuine republic, the people's sovereign authority is ongoing and continuous, manifested in the expression of public opinion. Once formed and settled, the voice of the majority is synonymous with public opinion.[53] As the expression of sovereignty, however, majority opinion is itself bound by the fundamental principles of right that justify its power.[54] Its authority derives from a sacred trust that imparts not only the right of a people to govern themselves, but their obligation to govern according to the principles that legitimate their rule. These principles are embedded in the constitutional charters they themselves make and which represent the highest expression of the sovereignty of public opinion.

As governmental power is to be dependent on the will of the society, the will of the society must be dependent on the "reason of the society."[55] Just as representatives are responsible to public opinion, the majority possesses a moral and constitutional responsibility to the minority.[56] "Every good citizen," Madison explains, must be "a centinel over the rights of the people."[57] The trespass on individual rights is in fact an encroachment on the rights of all. The end of government "is to protect property of every sort," which includes the common understanding of property as well as "that which lies in the various rights of individuals." In the second meaning—"its larger and juster meaning"—property "embraces every thing to which a man may attach a value and have a right, and *which leaves to every one else the like advantage.*"[58] In this sense, human beings possess a property in their rights, that is, in the free use of their faculties and in "the enjoyment and communication of their opinions," in which they have at least an equal if not more valuable property.

The most sacred of all property, Madison asserts, is conscience. The freedom of the mind to form opinions is a natural and unalienable right, all other rights of property being derivative and dependent on positive law. Every member of a republican society owes "a debt of protection" to every other member in the free exercise of his faculties. This is required "by the very nature and original conditions of the social pact" to which "the public faith is pledged."[59] In other words, every republican citizen possesses a positive obligation to respect the rights of his fellow citizens, a duty that is concomitant to his own assertion of liberties. "That alone is a just government," Madison declared, "which *impartially* secures to every man, whatever is his *own.*"

The men who fought and died in the American revolution so that a new land of self-governing citizens might become a political reality and a harbinger to the world, had not the fortune to receive the benefits accrued by their generation's mutual pledge of indebtedness. They knew they might not. In the knowledge that they might not live to share in the dream of America, they gave to their fellow citizens, and to all succeeding generations of Americans, the gift of freedom outright. To them and the irredeemable sacrifice they made for us, we are forever indebted.

ROBERT FROST'S MADISON

When Robert Frost delivered his talk to the graduating class of Sarah Lawrence College in 1956, he chose as his themes freedom and self-government. "I never have valued any liberty conferred on me particularly," he remarked. "I value myself on the liberties I take, and I have learned to appreciate the word 'unscrupulous.'"[60] There is a certain measure of unscrupulousness in bending a story one is telling, in not being a "stickler at trifles." I do not mean you should lie, Frost said, that is corruption, but you should leave out what you don't want to say. Like Toynbee "when he writes about the history of the world . . . you know, he leaves Vermont out—unscrupulous."

Frost believed that we should especially be unscrupulous in our thinking. Too much uncertainty is just so much timidity. There are some questions that we pick up in college or along the way, which are worth picking up again and again the rest of our lives. We should treat them like knitting that is kept to pick up at odd moments. We should pick them up not in a spirit of uncertainty and timidity, but to knit about, "to have ideas about." I don't mean just to opinionate about, Frost said. "Opinion is just a pro and con, having your nose counted." No, I mean things that you "have ideas about. That's something more."

Frost mused that one of the things he had been knitting about lately was this thing called "the dream." It gets "thrown in my face every little while, and always by somebody who thinks the dream has not come true." When I "pick it up," he said

> I wonder what the dream is, or why. And the next time I pick it up, I wonder who dreamed it. Did Tom Paine dream it? Did Thomas Jefferson dream it: did George Washington dream it? Gouverneur Morris?

"Lately I've decided," Frost told his audience, that "the best dreamer of it was Madison." Frost said he had been reading *The Federalist Papers* recently and wondered if Madison's dream was a dream for us today, and for future generations, or whether it was something that had gone by. "Can we treat the Constitution as if it were something gone by? "Can we interpret it out of existence?" he asked. Does it mean something different every day until it wouldn't mean anything at all to Madison?

In the course of his address at Sarah Lawrence College Frost recited two of his favorite poems, "The Gift Outright" and "Birches." The first poem, he tells us, is about the American Revolution; the second poem we have to interpret for ourselves. Having grown up in the Adirondacks on Lake Champlain, I feel I know the places Frost is talking about. I know the tempo and the accents of rural life that he is remembering from his youth. I know how the white birches are like nature's lights on a country road after dark. And I know what happens to birches in a New England ice storm.

In 1998 a devastating ice storm hit New England. My family lived through the storm, day after day without electricity, without heat, without news from the rest of America. All life seemed to stop and bow down before the enormous power. The birches knelt to earth under the hoary weight, prostrating themselves like novitiates at evensong. Later the sound came . . . not like any that could be described in earthly terms, my mother said. In Frost's language, with the returning sun the trees shed their "crystal shells. . . . Such heaps of broken glass to sweep away[,] You'd think the inner dome of heaven had fallen." Many of the birches, "dragged to the withered bracken by the load," "never right[ed] themselves." Still today in the Adirondacks, you may see them bent down on hands and knees, their trunks arching and their leaves trailing in the woods, "like girls . . . that throw their hair before them over their heads to dry in the sun."

"I should prefer to have some boy bend" the birches and ride them down and take the stiffness out, Frost wrote. A boy who

learned all there was
To learn about not launching out too soon
And so not carrying the tree away
Clear to the ground.
He always kept his poise
To the top branches, climbing carefully
With the same pains you use to fill a cup
Up to the brim, and even above the brim.
Then he flung outward, feet first, with a swish,
Kicking his way down through the air to the ground.

"So was I once myself a swinger of birches," Frost admitted. "And so I dream of going back to be." I think of climbing "black branches up a snow-white trunk *toward* heaven, till the tree could bear no more, but dipped its top and set me down again," he wrote.

You see, "the thing is, the measure," Frost told his audience.

The boy who swung on birches knew just how far he could bend the tree until it could bear no more. He was unscrupulous in his climb up. But he also knew the measure. He knew not to launch out too soon and bring the tree to its knees, but to let it dip and set him down again.

Madison's dream, like the New England boy's, was a dream of ascent into freedom. It was a dream not so much of liberty conferred as in liberties to be taken. He challenged Americans to a new and more noble course, to climb to the top with poise, and then to launch outward feet first, with a swish. He encouraged Americans to use their freedom to form ideas, not just to have opinions pro or con, but to craft ideas and knit them into the broadcloth of the public mind. Amongst his peers, Madison was indeed an unscrupulous democrat. But he always knew the measure.

"Measure always reassures me," Frost said. "Now I know, I think I know, as of today—what Madison's dream was. It was just a dream of a new land to fulfill with people in self-control. In self-control. That is all through his thinking." Madison's "dream was to occupy the land with character—that is another way to put it—to occupy a new land with character." Frost saw that there was perhaps a certain measure of American unscrupulousness in bending and shaping the land to our character. He admired it. Because, the thing is, the measure.

NOTES

1. Mark Van Doren, "The American Poet," *Atlantic Monthly*, June 1951.

2. Joshua Miller, "The Ghostly Body Politic: The Federalist Papers and Popular Sovereignty," *Political Theory*, 16:1 (Feb. 1988), 99–119.

3. See Robert A. Dahl, *A Preface to Democratic Theory* (Chicago: University of Chicago Press, 1956).

4. Gordon S. Wood, *The Creation of the American Republic 1776–1787* (Chapel Hill, NC: University of North Carolina Press, 1998), 562.

5. Alexander Hamilton, James Madison and John Jay, *The Federalist Papers*, ed. Clinton Rossiter (New York: New American Library, 1961), FP #50:319 (Hereafter cited as FP; all further references are to this edition).

6. See *FP* #10:81.

7. *FP* #10:81. See also Robert A. Rutland, et al., eds., *The Papers of James Madison*, 17 vols. (Chicago: University of Chicago Press, 1962–91), 10:213 (hereafter cited as *PJM*).

8. *FP* #49:315.

9. *FP* #10:53.

10. This is the problem Madison is virtually silent about in the pages of *The Federalist*, perhaps because it was not the appropriate venue for such a discussion, or perhaps because he did not believe that the generation of Americans who fought the Revolution were in particular need of a civics lesson on the principles of justice or the meaning of honor (though he does proffer a lesson directed at southerners on the unnatural institution of slavery in the 54th essay). Certainly, he continues throughout his life to be

concerned about the effect of the institution of slavery on American character—on both what it does to slaves as well as to freemen. He also frets about the future of America when the majority of citizens become landless, turning from agricultural pursuits to manufacturing.

11. *FP* #63:384.

12. *PJM* 14:198; "Notes on Government," *PJM* 14:160.

13. *PJM* 14:197–98.

14. *PJM* 14:372.

15. "Notes on Government," PJM 14:158.

16. *FP* #62:379. In *Federalist* 51 Madison asserts that if a majority is united by a common interest, the rights of the minority will be insecure. Nonetheless, in *Federalist* 14, 46, 52, and 58, he argues for the discovery of common interest in the society. See *FP* pp. 99, 297, 327, 357.

17. See the excellent discussion of Madison''s conception of "the practicable sphere" of a republic by Lance Banning in *The Sacred Fire of Liberty: James Madison and the Founding of the Federal Republic* (Ithaca, NY: Cornell University Press, 1995), 208–14. Banning argues that Madison's case for limiting territorial extension was not because of a concern for size, but because of a desire to achieve the "appropriate relationship between the people and their rulers" (210). I agree completely with this claim by Banning, and I certainly believe that the principle of federalism is a critical part of how Madison intended to achieve the "mean extent" and "practical" republican sphere. However, I would not place such singular emphasis on the federal principle as Banning does; rather, I interpret Madison's case for the practical sphere to be driven by his conception of the conditions necessary to achieve the kind of communicative activity that leads to the proper formation of public opinion and to the dependence of government on it. Federalism is a means that contributes to this end, as are a number of other factors, which together establish a milieu in which political communication supports and promotes the principles of republican government by republican means.

18. "Public Opinion," *PJM* 14:170; "Notes on Government," *PJM* 14:161.

19. *PJM* 14:170. Cf. *FP* #14:102–3.

20. "Public Opinion," *PJM* 14:170.

21. See "Public Opinion," *PJM* 14:170.

22. Madison to Benjamin Rush, 7 March 1790, *PJM* 13:93–94.

23. FP #55:342.

24. *FP* #63:387.

25. See *FP* #63:385–389.

26. *FP #* 63:386–389.

27. *FP* #14:100–101.

28. *FP* #14:102–3

29. See *FP* #58:360; "Notes of Government," *PJM* 14:165–66.

30. "Notes on Government," *PJM* 14:165–66.

31. *FP* #49:317; FP #50:319; FP #51:322–25.

32. See *PJM* 12:237.

33. See *PJM* 12:256, 236-37.

34. Marvin Meyers, ed., *The Mind of the Founder: Sources of the Political Thought of James Madison* (Indianapolis: Bobbs-Merrill, 1973), 336.

35. Madison to Benjamin Rush, 7 March 1790, *PJM* 13.93.

36. Meyers, 338.

37. *PJM* 14:168.

38. See my study of the eighteenth century French concept of public opinion and its influence on Madison's theory of republicanism in "Madison and the French Enlightenment: the Authority of Public Opinion," *William and Mary Quarterly*, 3rd Series, vol. LIX, no.4, October 2002.

39. Jacques Necker, *A Treatise on the Administration of the Finances of France*, 3 vols., Thomas Mortimer, trans. (London, 1785), I:lxv–lxvi.

40. *PJM* 14:162.

41. *PJM* 14:234.

42. *PJM* 14:170.

43. *PJM* 14:192.

44. Meyers, 433.

45. *FP* #49:317.

46. *FP* #39:240.

47. *PJM* 14:371.

48. *PJM* 14:138.

49. *PJM* 14:192.

50. *PJM* 14:192.

51. *PJM* 14:191.

52. *PJM* 14:170; See also PJM 162–63; Meyers, 221.

53. Meyers, 90.

54. See *PJM* 14:192. Theoretically, the majority relinquishes its moral and constitutional authority if it exercises its power licentiously.

55. *PJM* 14:207. See also *PJM* 14:234; *FP* #49:317; *FP* #50:319; *FP* #51:325.

56. Meyers, 504.

57. *PJM* 14:179.

58. *PJM* 14:266.

59. *PJM* 14:287.

60. Robert Frost, "A Talk for Students" (New York: Fund for the Republic, 1956). The original version of Frost's commencement address, overscored with revisions by the Fund for the Republic, can be found at Princeton University Library.

5

Is the Purpose of Civic Education to Transmit or Transform the American Regime?

JOHN FONTE

INTRODUCTION

THE MAJOR QUESTION facing America in the twenty-first century is this: Will the American regime—that is to say, American constitutional democracy and the American way of life—be *transmitted* to future generations of Americans or will it be *transformed* into something radically different? I am using "regime" in the traditional Aristotelian sense to include both the state and civil society; that is, the institutions, laws, and constitution on the one hand and the culture, mores, and way of life on the other hand.

For more than thirty years we have witnessed a great conflict between those who wish to *transmit* American citizenship, as it has been traditionally understood, and those who wish to *transform* it. This essay will address this conflict and examine what it means for American democracy.

Citizenship education in America's liberal democracy is ultimately about what we value as Americans—what we wish to affirm. It is about what Alexis de Tocqueville, called the "notions and sentiments of a people." In American schools (both public and private) and civic institutions (such as museums, associations, etc.) education for citizenship in our liberal democracy rests on a foundation of principles, values, concepts, and symbols that are both empirical or descriptive (what is) and normative (what ought to be). Nevertheless, in the final analysis, civic education is, by definition, normative; it is concerned with developing "good citizens," however that term is defined.

This essay is divided into three parts. The first part outlines the traditional approach to American citizenship and civic education. The ultimate goal of the traditional approach is to preserve, improve, and transmit the American regime to future generations of Americans. The first section examines the views of the American Founders and Abraham Lincoln, who consciously modeled his political theories on the Founding. The second section explores neo-traditionalist thinking during the past several decades.

The third section examines the challenge to the traditional framework of American citizenship that has developed during the last few decades. The challenge to the traditional framework of civic education is a root and branch attack on the basic principles of the American regime. What is at stake in this conflict is the survival of the American liberal democratic regime. Will it be perpetuated, improved, and transmitted to future generations or will it be transformed into a different type of regime, in effect, a counter-regime?

I. THE TRADITIONAL APPROACH OF THE FOUNDERS AND LINCOLN

The Philosophical Foundation of the American Regime
The second paragraph of the Declaration of Independence states the fundamental principles of the American political system with utmost clarity. First, "Governments are instituted among men" to "secure" unalienable natural "rights" and, second, these governments derive "their just powers from the consent of the governed." Hence, "natural rights" and "consent of the governed" are the twin pillars of the American political order.

The reference to "natural rights" in the Declaration means that governments cannot violate "unalienable rights;" governmental power, therefore, should be limited. Moreover, as the Declaration puts it, individuals are created equal and thus possess equal natural rights. The reference to "consent" in the Declaration emphasizes the principle of republicanism, democracy, or self-government. Governments are based on consent of the governed. In other words, a self-identified "people" has the right to rule themselves.

As University of Virginia political scientist James W. Ceaser explains, the American regime is a "fusion of two governmental principles." One of these principles is sometimes called "constitutionalism" and sometimes called "liberalism." This principle emphasizes the protection of individual rights and limited government. The other principle is sometimes called "republicanism" or more usually called "democracy." This principle focuses on the "interests of the people as a

whole (or the majority), not the interests of a select or designated minority."[1] From the fusion of these two principles of constitutionalism
(liberalism) and republicanism (democracy) comes the concept of constitutional democracy or liberal democracy. Thus, American liberal democracy means that self-government (democracy) is limited by natural rights that no government can violate.

While there are legitimate arguments over the different philosophical and moral influences on the American regime, there can be no doubt
that the American republic is based on such concepts as "the laws of
nature and nature's God," "self-evident truths," and "unalienable
rights" that are "endowed" by a "Creator." It is a regime built on universal moral principles and eternal truths, on the concept that there is
a natural moral order to the universe. Thus, it is a regime connected to
both the Enlightenment and the Judeo-Christian moral order—however many qualifications, tensions, and nuances might be attached to
those connections.

The regime of the American Founding rejected relativism and his-
toricism. That is to say, for the founders the "laws of nature and nature's
God" were truths applicable to the men and women of every period of
the historical past, and in the future. They were not considered to be
simply the perspective of eighteenth century "white male American
colonials." Thus, "unalienable rights" derive from a transcendent moral
order. These rights are natural to man; they are not artificial or "socially constructed." They are not artifacts of human will, but are inherent in the nature of man.

A Realistic View of Human Nature

Complementing their view of natural law and natural rights is the
Founders' concept of human nature, which is central to understanding
the philosophical basis of the American regime. Clearly, for the
Founders any successful political system would have to be built on principles consistent with human nature. An eminent historian of Eighteenth Century America, Bernard Bailyn, has noted that a realistic conception of human nature was widely held by almost all the leading
Americans of the day that included both the supporters (George Washington, Alexander Hamilton, James Madison) and the opponents
(Patrick Henry, George Mason, Richard Henry Lee) of the Federal
Constitution of 1787: "the antifederalists, no less than the federalists,
had a thoroughly realistic sense of human nature, and never deluded
themselves that any people could be entirely virtuous or that any political population could be principally animated by public spirit."[2]

This "realistic" view of human nature is expressed most significantly in *The Federalist Papers*, the eighty-five essays written by James Madison, Alexander Hamilton, and John Jay that argued for the ratification of the U.S. Constitution. Thomas Jefferson wrote James Madison that *The Federalist Papers* were, "in my opinion, the best commentary on the principles of government which ever was written."³ While George Washington wrote Alexander Hamilton, "that work [*The Federalist Papers*] will merit the notice of posterity because in it are candidly and ably discussed the principles of freedom and topics of government—which will be always interesting to mankind so long as they shall be connected to civil society."⁴

In *The Federalist Papers* James Madison explained that the entire edifice of the American regime was built on a realistic conception of human nature. In *Federalist 51* he wrote:

> Ambition must be made to counteract ambition. . . . It may be a reflection on human nature that such devices should be necessary. But what is government itself but the greatest of all reflections on human nature? If men were angels, no government would be necessary. If angels were to govern men, neither external nor internal controls on government would be necessary. In framing a government which is to be administered by men over men, the great difficulty lies in this: you must first enable the government to control the governed; and in the next place oblige it to control itself.⁵

In *Federalist 55*, Madison declared: "As there is a degree of depravity in mankind which requires a certain degree of circumspection and distrust so there are other qualities in human nature which justify a certain position of esteem and confidence. Republican government presupposes the existence of these qualities in a higher degree than any other form."⁶ That is to say, human beings possess many imperfections (they are "not angels"), but they are capable of self-government if a republican regime is constituted to complement instead of clash with human nature.

What Is Needed to Sustain the American Constitutional Republic?
The Founding Fathers developed a specific institutional framework and suggested a general cultural framework that would sustain an American regime based on "natural rights" (constitutionalism) and the "consent of the governed" (republicanism) that was consistent with their view of human nature.

Institutional Framework. For the Founding Fathers the main problem was to create and, more importantly, sustain a government based on "natural rights" (constitutionalism or liberalism) and "consent of the governed" (democracy or republicanism) that was consistent with natural law and human nature. They knew from their intense reading of history that almost all previous republics had failed. These old republics had failed because of the weaknesses of human nature. Unbridled passions, disorder, lust for power, the pernicious influence of demagogues, and finally anarchy followed by tyranny were too often the historical record of republican government. Problems arouse from both the governors and the governed. Republican governments had failed to secure either good government or liberty, at least for very long.

The Federalist Papers noted that in many cases weak democratic governments unable to maintain order had been replaced by tyrannies that extinguished liberty and ignored justice. Hence, the danger was that republican regimes could become too weak (and thus inept, unable to secure liberty or establish effective government) or too strong (and thus tyrannical or unjust).

The institutional framework that the Founders created to sustain the American liberal democratic regime was, of course, the Constitution of the United States. The Constitution established a series of institutional arrangements—a system of checks and balances, separation of powers, representation, federalism, and limited government—that created a framework for a regime that was neither too strong nor too weak, that was consistent with good government and the protection of liberty.

Cultural Framework. Crucial for the Founders was the issue of how to cultivate the qualities in human nature that would sustain and strengthen republican self-government. Although *The Federalist Papers* did not explore this question, it was addressed directly and clearly in one of the most famous documents in American history, George Washington's Farewell Address of 1796.

In this address, President Washington told his fellow Americans that the cultivation of education and of religion and morality is necessary to sustain a free society. Thus, Washington writes:

> Of all the dispositions and habits which lead to political prosperity, Religion and morality are indispensable supports. In vain would that man claim the tribute of Patriotism, who should labor to subvert these great Pillars of human happiness, these firmest props of the duties of men and citizens. The mere Politician, equally with the pious man ought to respect and cherish them. A volume could not trace all their connections with private and public felicity. Let it simply be asked where is the security for property, for

reputation, for life, if the sense of religious obligation desert the oaths, which are the instruments of investigation in Courts of Justice? And let us with caution indulge the supposition, that morality can be maintained without religion. Whatever may be conceded to the influence of refined education on minds of peculiar structure, reason and experience both forbid us to expect that National morality can prevail in exclusion of religious principle. 'Tis substantially true that virtue and morality is a necessary spring of popular government. The rule indeed extends with more or less force to every species of free Government. Who that is a sincere friend to it, can look with indifference upon attempts to shake the foundation of the fabric.[7]

In the very next paragraph in the Farewell Address, Washington turned to education: "Promote then as an object of primary importance, Institutions for the general diffusion of knowledge. In proportion as the structure of a government gives force to public opinion, it is essential that public opinion should be enlightened."[8]

Years earlier in his First Annual Message to Congress Washington explicated the significance of civic education in sustaining republican self-government:

There is nothing which can better deserve your patronage, than the promotion of Science and Literature. Knowledge is, in every country, the surest basis of happiness. In one in which the measures of Government receive their impression so immediately from the sense of the Community as in ours it is proportionably essential. To the security of a free Constitution it contributes in various ways: By convincing those who are entrusted with the public administration, that every valuable end of Government is best answered by the enlightened confidence of the people: and by teaching the people themselves to know and to value their own rights; to discern and provide against invasions of them; to distinguish between oppression and the necessary exercise of lawful authority; between burdens proceeding from a disregard to their convenience and those resulting from the inevitable exigencies of Society; to discriminate the spirit of liberty from that of licentiousness—cherishing the first, avoiding the last; and uniting a speedy, but temperate vigilance against encroachments, with an inviolable respect to the Laws.[9]

Also, in the First Annual Message, Washington's rhetoric emphasized transcendent morality and eternal truths in stating that ". . . the propitious smiles of Heaven can never be expected on a nation that disregards the external rules of order and right, which heaven itself has ordained. . . ."[10]

Over and again the Founders mentioned religion, morality, and education as bulwarks necessary to sustaining republican government.

Before the Constitution was enacted, Congress in 1787 passed the Northwest Ordinance to establish policies for the broad territories northwest of the Ohio River that would later form ten new states. The Ordinance stated clearly in Article 3, that "Religion, Morality, and knowledge, being necessary to good government and the happiness of mankind, Schools and the means of education shall forever be encouraged."[11]

Civic and Moral Education
Besides George Washington, other Founders, including John Adams, Thomas Jefferson, and James Madison wrote of the importance of civic and moral education for the perpetuation of American self-government.

Thus, John Adams insisted in 1778 that all Americans, rich and poor, needed civic and moral education, if the American constitutional republic was to be sustained:

> Children should be educated and instructed in the principles of freedom. Aristotle speaks plainly to this purpose, saying: "that the institution of youth should be accommodated to that form of government under which they live; forasmuch as it makes exceedingly for the preservation of the present government, whatsoever it be. . . ." The instruction of the people and every kind of knowledge that can be of use to them in the practice of their moral duties" as men, as citizens, as Christians, and of their political and civic duties, as members of society and freemen, ought to be the care of the public, and of all who have any share in the conduct of its affairs, in a manner that never yet has been practiced in any age or nation. The education here intended is not merely that of the children of the rich and noble, but of every rank and class of people, down to the lowest and the poorest. It is not too much to say that schools for the education of all should be placed at convenient distances, and maintained at the public expense.[12]

Thomas Jefferson, of course, devoted extensive thought to civic education. He personally developed plans for public elementary education in Virginia and created the University of Virginia. As a curricular framework for good citizenship he suggested that the study of the past would warn Americans of the misuse of power and ambition; thus he recommended that students should be: "acquainted with Graecian, Roman, English, and American history" so that they will "understand the experience of other times and other nations" and, most importantly, "know ambition under every disguise it may assume, and knowing it to defeat its views."[13]

Like Jefferson, James Madison believed that education would help

Americans understand and be wary of unscrupulous ambition and un-
limited power. Thus, Madison wrote: "Learned institutions ought to
be the favorite objects with every free people. They throw that light
over the public mind which is the best security against crafty and dangerous encroachments of the public liberty. . . ."[14] Lorraine Smith Pangle
and Thomas Pangle in a seminal work on the educational ideas of the
American Founding note that Madison emphasized federalism and the
role of the states in achieving sound education goals. The Pangles contend that Madison "hoped that the American resistance to centralized
authority might be turned to the advantage of education, by encouraging a healthy and productive competition between states. . . . [He] saw
the federal system rather as a laboratory that allowed controlled experiments in fields like education, limiting the scope of failures and
encouraging friendly rivalry in reaching common goals."[15]

Thus, the Founders were wary of the weaknesses of human nature, but hopeful of strengthening what Lincoln later called "the better
angels of our nature." They promoted religion, morality, and education as a cultural core that would work in tandem with the institutional framework of "checks and balances," federalism, and limited
government to sustain a regime that fostered both effective government
and liberty.

The Founders and Lincoln Affirm the American
Unum, American Patriotism, and the American Regime

For the American constitutional republic to exist at all it was necessary
to have an "American people." The opening words of the Declaration
of Independence refer to "one people" and the beginning of the Constitution refers to "the People of the United States." The affirmation
of the American people as one people joined in a national union is
central to regime's legitimacy. This message is exemplified in the motto
chosen by Congress, *E Pluribus Unum* ("out of many one"). Thus, the
concepts of one people, the union, and unity were affirmed again and
again in the early years of the republic and are repeated in times of
crisis today.

This affirmation of the *Unum* over the *pluribus*—of unity over
diversity—is particularly true for the two giants of America's past:
George Washington and Abraham Lincoln. For both Washington and
Lincoln at crucial moments in their careers placed the concepts of one
people and national unity at the center of their Presidencies and political thought. With different words and in different contexts, Washington in his Farewell Address and Lincoln in his Gettysburg Address ar-

gued that American unity was essential to the survival of liberty and self-government in America and throughout the world.

Matthew Spalding and Patrick Garrity in their book analyzing George Washington's political thought (*A Sacred Union of Citizens*) write that "Above all, the Farewell Address directs the American regime toward Union, or unity rather than diversity. America must be something more than a league of states or regions, a collection of various groups and interests."[16] Throughout the text of the Farewell Address, Washington emphasizes American unity in both the normative (what should be) and descriptive (what is) sense.

In the Farewell Address, President Washington tells Americans that "your Union ought to be considered as a main prop to your liberty, and that the love of the one ought to endear to you the preservation of the other." Indeed Washington insists: "The Unity of Government which constitutes you one people is also now dear to you. It is justly so; for it is a Pillar in the Edifice of your real independence, the support of your tranquility at home, your peace aboard; of your safety; of your prosperity; of that very Liberty which you so highly prize."[17]

Moreover, Washington warns that because "batteries of internal and external enemies will be most constantly and actively" directed against "this truth"—"it is of infinite moment that you should properly estimate the immense value of your national Union to your collective and individual happiness; that you should cherish a cordial, habitual and immovable attachment to it; accustoming yourselves to think and speak of it as of the Palladium of your political safety and prosperity. . . ."[18]

In the next paragraph, in one of the most quoted passages of the Farewell Address Washington declares:

> Citizens by birth or choice, of a common country, that country has a right to concentrate your affections. The name AMERICAN, which belongs to you, in your national capacity, must always exalt the just pride of Patriotism, more than any appellation derived from local discriminations. With slight shades of difference, you have the same Religion, Manners, Habits, and political Principles. You have in a common cause fought and triumphed together. The independence and liberty you possess are the work of joint councils, and joint efforts; of common dangers, sufferings, and successes.[19]

One could ask: what did Washington mean by the second last sentence of this paragraph? What was he attempting to affirm? Clearly, President Washington, the author of famous letters to the Hebrew Congregation of Newport, Rhode Island and St Mary's Catholic Church of Alexandria, Virginia, knew that Americans had different religions.

He also knew that they came from different ethnic backgrounds. However, his articulation of the idea that "with slight shades of difference you have the same religion, manners, habits, and political principles" affirmed the point that Americans essentially have (and need to have) what today we would call a "common civic culture" in terms of principles, values, customs, and mores.

Central to Washington's advocacy of a national university was his desire to strengthen American unity and patriotism. He worried that sending young Americans to Europe to study could result in "ardent and susceptible minds" becoming "too strongly and too early prepossessed in favor of other political systems, before they are capable of appreciating their own."[20]

To counter this tendency, Washington emphasized the benefits to unity and a common civic culture of students from all over America studying together in a national university. He declares:

> Amongst the motives to such an Institution, the assimilation of the principles, opinions and manners of our Country men, by the common education of a portion of our Youth from every quarter, well deserves attention. The more homogeneous our Citizens can be made in these particulars, the greater will be our prospect of permanent Union; and a primary object of such a National Institution should be, the education of our Youth in the science of Government. In a Republic, what species of knowledge can be equally important? and what duty, more pressing on a Legislature, than to patronize a plan for communicating it to those, who are to be the future guardians of the liberties of the Country?[21]

Further he insisted: "That which would render [the university] of the highest importance, in my opinion, is, that the Juvenal period of life, when friendships are formed, and habits established that will stick by one; the youth, or young men from different parts of the United States would be assembled together, and would by degrees discover that there was not that cause for those jealousies and prejudices which one part of the Union had imbibed against another part. . . ."[22]

Like George Washington, Abraham Lincoln throughout his career linked American liberty and American unity in an inseparable bond. His major speeches and writings continually affirm the two concepts and the linkage between them. Spalding and Garitty suggest that the Farewell Address "foreshadowed" the Gettysburg Address. They declare that Washington's ringing declaration in the Farewell Address: ". . . your Union ought to be considered as a main prop of your liberty, and that the love of the one ought to endear to you the preservation of the other" is a central point of the Gettysburg Address. That is, if American unity is destroyed liberty will not be preserved.[23]

At the same time, as Lincoln put it, "the great task remaining" is to ensure that the preservation of the American union completes the Founders' principles and goals of a regime based on natural rights and liberty. As political philosopher Harry Jaffa has argued, "The American Revolution and the Civil War were not merely discrete events," but constituted, "the first and last acts of a single drama" in the sense that the end of slavery fulfilled the natural rights promise of the Founding.[24]

The Patriotic Assimilation of Immigrants

There are basically two types of newcomers to American citizenship that the Founding regime's leaders had to consider. First, as noted, they had to think about the young. After all, children were not born republican citizens, but would have to be taught how to become citizens. Second, they had to think about immigrants. How best should these newcomers become American citizens? Their answer was clear and unequivocal: immigrants should be assimilated into American ideas and American common culture. Hence, the Founders regularly used words associated with ideas ("principles," "beliefs") and words associated with the common civic culture ("habits," "customs," "manners," "language," "laws," "our society").

George Washington in a letter to John Adams worried about large numbers of immigrants settling together in an area and therefore not becoming assimilated with the rest of the population:

> . . . the policy or advantage of [immigration] taking place in a body (I mean the settling of them in a body) may be much questioned; for, by so doing, they retain the language, habits, and principles (good or bad) which they bring with them. Whereas by an intermixture with our people, they, or their descendants, get assimilated to our customs, measures, laws: in a word soon become one people.[25]

In a 1790 speech to Congress on the naturalization of immigrants, James Madison stated that America should welcome immigrants who could assimilate, but exclude those who would not incorporate themselves into our society.[26] Both Thomas Jefferson and Alexander Hamilton saw advantages to immigration, but worried about the assimilation of newcomers, and insisted that civic integration was necessary for the preservation of the American republic. In *Notes on the State of Virginia*, Jefferson worried that a "greater number of emigrants" came from countries with "absolute monarchies," hence he feared:

They will bring with them the principles of government they leave, imbibed in their early youth; or if able to throw them off, it will be in exchange for an unbounded licentiousness, passing, as is usual from one extreme to another. It would be a miracle were they to stop precisely at the point of temperate liberty. . . ."[7]

Alexander Hamilton insisted that "The safety of a republic depends essentially on the energy of a common national sentiment; on a uniformity of principles and habits; on the exemption of citizens from foreign bias and prejudice; and on the love of country. . . ." Hamilton opposed granting citizenship immediately to new immigrants: "To admit foreigners indiscriminately to the rights of citizens, the moment they put foot in our country would be nothing less than to admit the Grecian horse into the citadel of our liberty and sovereignty." Instead, Hamilton recommended we should gradually draw newcomers into American life, "to enable aliens to get rid of foreign and acquire American attachments; to learn the principles and imbibe the spirit of our government; and to admit of a philosophy at least, of their feeling a real interest in our affairs."[28]

II. MODERN NEO-TRADITIONALISTS AND CIVIC EDUCATION

Obviously the core framework of the American regime (as articulated by the Founders and Lincoln) has been under severe ideological assault for decades. This challenge, that marches under an array of banners—multiculturalism, diversity, transnationalism, ethnic and gender group consciousness and the like—will be examined later in Part III. But first, I will explore a selection of neo-traditionalist writing that defends what could be called the traditional approach to American citizenship, civic education, and the affirmation of the regime (i.e., "the American way of life").

During the 1980s, 1990s, and in the current decade a group of thinkers have written vigorously in defense of an American regime defined in some broad traditional sense (with, to be sure, various qualifications). These neo-traditionalist thinkers include people such as William Bennett, Allan Bloom, Walter Berns, Arthur Schlesinger Jr., John Patrick Diggins, Harry Jaffa, Charles Kesler, Thomas West, Lynne Cheney, Dinesh D'Souza, Gertrude Himmelfarb, Irving Kristol, Norman Podhoretz, Midge Decter, Forrest McDonald, Wilfred McClay, Sidney Hook, Albert Shanker, Chester Finn, Paul Gagnon, Diane

Ravitch, Sandra Stotsky, Gilbert Sewall, Herbert London, Roger Kimball, Hilton Kramer, and others.

Most of the neo-traditionalists support the following core concepts of the American regime as articulated by the Founders and Lincoln: (1) the existence of an objective moral order (and conversely the rejection of relativism); (2) a realistic view of human nature (and, thus, opposition to utopianism and the idea that human nature is extremely malleable); (3) an affirmation of the American *Unum* (and thus a de-emphasis on diversity, multiculturalism, ethnic group consciousness, transnational concerns and the like); and (4) the promotion of an explicit civic, patriotic, and moral education (however defined), the purpose of which is to transmit the American regime and sustain and improve our free society of ordered liberty.

However, as much as they might agree on the practical issues facing civic education curriculum fights today, the neo-traditionalists are divided over first principles. They fall roughly into two camps: (a) the natural rights school and (b) the pragmatists.

(A) The Natural Rights School

The natural rights school adheres to the Founders' vision of natural rights and natural law. This wing of neo-traditionalism sees the regime through the Founders eyes. It, particularly, condemns the explicit rejection of natural rights and natural law in the late nineteenth and early twentieth century by progressives such as Woodrow Wilson, John Dewey, and Oliver Wendell Holmes.

The natural rights school is influenced by the thinking of political philosopher Leo Strauss. Its adherents are centered in several university political science departments and in think tanks such as the Claremont Institute, the American Enterprise Institute, the Hudson Institute, and the Heritage Foundation. Its leading theorists include Harry Jaffa, Walter Berns, Allan Bloom, Harvey Mansfield, Charles Kesler, Ken Masugi, Thomas West, and others.

Professor Thomas West of the University of Dallas, a scholar at the Claremont Institute, has been one of the most outspoken intellectual defenders of the Founding Fathers and the traditional framework of American citizenship. In his book, *Vindicating the Founders*, Professor West fashions a dichotomy. We must "choose," he insists, "between two competing visions of liberty and equality: the Founders' view and today's." He then asks provocatively why the Founders' view is always "put on trial," and why the question is not "whether we can justify our departure from the founding."[29]

Critics of the American Founding contend that the nation's foundation, its traditional framework, and its Founders are fatally flawed by the existence of slavery. Professor West begins his book by tackling the slavery issue head on. The Founders, West states, believed that "all men were created equal" in the sense that all human beings were by nature equal and therefore possessed equal rights to liberty. Thus, they were in principle opposed to slavery, thought it was morally wrong, and looked forward to the day when it would disappear. But West noted vested interests supported slavery, so "[t]here was little" the Founders "could have done about slavery at the [Constitutional] convention unless they were willing to risk breaking up the union."[30]

West attacks a leading college textbook, *American Government*, by Karen O'Connor and Larry Sabato, because the authors chided the Founders for not abolishing slavery at the time of the establishment of the Constitution in 1789 ("if the Founders had done what O'Connor and Sabato think they should have done, there would have been no union, the South would have been free to develop slavery without restraint and the eventual abolition might never have occurred"[31]).

Professor West argues that the Founders both condemned slavery and took definite steps to put the "peculiar institution," in Lincoln's words, "on the road to extinction." John Adams described slavery as an "abhorrence" and George Washington stated: "There is not a man living who wished more sincerely than I do, to see a plan adopted for the abolition of it."[32]

West notes that "at the beginning of the Revolution, slavery existed in each of the thirteen original states, and the slave trade with Africa was carried on without restraint." From the Declaration of Independence to the establishment of the Constitution six states abolished slavery; two more followed between 1799 and 1804; the slave trade was abolished in 1808; the Northwest Ordinance in 1787 forbade slavery in five future states; more than a hundred thousand Black Americans were freed by the end of the Founding era and many voted. [33]

West contends that these anti-slavery actions proceeded from the logic of the American Revolution and specifically from the Declaration of Independence, from the belief that "all men are created equal," and "endowed by their Creator" with "unalienable rights."

While American Southerners of the Founding era (Washington, Jefferson, Madison, Mason, Monroe, Henry, etc.) believed slavery was wrong and should be abolished when it was possible to do so, West explains that Southern elite opinion (as articulated by John C. Calhoun) changed in the 1830s.[34]

One of West's major arguments is that the Civil War completed the Founding. Abraham Lincoln is the chief agent of this restoration of "political health" and the completion of the Founding in principle. Thus, West quotes Lincoln in 1858 declaring: "[T]he fathers of this government expected and intended the institution of slavery to come to an end. They expected and intended that it should be in the course of ultimate extinction."[35]

West concludes his section on slavery with a ringing affirmation of the Founders and Lincoln, and a denunciation of the contemporary critics of the Founding period. He retorts:

> The Founders believed that their compromises with slavery would be corrected in the course of American history after the union was formed. The belief turned out to be true. . . . The Civil War fulfilled the anti-slavery promise of the American Founding. Lincoln was right and today's [academic] consensus is wrong. America really was conceived in liberty, and dedicated to the proposition that all men are created equal. Under the principles of the Declaration and the law of the Constitution, blacks won their liberty, became equal citizens, gained the right to vote, and eventually had their life, liberty, and property equally protected by the law. But today the founding, which makes all of this possible, is denounced as unjust and anti-black. Surely that uncharitable verdict deserves to be reversed.[36]

(B) The Pragmatists

The other wing of the neo-traditionalists, the pragmatists, do not accept the philosophical base of the American regime—*i.e.*, natural rights theory of the Founding Period—as something that is "true" in and of itself. For the pragmatists, the "natural rights" theory of the Founding is a historically based construct, connected to a particular time and place, the eighteenth century Western world. It is not a universal and timeless truth inherent in the nature of human beings. This means that for the pragmatists, the statement in the Declaration of Independence that all men are "endowed by their Creator with certain unalienable rights" is not literally "true," but is seen as the beginning of a political concept of "rights" and self-government that were created by men and are still evolving.

Nevertheless, although the pragmatists differ with the natural rights school on philosophical first principles, both wings of neo-traditionalism are in essential agreement on the necessity to defend the great bulk (although, not all) of the core cultural framework of the American regime discussed earlier, such as: (1) opposition to moral relativism (to be sure, there are obvious philosophical contradictions, but neo-traditionalist pragmatists also insist upon repudiation of moral relativism); (2) a realistic view of human nature; (3) affirmation of the American *Unum*; and (4) the promotion of a civic, patriotic, and moral education (again, however defined) that seeks to sustain and improve our constitutional democracy.

This means that despite philosophical differences they are usually allies against the multiculturalists and ethnic and gender studies advocates in the practical world of educational politics and curriculum fights.

The late Sidney Hook, an eminent American philosopher and public intellectual, exemplifies the pragmatic neo-traditionalist viewpoint. Hook was a leading philosopher of the "pragmatist" school, a self-styled "secular humanist," agnostic in religion, and a student of John Dewey, the bête noir of pro-natural rights philosophers. Nevertheless, Hook articulated a vision of American civic education that defended a large part of the cultural framework of the American regime as understood by traditional natural rights adherents.

Sidney Hook's NEH Jefferson Lecture of 1984

In May 1984, Sidney Hook delivered the prestigious Jefferson Lecture in the Humanities, awarded for outstanding scholarship by the National Endowment for the Humanities (NEH). In bold and forceful language, Hook used the occasion of the Jefferson Lecture to call for the revitalization of education for citizenship in American liberal democracy (". . . faith and belief in the principles of liberal democracy has declined in the United States. Unless that faith can be restored and revivified liberal democracy will perish").[37]

Throughout his lecture, Hook affirmed the civic-cultural framework of the American regime although he used pragmatic, rather than natural law, rhetoric and arguments. Nevertheless, his opposition to relativism and utopianism; his support for a realistic concept of human nature; his celebration of the American *Unum*; and his emphasis on civic education, patriotism, and loyalty to our liberal democratic regime are clear enough.

Hook outlined four main issues: (1) the core principles of American liberal democracy; (2) the type of education necessary to sustain that democracy; (3) the contemporary threats to our free society; and (4) finally, what must be done to preserve and perpetuate our liberal democratic regime.

First, Professor Hook explains the institutional framework of the American regime, i.e., that American liberal democracy was based on self-government and majority rule, but within the context of limited government. He quoted Jefferson's axiom that "the first principle of republicanism" is majority rule, but Hook noted that the modern conception of self-government (unlike the ancient republics) recognized limits to government power. Hence republicanism was united with constitutionalism and freedom of speech, press, association, and assembly and limits to government power were integral to our free self-governing society.

Second, in forthright normative language, Hook asked how "in the spirit of Jefferson" we should "devise an educational system that would indeed strengthen allegiance to our self-governing democratic society." He suggested that neither education in the sciences nor the humanities by themselves are sufficient to sustain allegiance in a free society. He noted that "the subject matters and techniques of the sciences can be mastered in any kind of society" and that they could become an "instrument of enforcing a cruel and ruthless despotism."

And while the humanities are central to education in every society because their subject matter is perennial and transcendent ("They take us out of ourselves and enable us to see with the eyes and minds of others"), Hook lamented, nevertheless, "we can not honestly maintain that the study of the humanities of itself generates allegiance to the free society." He noted that it was often students trained in the humanities in Germany, France, Italy, and Spain who "provided the intellectual shock troops for anti-democratic movements" and that from "Plato to the present" many of the "dominating figures in the humanistic disciplines" have been hostile to political democracy.

In his third and fourth points, Professor Hook continued to address directly the crucial, yet always controversial questions, of the role of civic education in inculcating allegiance and loyalty to the United States.

Thus, thirdly, Hook warned that America was in the throes of an "urgent contemporary crisis" that was "eroding allegiance to the ideals of a free self-governing society itself." He listed specific internal threats to the "democratic ethos in American life," including: (1) the vehement assertion of rights and entitlements without the acceptance of corresponding duties and obligations; (2) the invocation of group rights to justify overriding the rights of individuals; (3) the growth of violence, and the toleration of violence, in schools and local assemblies; (4) the open defiance of laws authorized by the democratic process, and the indulgence of courts toward repeated and unrepentant violators; (5) the continued invasion by the courts themselves into the legislative process; (6) the loss of faith in the electorate as the ultimate custodian of its own freedom.

Fourth, Hook outlined his prescriptions for preserving and perpetuating self-government in America. He declared that first and foremost, American students must examine the "basic elements of a free society." Moreover, instead of "relying primarily on the sciences and humanities to inspire loyalty to the processes of self-government," Hook insisted that "we should seek to develop that loyalty directly through honest inquiry into the functioning of a democratic community, by learning its history, celebrating its heroes, and noting its achievements." A free society will never be perfect and Hook explicitly eschewed "utopian" solutions to educational issues as well as political problems.

Hook stated that in the early years, education in *all societies* (free and unfree) is based on some form of indoctrination, including the "habits of character, hygiene, elementary sociality, and morality." However, the difference between a free society and an unfree society is that in a free society, as students mature, the methods of indoctrination give way to "methods of reflective critical thought at every appropriate level." On the other hand, in an unfree society non-rational and irrational indoctrination continues throughout "the entire course of study" and even after the completion of formal education because an "unfree society regards its subjects as in a permanent state of political childhood."

Finally, Professor Hook addressed immigration and the demographic changes in American life. He thoroughly rejected the core multicultural argument that demographic changes require drastically revising and diluting our nation's story in order to make the curriculum "relevant" to new (non-Western and non-Anglo) immigrants and native-born minorities. Instead, (like the Founders, Lincoln, and early twentieth century American leaders including Theodore Roosevelt and Woodrow Wilson) Hook called for the patriotic assimilation of all young Americans into the mainstream of our civic culture.

He declared that precisely because America is a "pluralistic, multi-ethnic, uncoordinated society" all of our young people native-born and immigrant alike, white, black, and brown, need "a prolonged schooling in the history of our free society, its martyrology, and its national tradition." He called on American public schools reinforced by colleges and universities to play this unifying role as they did in the days of mass immigration during the presidencies of Theodore Roosevelt and Woodrow Wilson in the early years of the twentieth century. Proper civic education, Hook insisted, was necessary for the "perpetuation" and, indeed, the "survival" of our free society.

The Education for Democracy Project
One year after Sidney Hook's NEH Jefferson Lecture, three associations, the American Federation of Teachers (AFT), the Education Excellence Network, and Freedom House launched The Education for Democracy Project. Evoking Hook's lecture as an inspiration, the project called for strengthening the normative principles of American civic education. In 1987 under the leadership of AFT President, Albert Shanker, the project published *A Statement of Principles: Guidelines for Strengthening the Teaching of Democratic Values*, a forceful, twenty-three-page manifesto.

More than a hundred prominent Americans from different ends of the political spectrum endorsed the *Statement of Principles* including: Jimmy Carter, Gerald Ford, Walter Mondale, Norman Lear, Marion Wright Edelman, Benjamin Hooks, Lynne Cheney, Barbara Jordan, Tipper Gore, Henry Cisneros, Baynard Rustin, Donna Shalala, and George Will.

It is significant that the document was endorsed by liberals and conservatives, and by leading thinkers of both a natural rights and pragmatist bent. Thus natural rights adherents Walter Berns and Rev. Richard John Neuhaus joined pragmatists Sidney Hook and Arthur Schlesinger Jr. in endorsing the *Statement*. Although these four thinkers disagree over natural rights and natural law, they are in general agreement with the realistic view of human nature articulated in *The Federalist Papers*. It is in this agreement on the Founders' realistic concept of human nature and rejection of utopianism that the natural rights school and the pragmatists find some common philosophical ground.

A Statement of Principles articulates a strong emphasis on the American *Unum*, political loyalty and the transmission of the regime to future generations. Thus it declares: "As the years pass, we become an increasingly diverse people, drawn from many racial, national, linguistic, and religious origins," but "our political heritage is one—the vision of a common life in liberty, justice, and equality as expressed in the Declaration of Independence and the Constitution two centuries ago." In clear language the *Statement* proclaimed: "We are convinced that democracy's survival depends upon our transmitting to each new generation the political vision of liberty and equality that unites us as Americans—and a deep loyalty to the political institutions our founders put together to fulfill that vision."[38]

Unlike the tepid and tentative prose of many consensus documents in education, the language of *A Statement of Principles* endorses civic education in vivid and prescriptive prose. Thus, the *Statement* insists that American students should "cherish freedom and accept the responsibility for preserving and extending it," and echoing Sidney Hook states that schools should impart an "informed, reasoned allegiance to the ideals of a free society." Moreover, civic virtues such as devotion to freedom, justice, equal rights, the rule of law, civility, truth, self-restraint, and personal responsibility must be "taught and learned" because children are not born with these qualities.

Like Sidney Hook's Jefferson Lecture (and the Founders and Lincoln), *A Statement of Principles* explicitly opposes moral relativism. The AFT document makes a crucial distinction between neutrality and objectivity. It rejects the former and advocates the later. As an example of "value-free" neutrality it criticizes a question on the NAEP (National Assessment for Education Progress) 1982 Civics text that found the Chinese Communist definition of "freedom" (the professed "right to a job, medical care, food," although, of course, these "rights" are not actually observed in practice) was simply "different" from the American definition of freedom (free press, free speech, free elections).

The *Statement* notes that under the NAEP approved Orwellian definition of "freedom" most slaves in human history could be classified as "free," since slaves had food, "a job," and medical care. Instead of value-free neutrality, the document calls for objectivity, analysis, and serious critical thinking—meaning a thorough historical examination of the human condition in societies past and present. Accordingly, students should learn about totalitarianism and concentration camps under communism and Nazism as well the tragedies (slavery, discrimination, etc.) and triumphs (expansion of freedom and democracy) of our own society.

A Statement of Principles is very clear about what is most important for American citizens (and thus students who will be future citizens) to know and why. "First, citizens must know the fundamental ideas central to the political vision of the eighteenth-century founders . . . the meanings and the implications of the Declaration of Independence, the Constitution, *The Federalist Papers*, and the Bill of Rights." Moreover, the *Statement* insists that students understand the Founders' realistic concept of human nature, thus in examining the Founding documents it states rhetorically: "What were the prevailing assumptions about human nature? About the relationship between God and themselves? About the origin of human society and the meaning and direction of human history?"

Furthermore, *A Statement* declares "To understand our ideas requires a knowledge of the whole sweep of Western civilization, from the ancient Jews and Christians—whose ethical beliefs gave rise to democratic thought—to the Greeks and Romans through the Middle Ages, the Renaissance and the Reformation, the English Revolution—so important to America—the eighteenth century Enlightenment, and the French Revolution, a violent cousin to our own."

Second, students should know the history of liberal democracy "dating back at least to the English Revolution, and forward to our own century's total wars; to the failure of the nascent liberal regimes of Russia, Italy, Germany, Spain, and Japan; to the totalitarianism, oppression, and mass exterminations of our time. How has it all happened?" Thus, like Sidney Hook's NEH address, the AFT *Statement* calls for a thorough study of the theory and practice of both democratic and undemocratic regimes throughout history and particularly in the twentieth century.

Finally, the *Statement* declares that a decisive improvement in education for American democratic citizenship will require a "sea-change in the typical curriculum." The signatories endorse a social studies curriculum that centers around history and geography and a "broader, deeper learning in the humanities, particularly in literature, ideas, and biography, so that students may encounter and comprehend the values upon which democracy depends." They call for "more attention to world studies, especially to the realistic and unsentimental study of other nations;" world geography; and "at least one non-Western society in depth." They call for active learning and critical analysis based on factual knowledge. And, they insist that, through such a social studies curriculum, moral education, properly understood, meaning education that is neither partisan nor value neutral can be restored to our schools.

The *Statement* concludes with a ringing normative declaration broadly consistent with the vision of the Founders and Lincoln:

> As citizens of a democratic republic, we are part of the noblest political effort in history. Our children must learn, and we must teach them, the knowledge, values, and habits that will best protect and extend this precious inheritance. Today we ask our schools to make a greater contribution to that effort and we ask all Americans to help them do it.

The Education for Democracy Project's Textbook Review
Besides the twenty-three page *A Statement of Principles*, The Education for Democracy Project sponsored an extensive review of American and World History textbooks. The two books, *Democracy's Untold Story: What World History Textbooks Neglect* (1987) and

Democracy's Half-Told Story: What American History Textbooks Should Add (1989), written by historian Paul Gagnon, provide extensive details on a desired curriculum and develop a clear normative framework for civic education.

At the same time that The Education for Democracy Project launched its textbook review, multicultural education started to achieve greater prominence and gain increasing support among K-12 educators, particularly in the social studies. Multicultural educators were critical of what they considered the traditional curricular emphasis on white males, Western civilization, great individuals, and political history and institutions. They called for transforming the curriculum by placing greater attention on minorities, women, non-Western cultures, ordinary people, and social history. The multiculturalists and other educational theorists argued that an emphasis on a Western Core was: (1) not appropriate for a society that was, through immigration, becoming increasingly non-Western and, hence, whose new inhabitants would not be able to "relate" to Western traditions; and (2) obsolete because the "information explosion" makes it more important for students to focus on generic skills and inquiry, that is, "to learn how to learn," rather than to study any particular set of core knowledge.

Anticipating these arguments, Professor Gagnon met them head on. In so doing he essentially re-cast in contemporary language the core arguments of civic/patriotic assimilation for both newcomers and the native-born dating back to George Washington's Farewell Address and the educational writings of John Adams, James Madison, and Thomas Jefferson discussed earlier.

First, Gagnon insisted that "In an increasingly multicultural society, it is imperative that adequate time be devoted to what we Americans have in common. For it is precisely our common political heritage—and its mainly Western intellectual, cultural, and moral sources—that allows us the freedom to be different from each other, that impels us to respect our differences, and that encourages us to live together in liberty and equality."[39]

He continued:

> Whether by past force or recent choice, the people of non-Western origins living in this country are now part of a community whose ideas and institutions, for good and ill, grow out of the Western experience. . . . And there is little hope that mainstream Americans can come to sympathetic understanding of strangers in their midst, or of foreign lands and cultures, without first facing up to the historical record of the best and worst in themselves. It simply makes no sense for our schools to start anywhere but with the Western experience. They must start from the beginning.[40]

Second, Gagnon argues that education for democratic citizenship means that the faster the pace of change, the "higher the flood of 'knowledge,' the more critical it will be for us to understand the ideas, institutions, and events that have shaped our society." Thus, the "ideas of the Declaration of Independence, the Bill of Rights, Lincoln's second inaugural address, the Atlantic Charter, the civil rights laws" will become "less obsolete" and "more relevant." He concludes by asking, "What can be obsolete about knowledge that tells us where we have come from and what we ought to be?"[41]

Indeed, as George Washington has written of *The Federalist Papers*, "when the transient circumstances . . . which have attended this crisis shall have disappeared, that work will merit the notice of posterity, because in it are candidly and ably discussed the principles of freedom and the topics of government—which will always be interesting to mankind as long as they shall be connected to civil society." And, as noted earlier, Thomas Jefferson described *The Federalist Papers* as: "The best commentary on the principles of government which ever was written." Jefferson's comments might be considered as true today as when he wrote these words to James Madison from Paris in 1787. Certainly, *The Federalist Papers*, and the Declaration of Independence and the other works of the Founders and of Lincoln stand up well against the utopian nineteenth and twentieth century theories widely celebrated by today's trendy academics including the works of Karl Marx, Friedrich Nietzsche, Antonio Gramsci, Jacques Derrida, Frantz Fanon, and John Rawls.

III. TO TRANSFORM THE AMERICAN REGIME AND ESTABLISH A COUNTER-REGIME?

Aristotle stated that the goal of civic education in any society is to transmit the "regime." To repeat, my definition of "regime" in this essay is the Aristotelian one, including both the state and civil society, the government and the culture, encompassing the institutions, ideas, values, mores, habits, customs, traditions, and "way of life" of a people. As we have seen from the Founders and Lincoln to the *Education for Democracy Statement*, leading Americans have been engaged in the work of perpetuating our "regime," i.e., our way of life to future generations of Americans.

At the same time, during the last several decades the cultural framework of the American regime has been subjected to a root and branch challenge on everything that matters. This challenge is total and is directed at the principles, values, ideas, and institutions of American liberal democracy, as they have been traditionally understood. That is to say, in the final analysis the challenge is to the American "regime" or to the American way of life itself.

The ultimate purpose of the challenge, usually implicit, although sometimes explicitly declared, is the transformation of the American regime and the establishment of a counter-regime. (The chart at the end of this chapter provides a snapshot of the warring concepts in the conflict between those who want to *transmit* the American regime and those who want to *transform* it: that is, between the regime and the counter-regime.)

Proponents of the American regime argue that American liberal democracy and our way of life are based on an objective moral order, universal principles, that are applicable to all men and women everywhere. The counter-regime tells us that there is no objective moral order, no universal principles, that principles or, as they prefer, "values" are "situated" or relative, that they depend upon one's circumstances, history, race, religion, ethnicity, and class. While the American regime insists that good government must be based on a realistic view of human nature, the counter-regime believes that "human nature" is socially constructed and can be altered through deliberate social change and thus the utopian transformation of human society is possible. The American regime affirms *e pluribus unum*, the American union, and the idea of one people. The counter-regime affirms "diversity," "multiculturalism," and "transnationalism." It emphasizes racial, gender, and ethnic group consciousness, decries "systemic injustice," and deliberately employs the term the American "peoples" rather than the American people.

The American regime insists that immigrants should be assimilated into American common culture. The counter-regime rejects the "Americanization" (or civic/patriotic integration) of immigrants and not merely describes but *advocates* a "multicultural mosaic," or "salad bowl" where newcomers to America retain the customs, languages, world views, and (in some cases) loyalties of their birth nations. In truth, the challengers favor the assimilation of immigrants into the counter-regime.

Civic education is thus a battleground between those who believe that the purpose of citizenship education is to preserve, improve, and transmit the American regime and those who believe that the purpose of civic education is, in the words of one of America's leading educators "to transform the United States from what it is, to what it can and should be." In other words, it is a battleground between the regime and the counter-regime.

The Advance of the Counter-Regime
The intellectual and moral foundation of the counter-regime rests upon a rationale that has been called the "demographic imperative." Briefly stated, the argument runs roughly as follows: Major demographic changes are (and will be) occurring in the United States during the next few decades as millions of new immigrants from non-Western cultures, their children, as well as record numbers of women and native born ethnic minorities enter the work force, public life, and the professions in record numbers. At the same time, the global interdependence of the world's peoples and the transnational connections among them will increase. All of these changes render the traditional framework of American citizenship education obsolete. The traditional model of civic education is premised on an individualistic, white male, Western worldview. It is not appropriate for immigrants, ethnic minorities, and women. It is outmoded in today's multicultural and transnational world of multiple loyalties and will be even more so in decades to come.

Joyce Appleby, a leading historian and the President of the American Historical Association (AHA) from 1997–1998, advanced the agenda of the counter-regime when she wrote in the early 1990s that:

> The demographic reconfiguration of the American population and the enduring vitality of ethnic differences make it increasingly clear that the exclusive dominance of European cultural forms [i.e., Western Civilization and American Founding principles] in the United States is now consignable to a specific time period, let us say 1676 to 1992 (a terminal date fittingly coincident with the Columbian quincentenary). It is no longer a question of whether Americans must work on a multicultural understanding of their past, but how. The very inevitability of this development raises the stakes in current discussions of national history.[42]

In other words, America's past must be "re-understood" as "multicultural" in order to serve the goal of transforming the American regime and creating a counter-regime.

Professor Linda Kerber, in her Presidential Address to the Organization of American Historians (OAH) in 1997 also forwarded the counter-regime perspective when she asked: "Do we need citizenship? We are embedded in postnational and transnational relationships that may be reconstructing the meaning of citizenship out of recognition."[43] About the same time, an anthropologist associated with the University of Chicago's prestigious Committee on Social Thought, Arjun Appadurai, suggested that "the United States is in transition" from being a "land of immigrants" to being "one node in a postnational network of diasporas."[44] Implicit in the comments of Kerber and Appadurai is the notion that American citizenship is obsolete and will be replaced with a "post-national" citizenship. Also implicit in these two remarks is the idea that the American national regime will be replaced by a "post-national" and transnational counter-regime.

What one hears in the voices of leading counter-regime academics like Appleby, Kerber, and Appadurai and from speaker after speaker at academic conferences is a clear message of demographic determinism. They are telling Americans that "demographic changes require you to radically transform civic education, citizenship, and the traditional concepts of the American nation-state—you don't have a choice." Advocates of the counter-regime, thus, purposefully avoid the normative issue (should we transform the American regime?) and argue that because of demographic changes the regime must be transformed. Thus, what Appleby and the determinists are implicitly saying is that the views of the majority of Americans—that is, "government by consent of the governed"—is irrelevant. They are telling us that Alexander Hamilton was wrong when he wrote in, *Federalist* 1, that the American regime was based upon self-government ("reflection and choice") not determinism ("accident and force").

Moreover, as we saw in last section neo-traditionalists such as Sidney Hook noted that demographic changes in the United States argued logically—not for an affirmation of culture group consciousness—but, instead for a renewed emphasis on America's common culture ("precisely because . . . America is a pluralistic, multiethnic, uncoordinated society . . . we need a prolonged schooling in the history of our free society, its martyology, and its national tradition").

The American "Peoples" Replace the American People

During the 1990s a group of ideological academics and administrators attacked the core concept of the American *Unum*, the idea that despite our wide ethnic and racial diversity we are one people, the American people. Instead, the main authors of the National History Standards, Professor Gary Nash of UCLA; the Commissioner of Education for the State of New York, Thomas Sobol; and educational administrators in Maryland and Colorado deliberately employed the term "American peoples" in the curricular documents they developed.[45]

The concept of American "peoples" suggests that the United States is a multinational state such as the former Austro-Hungarian Empire, the Soviet Union, or Yugoslavia composed of different "peoples" and nations" with their own separate languages, histories, and ways of life, without a common culture and historical narrative—not, as Abraham Lincoln put it in the Gettysburg Address "one nation indivisible." Indeed, the title of the New York social studies curriculum of 1991 ("One Nation, Many Peoples: A Declaration of Cultural Interdependence") could be characterized as a Black Mass of counter-patriotism, a mockery of the Preamble of the Constitution's "We the People of the United States" and the Declaration of Independence's "When in the course of human events it becomes necessary for *one people*..." (emphasis added).

The Deconstruction of America's British and Western Origins
As the distinguished scholar Samuel Huntington has written, the United States is a settler nation.[46] Its laws, institutions, language, religion, customs, traditions, mores, were brought to the North American colonies by settlers from the British Isles. The most popular author in the American colonies was Shakespeare and the most widely read book was the King James Bible. There were, of course, other ethnic groups present: Germans, Dutch, French, Spanish, Swedes, Irish, indigenous American Indians, and Africans brought to the new world as slaves. However, the dominant culture was clearly British (an estimated three quarters of all colonists were from the British Isles).

Nevertheless, the National History Standards described the culture of Colonial America and the Founding period, not as predominately British or even predominately Western but as a "great convergence" of three different civilizations: the Native American, the West African, and the European. Under the banner of "three worlds meet" the National History Standards tell us that "Native American, African, and European cultures" converged and created a "composite" American culture. The implication is that the cultures of these three continents contributed equally to America's Founding.[47]

This concept of "three worlds meet" used by the National History Standards is an ideological weapon of the counter-regime, an attempt to de-legitimize the British and Western foundation of the American regime. It is, of course, a lie.

A leading intellectual historian John Patrick Diggins points out that our core liberal democratic principles come from Western and British civilizations not from MesoAmerican Indian culture and the culture of West Africa. He argues that it is not possible to teach the political ideas and values of American liberal democracy and, at the same time, declare that the American regime is a "convergence" of non-Western and Western cultures.

Diggins writes:

> The glaring fallacy of the National History Standards is that it cannot teach such ideas and values [liberal democracy] to the extent that it has America "converging" with non-Western cultures rather than decisively departing from them. What do fifteenth century Africa and pre-Columbian America have to do with modern "democratic ideals"? . . . How can one arrive at the political values of the West by having students begin with the non-West, where rarely do values come into being as an act of choice rather than as an inheritance? Not since the Nazis has a document so minimized the importance of the Western Enlightenment and replaced political knowledge about human nature with cultural mystiques about races and racial heritages, whether black or white. No doubt Director Nash had a hand in emphasizing the priority of primitive cultures over political ideas.[48]

In a similar vein, prize-winning historian Arthur Schlesinger Jr. has said, "to deny the essential European origin of American culture is to falsify history." He notes: "It may be too bad that dead White European males have played so large a role in shaping our culture. But that's the way it is. One cannot erase history. Would anyone seriously argue that teachers should conceal the European origins of American civilization?"[49]

Federal Funding for the Counter-Regime

Counter-regime ideology is funded widely throughout the federal government. For example, during the 1990s the U.S. Department of Education's research branch funded the work of Bonnie Bernard of the Western Regional Center for Drug Free Schools and Communities.

In a paper entitled "Moving Towards a Just and Vital Culture: Multiculturalism in Our Schools," Bernard writes that most ethnic minority cultures (Native American, African-American, Latino, immigrant cultures, etc.) are characterized by the "values of cooperation, communality, sharing, group support, interdependence, and social responsibility." If minority youth become assimilated into the "dominant" or mainstream American culture they become alienated because this mainstream culture is "characterized by values of individualism, independence, competition, self over others, and non-sharing," resulting in greater drug abuse.

The proposed remedy is multicultural education for both majority and minority youth. Bernard writes, "we are concerned . . . with changing the hearts and minds of the dominant culture, beginning with pre-school children, to not only respect difference and appreciate other cultures, but to learn cross-cultural literacy."

Bernard directly attacks the perspective "advocated for example by Allan Bloom and E. D. Hirsch" that all children be "assimilated into the dominant Western European cultural tradition" because this will "result in increased marginalization of ethnic and minority groups." The goal should be a multicultural education that will "allow us to develop a truly culturally transformed society."[50]

Another well-known education professor who has been widely funded over the years is Fred M. Newmann of the University of Wisconsin. An open counter-regime ideologist, Newmann declares that the "ultimate social ideal and thus the purpose of education" is the "emancipation of all people." He declares that "almost all social practices" in the United States "serve the interests of dominant groups and repress the interests of others, especially minorities, the poor, and women." He calls for new educational research that will lead to a "more coherent vision of social alternative" to the present system.[51]

Professional Certification for Teachers or Counter-Regime Ideology?
A more subtle version of counter-regime ideology is presented by the National Council for Accreditation of Teacher Education (NCATE). This group is currently developing national guidelines for professional certification for K-12 teachers. The organization is supported by leading corporations, almost all governors, and many education associations. It seeks to set professional standards for teachers and become a type of American Bar Association or American Medical Association for elementary and secondary school teachers.

NCATE outlined its goals in a vision statement published by the American Association of Colleges for Teacher Education. The statement declared that because of the "profoundly political and moral purposes of education" values are central to the enterprise of teaching: "Just as lawyers learn the value of justice, and doctors learn to value human life," teachers "cannot avoid the intrinsic connection of values with the purposes and processes of the education profession."[52]

What are those values? "First and foremost, quality teacher units must be places of active conscience. The professional commitment to social justice and the power of equity and diversity in American culture must be palpable."[53]

The NCATE document explicitly emphasized the concepts of cultural diversity and global perspective:

> The values, norms, and dispositions that define the domains and judgments of professional conscience give life, meaning, and direction to NCATE's standards. For example, units promote cultural diversity, not

because it is imbedded in the standards, but because we professionally believe in diversity and recognize the match between that belief and the external reality of the publics we serve.[54]

Note that NCATE does not serve the "public," i.e., the American
people, but the "publics" connected with the promotion of "cultural
diversity."

Significantly, the document declares, "If we serve the larger cause
of social justice, we continuously reinvent the free society and its no-
blest aspirations."[55] Thus, the only mention of a "free society" in the
NCATE document is the need to reinvent it. In other words, in order to
achieve "social justice" (defined as "equity," "diversity," and a "global
perspective") our free society—that is our regime—needs to be transformed. In practice, the attempt to achieve "social justice," "equity,"
and "diversity" means—not equality of opportunity for individuals—
but the advocacy of ethnic, racial, and gender preferences and numerical quotas for "protected classes" until the day (which never arrives in
a free society) that actual statistical equality of result for these ascribed
groups is to be achieved.

The NCATE document is almost the mirror opposite of George
Washington's Farewell Address that emphasized what unites us as
Americans. In fact, there is little, if anything, in the NCATE manifesto
that would have been recognizable to America's Founders and Lincoln
as serious civic education. There is nothing that affirms American citizenship, American self-government, the American *Unum*, our constitutional principles, and our liberal democracy. There is nothing that
affirms the American regime and everything that suggests the need to
transform it and replace it with a counter-regime.

CONCLUSION

In the post-9/11 world the conflict between the American regime and
the counter-regime continues to rage. In the fall of 2003 the Albert
Shanker Institute endowed by the American Federation of Teachers
published another "Education for Democracy" document. Citing the
"sudden and brutal attack on our country" on September 11, 2001 the
new *Education for Democracy: Renewing Our Commitment* statement
declared:

> A new tyranny—Islamist extremism—confronted us, striking at the heart
> of our cities and symbols. The issue of defending our democracy was no
> longer an abstraction, the question of civic education no longer an option.

As more than one commentator observed, "We were attacked for being American. We should at least know what being American means."[56]

Once again, the AFT statement affirmed the American regime and challenged the ideology of the counter-regime. For example, the document notes that recent high school history textbooks have adopted the "three worlds meet" paradigm proposed by the National History Standards (the same standards that were condemned by the United States Senate 99–1 in 1995). Echoing the mid-1990s arguments of John Patrick Diggins, Arthur Schlesinger Jr., Robert Lerner, myself, and others,[57] the statement quotes Diane Ravitch's 2003 book, *The Language Police*:

> In the new textbooks, democratic values and ideals compete with a welter of themes about geography, cultural diversity, economic development, technology, and global relations. In order to show how "three worlds met," the texts downplay the relative importance of European ideas that gave rise to democratic institutions and devote more attention to pre-Columbian civilizations and African Kingdoms. . . . The textbooks . . . have nearly buried the narrative about the ideas and institutions that made our national government possible.[58]

While it affirms the American regime, the *Statement* rejects indoctrination and one-sided propaganda, declaring that students need a "full and truthful account" of American history. This "would not ignore its serious flaws, past or present. Students should learn about the Middle Passage, the Dred Scott Decision, the Fugitive Slave Law, and the degradations and inhumanities of slavery."[59]

Nevertheless, today, because of the advance of what this essay has characterized as the counter-regime, the statement complains: "In too many instances, America's sins, slights, and shortcomings have become not just a piece of the story, but its *essence*" (emphasis in the original).[60]

Once again the *Education for Democracy* manifesto was endorsed by a wide range of Americans including former President Bill Clinton, former Republican Governor of Michigan John Engler, the Democrat Governor of New Mexico Bill Richardson, author Norman Podhoretz, the President of the NAACP Kweisi Mfume, and Jeanne Kirkpatrick of the American Enterprise Institute.

And once again adherents of natural rights theory such as Walter Berns, Harvey Mansfield, and Michael Novak joined pragmatic neo-traditionalists such as Arthur Schlesinger Jr., Amitai Etzioni, and Alan Wolfe in signing the *Education for Democracy Statement*.

At the same time that the *Education for Democracy* document was published in 2003 a full-scale curricular conflict over state social studies standards was raging in Minnesota. The proposed new Minnesota standards emphasized America's liberal democratic heritage and institutions. Paul Gagnon welcomed the new standards that were praised by neo-traditionalist thinkers such as Diane Ravitch and Jerry Martin, the President of the American Council of Trustees and Alumni. Professor Ravitch wrote:

> The new standards will put Minnesota in the same league with other states that are widely applauded for the quality of their standards. States like Massachusetts and California, for example, have been hailed by rating agencies that span the ideological spectrum, including the American Federation of Teachers and the Thomas B. Fordham Foundation. If Minnesota adopts the new standards in something like their current form, it will be a huge step forward for teaching children in the state about the USA and other major civilizations of the world.[61]

And Dr. Jerry Martin declared:

> These are the first standards I have been asked to review about which I had no major concerns in both American and world history, in geography, and in economics. They are easily the best standards I have ever seen. They will be a model for the nation.[62]

Counter-regime ideologists launched a sustained attack against the proposed Minnesota standards. Social studies teachers were prominent among the critics. They complained that children in the early grades were required to learn patriotic songs such as God Bless America, the Battle Hymn of the Republic, and "A Grand Old Flag." One wrote in that "Patriotic Symbols, Songs, and Events represents (sic) the worst type of nationalistic propaganda and must be eliminated from the standards." Another wrote that "the song 'you're a grand old flag,' suggested for fourth grade, could be offensive to some who don't believe in pledging allegiance." Yet another declared, "the Battle Hymn of the Republic and God Bless America have clearly religious messages and ought not to be taught in school as expressing American ideals."[63]

At a more sophisticated level of criticism, a group of historians from the University of Minnesota complained that in describing interactions between European settlers and American Indians the standards used terms and concepts that are "[o]stensibly benign" such as "exploration," "movement," "migration," "colonization," "settlement," "expansion," "acquisition," and "annexation." They explicitly argued for "balancing" these "benign" terms with their preferred concepts of "conquest," "subjugation," "exploitation," and "enslaving."[64]

The "choice of language" is crucial, the historians maintained, because the use of what they refer to as "benign" terms such as "settlement," in their view, underestimated the "genocidal impact on the America's of the European incursions." The University of Minnesota historians are, of course, right that the choice of language often conveys an ideological agenda. In their case, it is instructive that the historians choose to use the term "genocidal impact" in describing the interactions between the European colonists and the American Indians.

"Genocide" is a powerful negative concept, evoking horrible images of the Holocaust, of Hitler and Stalin, Auschwitz, and the Gulag. Using the term "genocidal impact" is a demagogic way of associating the horrors of the death camps of World War II with the travails of the American Indians—it is a way of slyly implying, without directly saying, that Colonial Americans were little different from Nazis and Stalinists.

Genocide is usually defined as the *deliberate* attempt to exterminate an entire group of people because of the race, ethnicity, religion, or class that they were born into. Although many Indians died through wars and diseases after the arrival of British settlers in North America, there clearly never was any deliberate policy by the Mayflower or Jamestown colonists or their descendants (or by the Conquistadors in Latin America) to exterminate the indigenous Amerindian people. Nor was the "impact" genocidal: today, for example, the Pequot Indian tribe of New England is thriving in the casino business, having been awarded special privileges by American courts.

What is the purpose, one wonders, of the Minnesota historians evoking the inaccurate concept of "genocide," except to discredit and delegitimize the foundations and symbols of the American regime in order to deconstruct it and create a new counter-regime?

By the same token, it is also instructive that these same historians complained that the Minnesota curricular standards use the pronoun "us" in suggesting that Western Civilization influences "us" Americans. They state gratuitously, this means that all Americans "are presumed to be of shared [racial or ethnic] descent."[65] Of course, it means no such thing. It means that all Americans, whatever their ethnic background, inherit their political ideas from British and Western Civilization.

Despite the wide acceptance of the new *Education for Democracy* document (at least on the surface, through the diverse number of signatures), the intensity of the Minnesota curriculum controversy reminds us that the ideological war over civic education (and by implication over the American regime) will continue indefinitely.

This is true, in spite of the comforting and superficial observations by many journalists and commentators during the past few years that the "culture wars" are over. What the heralding of the culture wars' demise means in reality is that the attention span of the media is limited, and that it is difficult for mainstream journalists to sustain either an understanding of or interest in our nation's long and continuing intellectual and ideological conflict.

But for those whose job it is to develop history and social studies curricula in America's public schools (and for those parents who are reading for perhaps the first time in their children's textbooks of America's "oppressive" past and "unjust" present)—there is no doubt that civic education is—and will remain—contested, long into the foreseeable future. Furthermore, civic education is contested because, as we have seen, the existence of the regime itself is contested on all the major questions that lie at the core of regime transformation.

Whether the American regime will survive and be transmitted to future generations—whether it will be, as Lincoln put it in his First Inaugural Address, "perpetual"—or whether it will join the failed republics of history and be transformed into a very different type of counter-regime will, no doubt, be decided during the course of the twenty-first century.

Regime Transmission	Regime Transformation
American People	American Peoples
Emphasis on national unity	Emphasis on group diversity
Individual citizen	Culture/ethnic/gender group
Individual rights	Group rights
Voluntary associations	Ascribed groups
Civic/individual identity	Racial/gender identity
National identity	Culture group identity
Emphasis on political freedom	Emphasis on ethnicity/gender
Multiethnicity	Multiculturalism
Melting pot	Mosaic/patchwork quilt
Americanization/assimilation	Cultural pluralism
Realistic constraints	Utopian agendas
Free society	Diverse society
Majority rule/limited gov't.	Social justice for groups
Realism about human nature	"Nature" is socially constructed
Natural rights	"Rights" are socially constructed

Objective moral order	Morality is socially constructed
American achievements	Gaps between ideal and real
Europeans discover America	Three worlds meet
British constitutional heritage	Convergence of three worlds
Mayflower colonists land	Hunters cross the Bering Strait
Emphasis on West	Emphasis on Non-West
Political/Intellectual history	Social/Ethnic history
Free enterprise	Economic equality
Emphasize equal opportunity	Emphasize equality of results
Stories of soldiers at war	Stories of the home front
American citizen	Global citizen
Citizen (of U.S.)	Resident (of U.S.)
National interests	Transnational concerns
Patriotism	Transnationalism
America Is	America Will Be
Preserve our Constitution	Fulfill our "social ideals"
Improve American democracy	Create a genuine democracy
Transmit the American Regime	Transform the American Regime
American Regime perpetuated	Counter-Regime created

NOTES

1. James W. Ceaser, *Liberal Democracy and Political Science* (Baltimore: Johns Hopkins University Press, 1990), 8.

2. Bernard Bailyn, *Faces of Revolution: Personalities and Themes in the Struggle for American Independence* (New York: Vintage Books, 1992), 241.

3. Letter from Thomas Jefferson to James Madison, November 18, 1788. In the "Correspondence of Thomas Jefferson" on the website of the School of Cooperative Individualism, www.cooperativeindividualism.org.

4. Alexander Hamilton, James Madison, and John Jay, *The Federalist Papers*, introduction by Clinton Rossiter (New York: Mentor, 1961), vii–viii.

5. *The Federalist Papers*, #51, 322.

6. *The Federalist Papers*, #55, 346.

7. Mathew Spalding and Patrick J. Garrity, *A Sacred Union of Citizens: George Washington's Farewell Address and the American Character*, int. by Daniel J Boorstin (Lanham, MD: Rowman and Littlefield Publishers, Inc., 1996), 183.

8. Spalding and Garrity, *Sacred Union*, 183.

9. George Washington, "First Annual Message," January 8, 1790, *The Papers of George Washington*, The Avalon Project at Yale Law School, online at www.yale.edu/lawweb/avalon/presiden/sou/washs01.htm.

10. Washington, "First Annual Message."

11. Northwest Ordinance of 1787, article 3, in Philip B. Kurland and Ralph Lerner, eds., *The Founders' Constitution* (Indianapolis: Liberty Fund, 1987), 1:28.

12. Lorraine Smith Pangle and Thomas L. Pangle, *The Learning of Liberty: The Educational Ideas of the American Founders* (Lawrence, KS: University Press of Kansas, 1993), 96.

13. Pangle and Pangle, *The Learning of Liberty*, 116.

14. James Madison, Letter to Barry, 4 August 1822, *The Mind of the Founder: Sources of the Political Thought of James Madison*, ed. Marvin Meyers, rev. ed. (Hanover, NH: University Press of New Hampshire, 1981), 343–46.

15. Pangle and Pangle, *The Learning of Liberty*, 143.

16. Spalding and Garrity, *Sacred Union*, 171.

17. George Washington, "Farewell Address," 1796, *The Papers of George Washington*, The Avalon Project at Yale Law School, online.

18. Washington, "Farewell Address."

19. Washington, "Farewell Address."

20. Pangle and Pangle, *The Learning of Liberty*, 150.

21. George Washington, "Eighth Annual Message," December 7, 1796, *The Papers of George Washington*, The Avalon Project at Yale Law School, online.

22. Washington, Letter to Alexander Hamilton, September 1, 1796.

23. Spalding and Garrity, *Sacred Union*, 21–22, 149–51, *passim*.

24. Harry V. Jaffa, *How to Think about the American Revolution* (Durham, NC: Carolina Academic Press, 1978), 53.

25. Letter of George Washington to John Adams, 15 November 1794, *The Writings of George Washington*, ed. John C. Fitzpatrick (Washington, DC: US Government Printing Office, 1931–40), vol. 34, 23.

26. See Naturalization Act, *Documentary History of the First Federal Congress*, Vol. 6, ed. Charlene B. Bickford et. al. (Baltimore, MD: John Hopkins University Press, 1968).

27. Thomas G. West, *Vindicating the Founders* (Lanham, MD: Rowman and Littlefield Publishers, Inc., 1997), 153–54.

28. West, *Vindicating*, 154–55.

29. West, *Vindicating*, xiv–xv.

30. West, *Vindicating*, 15.

31. West, *Vindicating*, 18–20.

32. West, *Vindicating*, 5.

33. West, *Vindicating*, 10–11

34. West, *Vindicating*, 10.

35. West, *Vindicating*, 32–33.

36. West, *Vindicating*, 36

37. All the following quotes from Sidney Hook's Jefferson Lecture taken from a copy of original typed manuscript of the Jefferson Lecture in the Humanities, National Endowment for the Humanities (NEH), May 1984.

38. All the following quotes from *The Education for Democracy* booklet come from *Education for Democracy: A Statement of Principles: Guidelines for Strengthening the Teaching of Democratic Values* (Washington, DC: American Federation of Teachers, 1987).

39. Paul Gagnon, *Democracy's Untold Story: What World History Textbooks Neglect* (Washington, DC: American Federation of Teachers, 1987), 26.

40. Gagnon, *Democracy's Untold Story*, 38.

41. Gagnon, *Democracy's Untold Story*, 27.

42. Joyce Appleby, Lynn Hunt, and Margaret Jacob, *Telling the Truth About History* (New York: W. W. Norton and Company, 1994), 291–92.

43. Linda K. Kerber, "The Meaning of Citizenship," *The Journal of American History*, Vol. 84, No. 3. (December 1997), 851.

44. Kerber, "The Meaning of Citizenship," 851.

45. See *National History Standards for United States History: Exploring the American Experiment* (Los Angeles: National Center for History in the School, University of California at Los Angeles, 1994); "One Nation Many Peoples: A Declaration of Cultural Interdependence," Social Studies Framework (Albany: State Education Department of New York, 1991); Colorado Model Content Standards for History (Denver: Colorado Department of Education, 1995); Maryland School Performance Program: "High School Learning Goals," *Social Studies* (Baltimore, MD: Maryland State Department of Education, September, 1996).

46. See Samuel P. Huntington, "The Erosion of American National Interests," *Foreign Affairs* (September-October 1997), 28–35.

47. *National History Standards for United States History,* 39.

48. John Patrick Diggins, "Can the Social Historian Get It Right?" *Transaction: Social Science and Modern Society*, vol 34. no. 2 (January/February 1997), 14–15.

49. Excerpt from Arthur M. Schlesinger Jr., "The Disuniting of America," in *American Educator* (Winter 1991), 14.

50. All previous quotes from paper by Bonnie Bernard, "Moving Toward a Just and Vital Culture: Multiculturalism in Our Schools," Western Regional Center For Drug-Free Schools and Communities, Far West Laboratory, commissioned by the Office of Education Research and Improvement, United States Department of Education, Washington, DC (April 1991).

51. Quotes from paper by Fred M. Newmann, "The Radical Perspective on Social Studies: A Synthesis and Critique," *Theory and Research in Social Education*, vol. XIII, no. 1 (Spring 1985), 1–18. (By The College and University Faculty Assembly of the National Council for the Social Studies. Research supported by a grant from the National Institute of Education, United States Department of Education, Washington, DC.)

52. NCATE quotes from *Capturing the Vision: Reflections on NCATE's Redesign Five Years After* (Washington, DC: AACTE Accreditation Resource Series, American Association of Colleges and for Teacher Educa-

tion, February 1993), 7. The recent version of NCATE "Standards for Professional Development Schools" (Spring 2001) reinforced the original themes of emphasis on multiculturalism, cultural diversity, and global education.

53. *Capturing the Vision*, 5

54. *Capturing the Vision*, 9.

55. *Capturing the Vision*, 8.

56. *Education for Democracy: Renewing Our Commitment* (Washington, DC: Albert Shanker Institute, 2003), 3–4.

57. See, for example, John Fonte and Robert Lerner, "History Standards Are Not Fixed," *Transaction: Social Science and Modern Society,* vol. 34, no. 2 (January/February, 1997), 20–25.

58. *Education for Democracy* (2003), 20.

59. *Education for Democracy* (2003), 16.

60. *Education for Democracy* (2003), 18.

61. Diane Ravitch, Review of Minnesota Social Studies Standards, Minnesota Department of Education, online at www.education.state.mn.us/content/059712.pdf.

62. Jerry Martin, Review of Minnesota Social Studies Standards, online at www.education.state.mn.us/content/053193.pdf.

63. Public Comments Section, Minnesota Social Studies Standards, online.

64. Letter dated October 23, 2003 to Commissioner Cheri Pierson Yecke, Minnesota Department of Education, from Dr. Mary Jo Maynes, Chair, Department of History, and other members of the history department at the University of Minnesota. Letter in possession of author. Previously available on Minnesota Department website.

65. Letter dated October 23, 2003.

6

Closing the Racial Gap: Culture Matters
ABIGAIL THERNSTROM

THE STUDENT BODY of Cedarbrook Middle School in a Philadelphia suburb is one-third black, two-thirds white. The town has a very low poverty rate, good schools, and a long-established black middle class. But in an eighth-grade advanced algebra class that a reporter visited in June 2001, there was not a single black student. The class in which the teacher was explaining that the 2 in 21 stands for 20, though, was 100 percent black. A few black students were taking accelerated English, but no whites were sitting in the English class that was learning to identify verbs.[1]

The Cedarbrook picture is by no means unique. It is all too familiar, and even worse in the big-city schools that most black and Hispanic youngsters attend. Today, at age seventeen the typical black or Hispanic student is scoring less well on the nation's most reliable tests than at least 80 percent of his or her white classmates. In five of the seven subjects tested by the National Assessment of Educational Progress (NAEP), a majority of black students perform in the lowest category—Below Basic. The result: by twelfth grade, blacks are typically four years behind white and Asian students, while Hispanics are doing only a tad better. These students are finishing high school with a junior high education.

This is a problem that can be solved. There is no good excuse for the racial gap in skills and knowledge. That gap is not an IQ story. But meeting the demands of schools is harder for members of some racial and ethnic groups than others. Some group cultures are academically advantageous. On the other hand, the values, habits, and skills that we call "culture" are not impervious to change. Indeed, they are shaped and reshaped by the social environment, and good schools play an invaluable part in that process. In educating academically disadvantaged kids, they aim to do more than teach the core academic subjects. They are deeply engaged in a "civic education" whose purpose is to transform the culture of their students—*as that culture affects academic achievement.*

Culture matters—that which informs a school, and that which students bring to a school. "Talking about cultural influences on achievement makes Americans uncomfortable. . . . But cultures differ in many ways, including academic orientation," *New York Times* education columnist Richard Rothstein has written. "Nobody knows a good way to discuss this. . . ."[2]

True enough. And yet group cultural differences are certainly no secret. "Sometimes my friends say, 'Can I borrow your notes?' They want them because I'm Asian and they assume I'm really smart," Karissa Yee, a freshman at San Francisco's Lowell High School, told a reporter.[3] A Sikh immigrant student in a California high school says, "Every day [our parents] tell us: "Obey your teachers. Do your schoolwork. Stay out of trouble. You're there to learn, not to fight. Keep trying harder. Keep pushing yourself. Do your homework. After you have done that, you can watch TV."[4]

It's a stereotype, but it's roughly accurate. The story of Asian American success in school is extraordinary. They are a tiny minority (roughly 4 percent of the American population) but a big presence in all highly selective schools. In many respects they do far better academically than whites. Even taking social class—family education and income—into account, they outperform members of all other groups.

This remarkable academic accomplishment is the product of cultural attitudes that various Asian groups brought with them and transmitted from generation to generation over a very long time. The closest historical parallel is with East European Jews, who have also experienced rapid Americanization in the century since their arrival on American shores without losing their extraordinary drive for educational excellence.[5]

Central to those cultural attitudes is a belief in the rewards that come with academic success. Asian American students are more deeply engaged in their schoolwork than their non-Asian classmates. They take Advanced Placement courses at triple the white rate. They have embraced the American work ethic with life-or-death fervor. Their parents expect nothing less.

Those expectations are evident in the results of a 1987–1990 survey of 20,000 students in nine high schools in California and Wisconsin conducted by sociologist Laurence Steinberg.[6] An intriguing group difference emerged from a question asking students about the "trouble threshold" in their families. What was the lowest grade they thought that they could receive without their parents getting angry? The answers revealed real racial and ethnic differences, with Asian students much more worried than black and Hispanic youngsters about the response of their parents to bad grades. Asian youths were successful, Steinberg writes, "not because of their stronger belief in the payoff for doing well, but because they have greater fear of the consequences of not doing well."

Weren't Asian parents being unrealistic in demanding that their children always get A's? Many Asian youths, they must have understood, are merely average or below average in their abilities. But Steinberg made a fascinating discovery: Asian parents and their children had a set of distinctive attitudes. They did not think in terms of innate ability. Nor did they see luck or teacher biases as playing a part in their grades. Academic success or failure did not (in their view) depend upon things "outside their personal control."[7] They believed instead that their academic performance depended almost entirely on how hard they worked; their performance was within their control. A grade below an A was evidence of insufficient effort.

The basic reason why Asian-American students today are outperforming American whites in school is thus somewhat ironic, as Steinberg notes. The children of immigrants are typically beating the competition because they are the true descendants of Benjamin Franklin. These American newcomers are the group that has most intensely embraced the traditional American work ethic.

Asians are not the only group to deliver cultural messages to their offspring, of course. But when we look at the education of Hispanic Americans, we see that these messages do not always mesh so well with the objectives of the school. The Hispanics who are flooding into American schools today are very much like Italian immigrants circa 1910. For those Italian peasants, school was not a high priority; they expected their children to enter the workplace as soon as possible. Like the Italians before them, many of the problems affecting the school performance of Latino children are rooted in their immigration background, in their movement back and forth across the border, and in the specific cultural and economic characteristics of the families who choose to migrate and often had to settle for low-skilled jobs in the Southwest that kept their children either working in the fields or bouncing from school to school.

Black academic underachievement also has deep historical and cultural roots. The first signs of underachievement appear very early in the life of black children, and although scholars have not been able to pinpoint the precise reasons, they can identify some of the risk factors that seem to be limiting their intellectual development. Among them: low-birth weight, single-parent households, and birth to a very young mother. There seem to be racial and ethnic differences in parenting practices that perhaps play a role in academic underachievement.

African American children tend to be less academically prepared when they first start school and are less ready, as well, to conform to behavioral demands. As a consequence, black students have disciplinary problems throughout their school careers at much higher rates than members of any other group. There are those who see racism at work in this pattern; there is no convincing evidence for the charge, however.

Doing well in school requires time on task and concentration, but black students spend an astonishing amount of time on their "social homework"—namely, watching television. They claim to be spending the same time on the homework assigned by their teachers as their classmates, but—given the hours devoted to TV—at best their attention is divided. That may be one reason why they are less likely to complete the school assignments. The special role of television in the life of black teen culture may also explain why they are willing to settle for low grades.

The process of connecting black and Latino children to the world of academic achievement isn't easy in the best of educational settings. But good schools show that it can be done. Their unstated goal, it might be said, is to replicate the culture that has served Asian families so well—within the schoolhouse walls, however. They aim to instill the same work ethic, to convince the children that academic success is the key to their future, and that hard work (not innate ability) will determine their acquisition of the skills and knowledge they absolutely must acquire to thrive in a competitive economy.

Good schools that put highly disadvantaged kids on the road to academic success do exist; there are just too few of them. The list is thus relatively short, but includes the KIPP Academies in New York, Houston, and elsewhere; North Star Academy in Newark, New Jersey; the South Boston Harbor Academy in Boston, among others. In the remaining pages of this chapter, I attempt to provide a close look at the "civic education" that is central to the instruction these schools offer.

The schools I came to admire all offer a first-class academic education, which focuses relentlessly on the core subjects during long school days, long weeks (Saturday classes too), and long years. But their attention to habits and skills beyond the academic subjects is evident in their own descriptions of the schools. The web site of the Amistad Academy in New Haven, for instance, contains a section called "Pillars of 'Harder and Smarter' Instruction." "Behavior," it explains, "should be thought of in the same way as academics—it must be taught. Effective behavioral instruction, like effective academic instruction, must be modeled, practiced, and reinforced."[8] "Are we conservative here?" Gregory Hodge, the head of the Frederick Douglass Academy asks us rhetorically. "Of course we are. We teach middle class values like responsibility."

In 1997 the College Board organized a "National Task Force on Minority High Achievement." The group consisted of representatives of mainstream civil rights groups, and the College Board itself tends to stick to very safe ground. And yet its report, *Reaching the Top*, which was released in October 1999, courageously placed considerable stress on the culture of the home, drawing a sharp contrast between East Asians and non-Asian minorities.[9]

Reaching the Top described the problem of underachievement as emerging "very early" in a child's life, and it referred to the "cultural attributes of home, community, and school," talking at length about the views toward school and hard work that Asian parents transmit to their children. "East Asian American high school and college students . . . spend much more time on their studies outside of school and are more likely to be part of academically oriented peer groups. . . ." In addition, "East Asian parents are more likely than Whites to train their children to believe success is based on effort rather than innate ability," and thus they instill in their children the values of hard work, "diligence, thoroughness, and self-discipline."[10] It was a point that Laurence Steinberg, in *Beyond the Classroom*, had made three years earlier. "In terms of school achievement," his study found, "it is more advantageous to be Asian than to be wealthy, to have nondivorced parents, or to have a mother who is able to stay at home full-time."[11]

"Culture" is a loose and slippery term that has been used in a great many different ways. It is sometimes taken to mean a fixed set of group traits that are passed on from generation to generation, an inheritance that is fairly impervious to changes in the social environment.

This is not how we use the term. In arguing that cultures of racial and ethnic groups strongly influence the educational performance of youths, we are simply saying that children first develop values, attitudes, and skills as a result of their experience in the families that raised them. But those values, attitudes, and skills continue to be shaped by their interaction with their peers, teachers, neighbors, and other aspects of their environment. In part, a common American culture influences American children in general. But some cultural patterns vary with social class or region. And some vary systematically along racial and ethnic lines. These differences are not identical to those that could have been identified a century or two centuries ago. The cultures of these racial and ethnic groups have altered as a result of changes in the social environment, and they will continue to change in the future. Good schools can become an enormously important element in that environment.

One further comment about what we mean by "culture." It is in part group differences in values. But it is also, as sociologist George Farkas has argued, "a tool kit of *skills*, the means by which strategies of action are constructed." Low-income parents, he notes, do value education, stable marriages, steady jobs, and other "middle class" objectives. But they differ in the "culturally-shaped skills, habits, and styles" that facilitate the realization of those aspirations.[12] The College Board referred to the problem of counter-productive "culturally-shaped skills, habits, and styles" that made for academic underperformance. What should schools do? Except for its advocacy of after-school and other supplementary educational programs, *Reaching the Top* skirted the question.

None of the schools of which we have spoken skirt the issue, however. Indeed, they confront it head on. The habits of "diligence, thoroughness, and self-discipline" are precisely those they try to instill, a daunting task in dealing with inner city youth. KIPP's South Bronx black and Hispanic students all reside in a neighborhood in which, as the school's literature puts it, "illiteracy, drug abuse, broken homes, gangs, and juvenile crime" are rampant. It is equally true of the other schools we describe.

"We are fighting a battle involving skills and values," David Levin, founder of the South Bronx KIPP Academy, notes. "We are not afraid to set social norms." In effect, he has adopted James Q. Wilson's "broken windows" theory and applied it to schools. To ignore one piece of trash on the floor ("I hate trash," Levin remarked on our first visit to the school), one shirt improperly tucked in, one fight between kids, one bit of foul language would send a disastrous no-one-cares message. And thus, at KIPP, the staff responds to every sign of disorder—

however slight. The result: even in the lunchroom, students talk quietly and need the supervision of only one staff member.

At North Star a few years back, a student had pencilled what a reporter called a "rather benign four-letter word" on a hallway wall. The co-director, James Verrilli, called an emergency meeting of the student body. "Somebody here does not belong with the rest of us. Somebody here wants to live amidst trash," he shouted. [13] Making a big deal over small infractions prevents larger problems from happening. The same point is made in the South Boston Harbor Academy brochure. "SBHA addresses each and every incident of inappropriate behavior, fostering in students the real connection between actions and consequences," it reads.

Chaos and violence disrupt learning. But these schools aim for something more than a safe and orderly environment. "Teachers need to teach ethics, morals, and responsibility to the kids. Those are the things I think are lacking our curriculum," famed teacher Jaime Escalante said in a 1993 interview. "We need . . . to develop the simple concept of responsibility in our kids." [14]

At North Star, students pledge to abide by the "Core Values of Community—Caring, Respect, Responsibility, and Justice. "Amistad Academy will graduate students who can do well—and who will do good," the school's program statement states. "We really wanted these kids to understand what it means to be a citizen of a society," Dacia Toll, the principal, adds. [15] Amistad students are expected to demonstrate consistent adherence to the norms embodied in REACH: Respect, Enthusiasm, Achievement, Citizenship, and Hard Work.

Both schools start their mornings with all the students gathered together in a circle. Individual students step forward to apologize to the group when a social norm has been broken, when behavioral expectations have not been met—including the expectation of arriving at school on time. The apologies are a recognition that students who break school norms have chosen to do so. Those who adhere to those norms have also made a choice, and that choice is rewarded in a variety of ways.

Respect for teachers is a prerequisite for a disciplined and focused academic environment. At the schools we admire, a bright line is drawn between teachers and students. Teachers are friendly, but they are not the students' friends and most are called by their last names. Indeed, at KIPP DC: KEY Academy, the principal, Susan Schaeffler, recalls having to tell a mother that her daughter needed a mom, not a pal. Mothering means setting behavioral standards.

Students at these schools learn to speak politely to teachers and the principal, as well as strangers. It's another invaluable skill. In a seventh grade class we watched at Amistad, students said "thank you" as the teacher handed out work sheets, and she replied, "you're welcome." At North Star, we found ourselves shaking the hand of a stream of students who told us their names, looked us in the eye, smiled, shook our hands firmly, and welcomed us to their school. At many of the schools we visited, youngsters brought in extra chairs on which we could sit to watch a class.

Rafe Esquith is one fifth grade teacher in a large elementary school in Central Los Angeles, but his classroom is, in effect, a one-room schoolhouse. He, too, insists that his inner-city Latino and Korean students learn the basic social rules that many more affluent kids are no longer taught. And thus Esquith has his youngsters write individual thank you notes to visitors.

A 1992 survey of a representative sample of the metropolitan Detroit population found that young unemployed blacks failed to grasp the importance of dress and appearance to potential employers.[16] Those are not skills overlooked at the schools we celebrate. KIPP's education in "self-discipline" includes learning how to dress for success, how to sit in a classroom chair (no heads on desks), the importance of looking directly at the person to whom you are talking, and the point of standing when greeting someone.

KIPP has a dress code, although there aren't uniforms. That code includes closed shoes, shirts with sleeves, skirts to the knees, no big earrings or other jewelry, no tight clothing, and belts for the boys. At most of the other schools, though, students did wear uniforms—green shirts tucked in, khaki pants or skirts, dark shoes (no sneakers) at North Star, for instance. At none of the schools were students allowed to use clothes as a means of self-expression; no baggy pants with waists dropped to hip level, no untied shoes, no revealingly-worn shirts or blouses.

Students at both KIPP and North Star spend the beginning of the fifth-grade (their first year) learning the school's code of behavior. At all these schools teachers are role models; they, too, dress professionally and are invariably courteous. All the principals at our favorite schools know the name of every student. David Levin is not alone in never walking by a kid without saying hello. Civility and decorum permeate these schools. "Who are you to set behavioral standards?" Levin has been asked. "I'm the boss," he replied.[17] Understanding who's in charge (in any school and most jobs) is also integral to a good education.

Esquith, as the lone teacher in a contained classroom, doesn't need a dress code, but he does expect perfect behavior. A student from another teacher's class comes to his early morning math lessons. "Everything is noisy and rude in my classroom," he says. Esquith takes his kids to concerts, ballgames, and restaurants. Before they go, they learn to sit quietly at the concert, and to clap at the right time. Their presence at a restaurant never disturbs the other patrons; they talk quietly. "Teachers can't say at the last minute [before a field trip], I want you to be on your best behavior," Esquith explains. "By then, it's too late." "Best behavior" takes practice.

Visit any classroom in any school, and it's immediately clear whether students are engaged in learning. In schools with a culture of work, no one is slouching in a seat, staring into space, doodling, eating, whispering to classmates, fixing a friend's hair, wandering around the room, or coming and leaving in the middle of class. Teachers are teaching; chaos is not an ever-present threat.

Disciplined behavior and disciplined work go hand-in-hand. "Oh Steven, you weren't listening? Sorry to bother you," Esquith said to a student who can't answer a question because his attention had wandered. Esquith was delivering two simultaneous messages: zero tolerance for inattention, and civility works better than anger. Total attention, diligence, and thoroughness are also expected when the students participate in sports. On one of our visits, Esquith was teaching volleyball. For two months, his class practiced handling the ball and moving properly, but without any net in place. Students play the actual game when they're ready to do so well. Good athletes, they learn, pay meticulous attention to their craft; excellence in every endeavor requires discipline.

At KIPP students chant rules in unison—

We "slant" at all times.
We listen carefully at all times.
We follow the teachers' instructions
We answer when given the signal.
We stay focused to save time.
We will always be nice and work hard.

"Slant" is an acronym for: Sit up. Listen. Ask and answer questions. Nod your head so people know you are listening and understanding. Track your speaker by keeping your eyes on whoever is talking.

KIPPsters learn to avoid wasting work time by walking down halls rapidly and quietly in orderly lines, and sitting in their classroom seats immediately. They are taught small habits that make a big difference—like using a finger on their left hand to keep track of their place in a book while the right hand is raised to ask a question. They learn to organize their pencils, notebooks and assignment sheets; six rules for notebook organization are spelled out on a handout. "God wants you to be organized, whatever God you believe in," Levin tells a class. At Houston's KIPP the students pick up worksheets containing math, logic, and word problems as they walk into school; they do them in their spare minutes in the day. "If you're off the bus, you're working," Mike Feinberg, the director, says.

Ronald Ferguson, who has been studying middle class black students in Shaker Heights and elsewhere, has found that 21 percent of black males in the lower track in school say, "I didn't try as hard as I could in school because I worried about what my friends might think." He also notes the "misguided love" of many teachers who "are a little too sympathetic . . . [letting] the blacks kids in elementary school get away with more, just relax, doze off in class, or not pay much attention."[18]

Teachers whose definition of "love" is letting kids doze off should be fired. Or not hired to begin with, although only charter schools are truly free to pick their staff and fire those who don't work out. Good teachers aren't tempted by racial double standards in judging academic work. But they also know that nurturing an alternative peer culture in which high academic achievement earns respect is essential.[19]

In the Detroit survey, young blacks (both employed and unemployed) underestimated the degree to which employers expected those whom they hired to be a "team player."[20] Esquith has created a supportive and nurturing community within his classroom. "Who has a compliment to give someone today?" he frequently asks. "We're a team," a KIPP teacher says. "Everyone ready? We wait until they are." To an incoming group of fifth-graders, Levin explains: A team is a family. We don't make fun of teammates. If you make other students feel bad, they won't concentrate in class. They'll be thinking about how to get back at you. And that will make you feel terrible, and around and around it will go. At the end of the year, that's what you will have spent your time on. But there will be no questions on the state test about being mean. "You are all KIPPsters," he concludes. "We're only worried about everyone moving ahead together." The stress on teamwork is a strategy to alter both behavioral norms and the academic culture. The student who can't spell a word is letting the "family" down. The youngster who thinks schoolwork is nerdy can't be part of the team.

Who wants to be left off a team? Other schools, too, nurture a sense of belonging to a special (and academically serious) group. The morning circles at North Star and Amistad are a daily reminder of the students' membership in a culture so different from the one to which many of the neighborhood peers belong. "Why are you here?" a teacher asks in a "call-response" chant that students run through in the morning circle. "To get an education," the students reply. "And what will you have to do?" Part of the students' response: "Take care of each other!" Teammates "take care of each other," and take care of their special place—which the school becomes.

At North Star and KIPP, we noticed students picking up trash when they saw it; they viewed the school as their second home—for some, their first home. They are expected to wipe their own lunch tables clean. Rafe Esquith's fifth-graders constantly scrub the tables, sweep the floor, and put things away, making the place look orderly. They don't need to be asked to do so; it's a routine part of their magic life in his one-room schoolhouse. And it's inseparable from the habit of hard academic work to which the "team" becomes committed.

Levin is "trying to break a complicated cycle" (as he puts it) in which the kids who start behind stay behind. In effect, the school is the employer they will later encounter. There are weekly paychecks in KIPP dollars that reflect such qualities as attendance, promptness, organization and neatness, hard work, behavior outside of class, and the respect given other "teammates." Checks are given out on Mondays, must be co-signed by parents, and can be used to purchase school supplies and other items in the KIPP store. Those whose paychecks maintain a certain average are eligible for trips to places like Utah, California, and Washington, DC.

In the real world, irresponsible decisions can be costly. At the KIPP DC: KEY Academy one of the students broke a window. Either the school pays for it or your mother pays and she can't afford it, Susan Schaeffler, the principal, told the student. She offered a deal: double dollars on the student's paycheck, but everything he earned would go towards replacing the window. At every KIPP Academy, the connection between hard work, good behavior, and rewards in life is very clear.

Grades don't figure into the KIPP Bronx paychecks, but there are plenty of rewards for academic accomplishment: a Wall of Honor in the hallway, award assemblies, "students of the week" listed on the classroom walls, along with "Homework Champs" and "Reading Champs" and samples of excellent written work.

Esquith, too, has a complicated system of points, awards, and paychecks. In class, students lose more points by giving a wrong answer than they gain by a correct one; he wants them to think before speaking. Trips to DC, California's Muir Woods, Philadelphia, the Oregon Shakespeare Festival, and elsewhere have long been integral to the education he offers; they reward mature behavior. A role in a Shakespearean production is also earned, in part by a willingness to spend countless hours working on the play, putting the classroom in order after hours, and so forth.

Paychecks in Esquith's class—unlike those at KIPP—reflect both academic and other work, as well as behavior. Every student in his class has a job, some more demanding and paying better than others. For instance, the attendance monitor, who keeps track of student absences, earns less than the janitors who are responsible for keeping the room spotless. Students have checking accounts, with the amounts recorded in ledgers by bankers, hired for their reliability. On top of their regular pay, students earn money by getting a perfect score on a test, having perfect attendance for a month, coming to school for the 6:30 a.m. math class, joining the orchestra, or staying after school for Shakespeare. On the other hand, they are fined for being late to school, having a messy desk, and breaking other classroom rules. Once a month there is an auction in which the students bid on such items as pens, calculators, and chess sets.

Property, as well, is bought and sold at Esquith's auctions. Classroom seats are real estate—with some locations worth more than others. The students pay rent, but if they have earned and saved enough, they can buy their seat as a condo. In fact, they can buy other students' seats, at which point rent is paid to them. (The kids know that if they are profligate and can't pay rent, they could be "homeless" and find themselves sitting on the floor, although we saw everyone safely in their chairs.) All students pay income taxes, and seat-owners pay a property tax as well. "This is like Monopoly," one youngster notes. To which Esquith answered, "Buddy, this is real life." His kids are learning the rules of the American game—which they can choose to join or reject.

Other schools attempt to acculturate the students to the larger world they will be entering in a variety of ways. At Amistad, for instance, every student participates in the school's "microsociety." Some students own their own "businesses," and there is a student-run bank, newspaper, museum, police force, court system, and legislature. The teachers pick the managers, but the managers choose the employees who apply for the jobs and are paid in Amistad dollars. Students who interview poorly (mumbling, failing to ask questions, and so forth) are not likely to be hired, and may end up in the ranks of the unemployed, with no income. If they've already been lawyers in the sixth and seventh grades, these children learn to think, "I can be a lawyer," Dacia Toll, the director notes.[21]

A variety of messages are intertwined in the education we have been describing.

In a KIPP phonics class, the teacher asks, "What room is this?" The students chant the answer: "This is the room that has the kids who want to learn to read more books to make a better tomorrow." "We are giving the kids the skills and confidence to take them to someplace better," David Levin says.

"Someplace better": the world of opportunity that awaits them if they are ready to take advantage of it. Getting ready is the point of working so hard. "Good things happen," Levin says, letting the students finish the sentence: "when you do the right thing." He goes on: "You never know when good things are going to happen. You want to be in a situation in which nothing is ever denied you."

On one of our visits, Levin has extra tickets to a Yankees game. They go to the students with the highest paycheck averages—the students who have met the behavioral demands of KIPP. And while grades aren't part of the mix, hard work (essential to learning) is. In a "Thinking Skills" class, Levin rhetorically asks: "Why do you have to finish work at home that you didn't finish here?" The answer: "You want knowledge." KIPP, it's important to recall, stands for "Knowledge is Power Program." Knowledge provides the power to get you to that better place.

Rafe Esquith, the KIPP Academies, North Star, Amistad, and other schools, in a multitude of ways, remind the students of what they're striving for. "Where are you headed?" a North Star teacher asks the students in the morning circle. "College!" they answer, pointing upward. North Star and KIPP name classrooms after various colleges. "Every day, starting in fifth grade, we heard about college, college, college," a KIPP alumnus remembers.[22] Esquith has long had college banners from elite schools decorating his walls, with the names of the students admitted to them underneath. When he takes his kids on trips, they stay at good hotels and eat at good restaurants. "I want to show them what they're working for," he explains. "In our neighborhood, you look outside your window and you see burned buildings," one of his students has remarked. But, she went on, he "teaches us that there is more to life than just [what's] outside the window."[23]

The schools we saw are helping their students get ready for a life beyond the burned buildings, but they can't do the job for them. They must take responsibility for their own lives. "We do everything we can to help, but we place the burden on them to get the job done," Gregory Hodge, the principal at the Frederick Douglass Academy in Harlem, explains.[24] "You've got to be ready in life," Levin tells his KIPPsters. "We will help you get ready; that's what we're trying to do." "My job is to open a lot of doors for these kids," Esquith says. "Their job is to choose which ones to walk through." They make choices, and choices have consequences. "It's not my job to save your souls," he tells his class. "It's my job to give you an opportunity to save your own soul."

It's an optimistic message about America, and about the rules that govern social mobility—the climb out of poverty to greater affluence. "There Are No Shortcuts" on the road to success, although doors are open for those determined to walk through them. Neither KIPP nor Esquith promise a rose garden—a future in which race and ethnicity will not matter. But the opportunities outweigh the barriers, they suggest; skills and persistence will pay off.[25]

In any case, barriers too easily become an excuse for failure. In May 2001, the *New York Times* quoted a Massachusetts teacher, James Bougas, on the subject of the statewide testing to which he objected. "Low scores," he said, "can reflect family hardship, not lack of effort or teaching."[26] It's a very different philosophy from that which informs KIPP. "You live in a world in which things are often not fair," Levin tells a sixth grade class. But the road to success is not paved with excuses. Or second chances.

At all the schools we admired, if a student goofs off or violates the rules of behavior, there are predictable and immediate consequences. No sob stories could persuade Levin to let a student go to the Yankee game unless he or she had earned a ticket. "You can't argue your way into privilege," Levin tells the sixth-graders. "You've got to earn it step-by-step." A disruptive student asks Esquith, "Can we talk about it?" "No," he replies without hesitation. A young girl is not listening to a classmate reading King Lear. "Tomorrow if you're not listening, what's going to happen?" he asks. "I'll have to leave," she whispers. "Yes, and how long will you be outside? The rest of the year, yes." They know he means it.

There are plenty of middle class kids who need to hear the same message, but, as with inadequate instruction in math and other core subjects, when schools fall down on their job, those who suffer most are the students who arrive with the least. Much is made of the fact that more affluent children have parents who read to them, and start school with larger vocabularies and a knowledge of numbers, letters, and colors. Those from low-income families certainly need help in beginning to acquire academic skills at an early age. But arguably the more difficult job is to teach "desire, discipline, and dedication," the watchwords painted in red and blue letters on sidewalks throughout Houston's KIPP. The students need to believe, just for starters, that indeed they can go "someplace better."

"We want students who, when we say, run through that wall, will run because they believe something is good on the other side," Levin tells a group of goofing-off students. "Fire, trust, the will to succeed is what we want to see. If you have that fire, it should show every day." It's hard to find that "fire" in many youngsters in any schools—whatever their demographic profile. Analyzing a survey of 20,000 teenagers in nine high schools in the decade 1985–1995, Laurence Steinberg found widespread disengagement from academic work.[27] But, again, the consequences are particularly severe for those students who do not come to school with the "tool kit" of "culturally shaped skills, habits, and styles" they need to succeed.

The effort to put disadvantaged youngsters on the traditional ladder of social mobility has another component, never explicitly articulated. Both Esquith and KIPP—but not every school we visited to the same degree—introduce their students (black, Hispanic, and Korean) to great writing, great music, and great documents. The Declaration of Independence, the words to "America, My Country 'Tis of Thee," and quotations from Henry David Thoreau and Oliver Wendell Holmes Jr.— as well as Michael Jordan and others—decorate the walls in the KIPP Academies in Houston and New York. Esquith's class is known as "The Hobart Shakespeareans," but on one of our visits the students were reading *Huck Finn* out loud, and on another, *Animal Farm*. The class discussion, as they read along, had everyone (nine- and ten-year olds) mesmerized.

Esquith and KIPP are guiding their students down the road that Ralph Ellison walked almost seven decades ago. "In Macon County, Alabama," Ellison wrote in 1963, "I read Marx, Freud, T. S. Eliot, Pound, Gertrude Stein, and Hemingway. Books which seldom, if ever, mentioned Negroes were to release me from whatever 'segregated' idea I might have had of my human possibilities. I was freed not by propagandists . . . but by composers, novelists, and poets who spoke to me of more interesting and freer ways of life."[28]

Even in the Jim Crow South, Ellison thought of himself as a writer and an American. "The values of my own people are neither 'white' nor 'black'; they are American," he wrote.[29] It is not how most educators think about black and Hispanic youngsters, it appears. They offer minority children a "segregated" idea of their potential.

A majority of both black and Hispanic adults in the nation want schools to "promote a common culture."[30] And yet many of the schools we saw—some we liked and many we did not—stressed racially-linked cultural differences. Students were kept on a very heavy diet of literary and historical material that stressed America's moral failings and the importance of racial identity. Their walls were decorated exclusively with pictures of African Americans, Malcolm X being most popular. Posters featured "African Americans in the Arts," alleged African sayings, Michael Jordan, Paul Robeson, and some quite obscure figures such as the first African American woman to receive an international pilots license. In one school, classrooms were given Kwanzaa names. At another, students recited "A Pledge for African People" that runs, in part: "We are an African People. . . . We will struggle to resurrect and unify our homeland; we will raise many children for our nation. . . . We will be free and self-determining; we are an African People."[31]

What, precisely, is the "homeland" or the "nation" to which this pledge referred? "I am as American as any," the well-known writer Richard Rodriguez has said.[32] African Americans—with the exception of recent immigrants—are *more* American than most of the nation's residents; unlike that of Rodriguez, their families go back centuries. "We feel that for too long our history was not told. They see whites on television," one principal said to us. "They want to read about issues relevant to them," another argued.

Fair enough. Until roughly the early 1970s, American history was mainly white history. It is also true that many black children remain too racially isolated; whites are strangers in their daily life. But too heavy a dose of African American history and literature arguably reinforces the isolation. Perhaps the very fact of racial isolation makes the stress on black history and literature particularly "relevant," but Ellison's view is worth remembering. In the brutally segregated South, he could never forget that he was black. He was also an avid reader of black literature. And yet it wasn't mainly black writing that spoke to him "of more interesting and freer ways of life." In fact, his discovery of T. S. Eliot's poem, "The Wasteland," was the intellectual turning point that sent him on the road to his emergence as a writer.[33]

There are magnificent books whose authors are not white, and of course all students should be exposed to them. Ellison's own master-piece, *Invisible Man*, is an obvious example. It's not *black* literature; it's American literature—about the black experience that is so central to the nation's history. "The price of being a brown author is that one cannot be shelved near those one has loved. The price is segregation," Richard Rodriguez has said. You are "shelved south of the border with the other writers who write about growing up Puerto Rican, and that's your section and you are so far away from James Baldwin, the writer who so influenced you when you were growing up."[34]

This is not an easy issue, however. Color has something to do with most people's sense of identity—more or less, depending on the individual and on the particular racial or ethnic group. But where, precisely, is the line between what Ellison called "propaganda" (and Rodriguez calls "segregation") and material on Hispanic history, for instance, that is perhaps especially inspirational for Hispanic kids? Particularly for black students, there is still no escape from racial identity. In the morning circle at North Star, three students beat West African-style drums. And yet that did not seem like "propaganda" to us, in part because the central message of the school is so very clear: Racial identity is not destiny.

The notion of race-as-destiny, Ellison argued, stifles the development of individuality and nurtures "that feverish industry dedicated to telling Negroes who and what they are"—an industry that "can usually be counted upon to deprive both humanity and culture of their complexity."[35] The "industry" to which he referred was populated by both blacks and whites.

"If white society has tried to do anything to us," he noted in the 1970s, "it has tried to keep us from being individuals"—to deprive blacks of the understanding that "individuality is still operative beyond the racial structuring of American society."[36] The best classes that we saw try to teach children the lessons that Ellison had to figure out in terrible racial circumstances. The extraordinary amount of time their students spend in school, the serious academic demands made upon them, and what they read are all aimed, in part, at helping students define themselves as individuals and Americans in a society rich with opportunity.

If these students come to think of themselves as unique, free to choose their identity, to emphasize their racial and ethnic group ties as much or little as they wish, and if they come to understand that they belong in the country in which they live, they will have an excellent chance of going far if they acquire solid skills. This is not a truth confined to racial and ethnic minorities. The traditional ticket to social mobility in America has been the ability of individuals to define themselves apart from the group (as defined by social class, geographical location, and a variety of other indicators) into which they were born.

"One of the kids asked me how I define freedom. And I told him that freedom is the power to choose to make a change in the right direction," Jaime Escalante has said.[37] But that freedom to choose requires both academic skills and an understanding of what the writer Jonathan Rauch once called "Main Street Codes"—the "rules for public behavior," the social norms that most Americans understand.[38]

Freeman A. Hrabowski III, the president of the University of Maryland Baltimore County, is nationally known for his work with black students. "Unless we have some interventions in settings where you have large numbers of poor people, poor children will not rise to the top," he said in an April 2002 interview. "[We must] give them the support to get the values they need. . . . I'm talking about values like hard work, respect for authority and willingness to listen to teachers. Many parents don't know how important these things are."[39]

Many schools don't understand their importance, either, although KIPP, North Star, the South Boston Harbor Academy, and others we have described certainly do. It's a point, however, not often articulated. It makes most people astonishingly nervous. Aren't these "white" values that President Hrabowski (black, himself) is pushing?

No. And Hrabowski is not the only black voice finally making that clear. In the summer of 2002, the Boston headquarters of Verizon was host to a dozen interns from Dorchester High School, where 70 percent of the students are African American and 25 percent are Hispanic. The summer interns came (in the words of a *Boston Globe* reporter) "sporting the styles and languages of school hallways and street corner hangouts." But they heard some tough talk from Karen Hinds, a West Indian immigrant who went to Dorchester High herself.

If you're interested in good jobs, you "have to know how to speak proper English," she admonished. Ignore those who say you are "acting white" or "sucking up," she went on. Your large hoop earrings, hip-hop styles, and inner-city walk have to go—when you're in the workplace, that is. Hinds's message was reinforced by an African American attorney from a prestigious law firm. "I don't think it is unreasonable to expect that you know how to speak with correct grammar when you walk into my office," Harry Daniels said to the assembled teenagers.[40]

It isn't a message that goes down well with everyone. In 1998, a school board member in majority-black Prince George's County, Maryland, suggested that teachers should correct the English of their students. Asked about the issue, the chairman of the English Department at the University of Illinois, Champaign-Urbana, responded: "Does the school board want [students] to start sounding less black?"[41]

"If you know how to do your job, it shouldn't matter what you look like or how you talk," said Kiara Robinson, one of the students at the Verizon meeting. "I don't think it's fair." In fact, it's not "fair" to students when schools fail to teach the rules of success—including standard English and the dress code of most well-paying jobs.[42] "The greatest problem now facing African-Americans is their isolation from the tacit norms of the dominant culture, and this is true of all classes," the sociologist Orlando Patterson has written.[43]

The best schools understand that fundamental point. Standards, testing, accountability—they are all essential. But the schools that are truly rescuing America's most academically disadvantaged kids are doing something more. They are providing a civic education in the values that make for life-long success. They are ending the students' isolation from the "tacit norms of the dominant culture," as Patterson has urged.

NOTES

[This essay has been adapted from Abigail Thernstrom and Stephan Thernstrom, *No Excuses: Closing the Racial Gap in Learning* (New York: Simon and Schuster, 2003).]

1. Dale Mezzacappa, "Facing an issue few want to touch," *Philadelphia Inquirer*, June 17, 2001: A01.

2. Richard Rothstein, "On Culture and Learning," *New York Times*, October 11, 2000: B10. No scholar has contributed more than Thomas Sowell to an understanding of "cultural influences on achievement." Among his many books, see particularly *Ethnic America: A History* (New York: Basic Books, 1981) and *Race and Culture: A World View; Migrations* and *Culture: A World View*; and *Conquests and Cultures: A World View* (New York: Basic Books, 1994, 1996, 1998).

3. Julian Guthrie, "Not geeks, gangsters at schools; Asian American parents, students meet in S.F. to find solutions, end myths about their culture," *San Francisco Examiner*, May 14, 2000: C1.

4. Margaret Gibson, *Accommodation without Assimilation: Sikh Immigrants in an American High School* (Ithaca, NY: Cornell University Press, 1988), 132.

5. For a searching and subtle analysis of the educational achievement of Jews in Providence, Rhode Island in the first third of the twentieth century, see Joel Perlmann, *Ethnic Differences: Schooling and Social Structure among the Irish, Italians, Jews, and Blacks in an American City, 1880–1935* (New York: Cambridge University Press, 1988), ch. 4. Perlmann analyzes group differences with the most elaborate controls for social and economic background, and finds large residual variations that can only be explained by what he terms "pre-migration cultural attributes."

6. Laurence Steinberg, *Beyond the Classroom: Why School Reform Has Failed and What Parents Need to Do* (New York: Simon and Schuster, 1996), 91, 161.

7. Steinberg, *Beyond the Classroom*, 91–94.

8. www.amistadacademy.org/about.modelschool.behavior.html

9. The College Board, *Reaching The Top: A Report of the National Task Force on Minority High Achievement* (New York: College Board Publications, October 1999)

10. College Board, *Reaching the Top*, 7, 14, 17, 18.

11. Laurence Steinberg, *Beyond the Classroom*, 86.

12. On this perspective, see Anne Swidler, whose views are summarized and applied to schooling issues in George Farkas, *Human Capital or Cultural Capital? Ethnicity and Poverty Groups in an Urban School District* (New York: Aldine de Gruyter, 1996), 11–13.

13. Lisa Coryell, "School's Success Rooted in Order," *Trenton Times*, May 20, 2001.

14. Carol Novak, Interview with Jaime Escalante, *Technos Quarterly*, Spring 1993, vol. 2, no. 1, www.technos.net/tq_02/1escalante.htm. Escalante is best known from the 1988 feature film *Stand and Deliver*, which told the remarkable story of the academic success of his math students in a predominantly Latino East Los Angeles public school with an abysmal academic record.

15. The Dacia Toll quotation is from Jodi Wilgoren, "In a Society of Their Own, Children Are Learning," *New York Times*, February 7, 2001: B9.

16. Reynolds Farley, Sheldon Danziger, and Harry J. Holzer, *Detroit Divided* (New York: Russell Sage Foundation, 2000), 142.

17. Levin told the "I'm the boss" story at a forum at the Massachusetts Department of Education, October 17, 2000.

18. Unpublished transcript, Brookings Papers on Educational Policy, Conference on National Standards, May 15–16, 2000; Brown Center on Education Policy, Brookings Institution, Washington, DC.

19. An alternative peer culture has the additional benefit of steering students away from neighborhood gangs. For a good recent description of the hazards of gang life for young black males, see Orlando Patterson, *Rituals of Blood: Consequences of Slavery in Two American Centuries* (New York: Basic Civitas, 1998), 137–45.

20. Farley, *Detroit Divided,* 142.

21. Wilgoren, "In a Society of Their Own," February 7, 2001: B9. See also the Amistad web site.

22. Marcos Maldonado, quoted on the KIPP web site www.KIPP.org/achievemt/day, viewed in May 2002.

23. Sandy Banks, "Disney Awards Teacher with a Touch of Class," *Los Angeles Times,* December 6, 1992: B1.

24. Samuel Casey Carter, "No Excuses: Seven Principals of Low-Income Schools Who Set the Standards for High Achievement," The Heritage Foundation, undated, 15.

25. In a 1990 study, Roslyn Mickelson found that black students do believe that "achievement and effort in school lead to job success later on." But they were more doubtful when asked about the likelihood of fair treatment in the work place; cited in Ronald F. Ferguson, "Teachers' Perceptions and Expectations and the Black-White Test Score Gap," in Christopher Jencks and Meredith Phillips, eds., *The Black-White Test Score Gap* (Washington, DC: Brookings Institution Press, 1998), 292–93.

26. Quoted in Richard Rothstein, "The Growing Revolt Against the Testers," *New York Times,* May 30, 2001: A19.

27. Steinberg, *Beyond the Classroom, passim.*

28. Ralph Ellison, "The World and the Jug," in John F. Callahan, ed., *The Collected Essays of Ralph Ellison* (New York: Modern Library, 1995), 164.

29. Ellison, "The Shadow and the Act," in Callahan, ed., *The Collected Essays,* 299.

30. Terry M. Moe, *Schools, Vouchers, and the American Public* (Washington, D.C.: Brookings Institution Press, 2001), Table 2–6. The survey was conducted in 1995. The black percentage was 57, the Hispanic 54, but (mysteriously) only 35 percent of whites signed on to the notion.

31. The web site of the Millwood public school district in Oklahoma City, www.millwood.k12.ok.us/Students.htm, viewed on March 22, 2002, contained "The Black Pledge of Allegiance," labeled as possibly "pertinent or relevant." That Pledge speaks of "One nation of Black people. . . . Totally united in the struggle for Black Love, Black Freedom, and Black Determination."

32. Robin Dougherty, "The Browning of America, Interview with Richard Rodgriquez," *Boston Globe*, April 14, 2002: E4.

33. Lawrence Jackson, Ralph Ellison: *The Emergence of Genius* (New York: John Wiley and Sons, 2002), 151.

34. Dougherty, "The Browning of America:" E4.

35. Ellison, "The Shadow and the Act," 57.

36. Ellison "Indivisible Man," first published in 1970, in Callahan, ed., *Collected Essays*, 394; and "'A Completion of Personality': A Talk with Ralph Ellison," in Callahan, ed., *Collected Essays*, 799.

37. Novak, Interview with Jaime Escalante.

38. Jonathan Rauch, "Courting Danger: The Rise of Anti-Social Law," Bradley Lecture, American Enterprise Institute, December 11, 2000.

39. "Never Let Them See You Sleep," interview with Karin Chenoweth, *Washington Post Magazine*, April 7, 2002: 14.

40. Megan Tench, "Straight Talk: Urban Teens Advised On What It Takes to Get Ahead," *Boston Globe*, August 5, 2002: B1.

41. DeNeen L. Brown, "A Good Word for Grammar: Pr. George's Schools Urged to Get Tough," *Washington Post*, March 16, 1998: 1.

42. Ellison attended Tuskegee from 1933–1936. According to Lawrence Jackson's biography of the great writer, the students were taught that their "ability to transcend jim crow would operate in proportion to their use of 'Good English,'" Ralph Ellison, "Shadow and Act," in Callahan, ed., *Collected Essays*, 110. Much of the education Tuskegee offered was relentlessly hostile to black culture, but this was an invaluable message to Ellison. The 1996 fight in Oakland, California over the school board's recognition of "Ebonics" as the primary language of African American children was pre-

cisely about the legitimacy of insisting that black children learn to switch to standard English, when appropriate, of course. For a balanced discussion of the issue, see John H. McWhorter, *The Word on the Street: Fact and Fable about American English* (New York: Plenum Publishing, 1998), chs. 6–8.

43. Orlando Patterson, "What to Do When Busing Becomes Irrelevant," *New York Times*, July 18, 1999: 17. Patterson is right to say the problem crosses class lines, but obviously it is more true of some African Americans than others. In an article on life in the Robert Taylor Homes in Chicago, the *Wall Street Journal* (December 19, 2000: 1) described the special isolation of the underclass: "Unemployment and a sense of alienation from mainstream society grew more pronounced until public housing life became like life nowhere else."

7

Should Felons Vote? A Paradigmatic Debate over the Meaning of Civic Responsibility

Thomas L. Pangle

WHAT FOLLOWS IS NOT a discussion of civic education, but rather an exercise in it. I elaborate an account of a paradigmatic contemporary issue that provides fruitful stimulus to argument that delves deeply into major questions of civic responsibility. The issue is, whether or not convicted felons ought to have the right to vote. I am not going to write as advocate of one side or the other. Instead, I shall present the strongest arguments on both sides of this controversy: by thus articulating a kind of dialogue, I mean to show how this debate takes us to the heart of questions we need to think about in regard to civic responsibility—and how this debate is an excellent one to present to students, young and old, to induce them to grapple with puzzles that deepen our awareness of the conflicting dimensions and goals of civic responsibility.

The question of voting rights of felons has become timely, in both Canada and in the United States. In Canada, this has in the past few years become a federal case, making its way through the appeals process—and decided finally, by the Supreme Court of Canada, in a tight 5–4 split decision, at the end of October 2002, with 265 pages of judicial opinions.[1]

But the issue has also been emerging as a subject of some discussion and agitation in the United States, especially in law and in prisoner advocate journals.[2] Why? Chiefly because this country now has an unprecedented number and percentage of convicted felons in the voting age population—enough to make not only the question of their rights, but also the question of their possible impact, as voters, loom larger. In the last generation, the number of prison inmates has grown from about 200,000, to around 1.2 million; the number of parolees from roughly 150,000, to approximately 700,000; the number of those on probation from one million, to three and a half million. A 1998 report by Human Rights Watch estimated that almost four million Americans, or 2 percent of the voting age population, are currently disenfranchised as a result of these laws.[3] One third of these disenfranchised are African-Americans. Three-quarters are persons who are not incarcerated—1.4 million are ex-felons and 1.5 million are on probation or parole.

Now to appreciate what the impact of these numbers might be, consider that just before the midterm elections of 2002, some major observers were saying that a total of only fifty thousand votes, across the country, might settle the question of which party controlled congress in the next term. Two years earlier, in the contested Florida recount in the presidential election, one major charge put forward by Republicans, with apparent evidence to back it up, was that in some districts, the results may have been seriously affected by the fact that numerous persons with records of past felonious conviction were allowed to vote, contrary to law; and on the other side, Democrats contended that many of the lists used to deny citizens the right to vote on account of their criminal records were in fact inaccurate and discriminatory. We were all thus reminded of the fact that in Florida, convicted felons lose forever their right to vote (under art. 6, sec. 4 of the state constitution). In addition, the particular districts in Florida where this charge of voter fraud was lodged were chiefly districts with large African-American populations; and we should also thereby have been apprised of the fact that the disenfranchisement of felons affects disproportionately the numbers of African-American male voters.

But the question of whether felons should lose their voting rights—and why they should, or why they should not—is a practical question that can also help us to clarify, by concretizing, a deep and abiding controversy in democratic political theory. I refer to the dialogue (the tension-ridden dialogue) between the more classical, civic-republican, and (on the other hand) the more modern, liberal-individualistic, conceptions of citizenship and statesmanship and freedom and responsibility. This theoretical controversy, between two differing but not wholly contradictory ways of conceiving the nature of republican government and citizenship, predates (and informs) the tradition of American political thought; but it also lives and develops within our tradition.

Now, the legal situation in the U.S. is a bit complicated: let me sketch it briefly. Though the right to vote is nowhere specifically mentioned in the original American Constitution or the Bill of Rights, it has been upheld by the courts as being an implicit fundamental right of citizens—subject to reasonable qualifications, including age and residence requirements that affect everyone.[4] But the legislative enactment and the administrative policing of this, as well as the rest of election law, has been understood to be left to state jurisdiction. The federal government has intervened only where state action has been held to be unconstitutionally discriminatory, especially after the enactment of crucial amendments to the constitution:

- the fifteenth amendment, prohibiting denial of voter rights on racial grounds;

- the nineteenth amendment, prohibiting denial of the right to vote on grounds of sex;

- the twenty-fourth amendment, prohibiting denial of the right to vote on grounds of failure to pay taxes;

- and the twenty-sixth amendment, prohibiting denial on grounds of age, of those eighteen or older.

State restrictions on the right to vote can and have also been challenged, sometimes successfully, on the basis of the equal protection of the laws clause of the fourteenth amendment. And it was chiefly on this basis that the lifetime disenfranchisement of felons, in the state of California, was challenged in the leading case that has come before the Supreme Court, decided in 1974: *Richardson v. Ramirez*, 418 U.S. 24. (The disenfranchisement has also been challenged under the eighth amendment, as a cruel and unusual punishment—the importance of which we'll see in a moment.) In this 1974 case, the Court's opinion (written by Rehnquist) upheld California's permanent disenfranchisement of convicted felons, as a valid exercise of state legislative authority—but did so on very narrow grounds, with almost no discussion of the broader and deeper issues of justice involved. For the court observed that this authority is explicitly granted to the states by the fourteenth amendment, in the previously very obscure section two.[5]

This section had previously been a dead letter in the law, because it enunciates a formula that was an unsuccessful attempt to try to force southern states to allow African-Americans the vote—a formula that was obviated three years later by the ratification of the fifteenth amendment, which explicitly guarantees to all citizens the right to vote. But three words in the otherwise dead section were held by the Court in the 1974 decision to be a clear indication of the intent of the framers to allow for the denial of the vote to those who have committed any crime.

Present state law, as one would expect, varies considerably by state—and most are not as harsh as California. As of Spring 2000:

• all states (and the District of Columbia) disenfranchised prison inmates while serving time, except for three states (Maine, Massachusetts, and Vermont: a fourth state, Utah, *used to* allow inmates to vote until 1998, when that was repealed by referendum);

• thirty-two states also, in addition, disenfranchised parolees;

• fourteen states, including California, disenfranchised felons for life—though some of these states, like Mississippi, disenfranchised only those who had committed specified very severe crimes (and also, most states have some procedures—usually very difficult—for rare reinstatement of voting rights).

Now, given the 1974 Supreme Court decision in the Ramirez case, the issue has pretty much ceased to be a federal constitutional issue in America: but it remains an issue of state as well as federal public policy and law. In other words, granted that the U.S. Constitution allows states to disenfranchise felons, *ought* states to do so?—and if so, for what valid reason?—and in what way or to what degree?

Or, is this disenfranchisement simply ill advised or even wrong, unjust, contrary to the basic principles of a free and democratic society—as has now been argued by the narrow majority in the case recently decided by the Canadian Supreme Court?

In Canada, this question, of justice or rightness, is a federal constitutional issue, because of the very different way such issues are framed under the Canadian Constitution. For in the Canadian Constitution's Charter of Rights, the right to vote, like *all* rights under the Canadian Charter of Rights, is declared under or after a primary blanket proviso of qualification stated in article one of the Charter.[6] That blanket proviso has been interpreted as forcing the courts continually to raise and consider the question: which restrictions on rights are justified by the basic principles of freedom and democracy?

Whether or not the plunge into such questions of political philosophy is a good idea for judicial practice, it is fruitful for political thought, including democratic theory. For this sort of far-reaching inquiry, applied to felon disenfranchisement, takes us to two fundamental questions:

• the first is, how are we to understand the moral basis, or meaning, of voting—and hence the moral qualification for voting, in a modern democracy such as ours?

• the second is, what ought to be the nature and goal of the loss of the right to vote as part of criminal punishment, under a democracy such as ours?

In other words, we need to note that the disenfranchisement of felons falls under two different legal rubrics, or may be conceived as being instituted with a view to two different, though not mutually exclusive, broad civic purposes:

On the one hand, the disenfranchisement may be conceived as chiefly a form or part of the punishment of the inmate.

But on the other hand, the disenfranchisement may be conceived as chiefly a disqualification of the inmate (parallel, say, to the disqualification from voting of fifteen year olds).

The argument *against* the disenfranchisement, which I am going to lay out first, is an argument that is couched largely, but not solely, in terms of more liberal-individualistic republican theory; and this argumentative perspective focuses on the *punitive* aspect as the more substantial, if not the sole, apparently liberal rationale for disenfranchisement.

THE ARGUMENT AGAINST DISENFRANCHISEMENT

Precisely as punitive, the disenfranchisement of felons, it is argued, reflects outmoded and unreasonable notions of what should be the goals of punishment in a liberal order, and of how best to achieve those goals. It is true of course, the opponents of disenfranchisement of felons concede, that this disenfranchisement is a very old and widespread practice throughout the world. But that should not necessarily make such disenfranchisement respectable. In fact, that should make the penalty suspicious in our liberal-progressive eyes. Our traditional disenfranchisement of felons has its historical roots in the English common law emerging out of the feudal period, where felony entailed what was called "civil death": in effect, a felon ceased to be considered a member of society; a felon lost all rights, not only to vote and participate, but to sue in the courts, to have legal protection of his property, or even to remain resident. Now it is a leitmotif of the liberal political philosophers of the Enlightenment, starting with Hobbes, and continued in Locke and Montesquieu—and their followers like Beccaria—to call into question the rationality of the harshness of much traditional punishment, as expressive of retaliatory passions in the populace that serve little constructive purpose, while effecting needless cruelties. Retribution as traditionally conceived, it is argued by these philosophers (most explicitly and sharply Hobbes[7]), is essentially reactive, seeking a remedy for suffering that lies irremediably in the past; reason dictates, on the contrary, forward-looking penalties targeted at prevention of future suffering from crime—through deterrence and rehabilitation.

So: if instead of simply accepting this tradition of criminal disenfranchisement, we ask the critical liberal question, how does this disenfranchisement contribute to deterrence?—we can see that the answer is: not much, or not very plausibly. It is not credible that persons prone to commit serious offenses will be stopped or even swayed by the thought that as a consequence they will lose the franchise. The loss of voting rights would be at most a tiny marginal addition to the other, far more directly onerous burdens of incarceration. But this tiny addition to deterrence is purchased at a very great cost to rehabilitation, which is the most constructive goal of punishment—even if we grant that it is the least likely to meet with great success in most cases.

Rehabilitation proceeds by trying to habituate prisoners in activities that will allow them to function successfully in society, after release, without resort to crime. Rehabilitation seeks to instill in prisoners an appreciation for the satisfactions of being respectable and honest members of a community to which they can conceive of themselves as contributing something. Now, if we deprive prisoners of the vote, we are cutting them off from participation in the political process, and thereby diminishing the chances that they will take an active interest in the affairs of the community during their prison time. If, on the other hand, we allow them to vote, it is at least a bit more likely that they may begin to occupy their enforced idleness by attending to the political scene, beginning to think about and take a partisan interest in electoral contests, and thus beginning to have a concern and an appreciation for the process of self-government that produces the laws which we are trying to teach them to respect.

Finally, though, we may have to grant that society also legitimately wishes to exact retribution from the criminals, if only out of overwhelming compassion for the human (if not wholly rational) feelings and thus sufferings of victims; for this reason, society aims to make convicted felons suffer, not only as a preventative of future or repeated crime, but also as a payment of the "debt to society" (as we say) that they incurred through their enjoying the fruits of their acts of lawless exploitation of their fellow citizens. But this particular punishment— namely, disenfranchisement, often for life—is an unfairly designed form of retribution. The principle of retributive justice is that "the punishment should fit the crime," and this means that the degree and kind of punishment should be lighter or heavier in proportion to the seriousness of the offense. But under most forms of legal disenfranchisement, all felons, or at least all inmates, equally lose the right to vote.

Now, what about the other purported purpose of disenfranchise-ment of felons—as a reasonable disqualification, parallel to the dis-qualification of the insane or of children? Well, it is true, the oppo-nents concede, that in most republics throughout history, the right to vote has been granted to only a portion of the sane adult citizenry, usually on the grounds that the right required, for its proper, public spirited, and responsible exercise, some sort of special qualifications of character. But: almost every other one of these criteria of disquali-fication, including (most prominently) gender, race, religion, property, and literacy, have been abandoned in modern democracy, and for good reason. While *some* of these disqualifications may in some measure have served their stated purpose under earlier forms of society, none continue to serve that purpose in modern conditions of society, and all involve some degree—and in contemporary conditions of society, an unacceptable degree—of arbitrary, unjust discrimination. The exclu-sion of some portion of the sane adult population from the vote has always in some degree been a mark of the fact that government, while claiming to be for the sake of all, has been in fact in the interest of a part—at the expense or through the exploitation of the excluded or marginalized. It has been one of the steady advances of modern de-mocracy that it has opened up full citizenship, including the voting right, to more and more of the adult citizenry, thus creating a more and more inclusive society, or a society that can more truly be said to give voice to, and thereby to attend to the interests of, all rather than only of a part. Should not that advance be continued, and extended to felons? In a truly just, truly free and democratic, society, even convicted citizens should be removed from society only temporarily, and as little as possible, consistent with their punishment.

What is more, this argument on grounds of universal liberal prin-ciples takes on poignant force when we observe, that in the United States in particular, the disenfranchisement of felons in practice means a dis-proportionate disenfranchisement of specific groups—primarily Afro-American males, but secondarily Hispanic males—who represent his-torically exploited and marginalized sectors of the population. How-ever well-intentioned the disenfranchisement of felons, is the policy not in effect a continuation of this marginalization?

It is true that we do exclude from the franchise young people un-der the age of eighteen, and it is true that this exclusion is reasonable and implies that we do think that some substantial maturity is required for the proper independent exercise of the vote. But this need not necessarily imply that any special moral character is required; it may be taken to mean nothing more than that voting requires a certain level of intellectual development—in other words, a certain practical experience of life, be that experience moral or immoral.

Besides, even if it is true that some convicted felons are likely to exercise their vote in a destructively malicious or irresponsible manner—Mafiosi voting for Mafiosi for example—there is no good reason to suppose that this is true of all, or even most felons (there is no hard evidence here, one way or the other).

THE ARGUMENT FOR DISENFRANCHISEMENT

Let us turn now to listen to the other side in this debate or dialogue. The most persuasive arguments on the other side, *against* the more liberal-individualistic arguments that I have just laid out, and in support of the justice of disenfranchisement of felonious inmates, take a fundamentally different approach to the whole issue, inspired by the more classical republican civic perspective. This argument reverses the emphasis, in interpreting the meaning and intention of the law of disenfranchisement. This argument contends that the disenfranchisement is chiefly intended not as a punishment, or as part of punishment, but, rather, as means to the fostering of responsible voting. One clear testimony to this, is the fact that the disenfranchisement of inmates is typically not part of the penal code, but is instead a part of the electoral laws (in both Canada and the U. S.).

If we approach the question from this interpretive perspective suggested by the classification of the disenfranchisement laws, we need to begin by considering this particular form of disqualification in the context of the other sorts of disqualification that characterize electoral laws in modern free and democratic societies. For in a free and democratic society, the right to vote is always qualified by law: some citizens are always lawfully disqualified from voting. No one thinks three year old citizens, or the helplessly insane, should be allowed to vote.

Now why not: what is the most reasonable rationale of all such disqualifications? Those who oppose disqualification have not yet faced the most important justification when they leave things at a rebuttal of worries about felons voting in a way that would adversely or corruptly affect the outcome of elections. That is, to be sure, one concern; but the concern with felons corrupting the outcome is not the most important concern, in the case of this class of disenfranchisement. The worry about how the votes of those to be disenfranchised might affect the outcome of elections is more of a concern as regards age qualifications; it is not so big a concern here, in regard to disenfranchisement of felons. Here, our major concern or aim should be the implications for the laying down of minimal standards of voters' moral responsibility, thereby defining and affirming, in solemn public law, and thereby educating the whole citizenry in, that minimum specific civic virtue that is required for and is realized in proper participation in the democratic procedure of electoral voting.

In other words, our biggest concern is or should be the educative message we send, through the law, to all of us—expressing who we are and what we expect of one another as a democratic community. What is sometimes called the "expressive" function of the law is given its most famous expression in Plato's *Laws*. There, the somewhat utopian notion is elaborated of promulgating explicit "preludes" to all major laws; these "preludes" are envisaged as pithy explanations, integral to major legislation, but preceding the rules or commands, and meant to instruct the citizenry in the purpose and meaning of each set of rules— and also meant to compel the legislators to reflect more thoroughly on what they are doing.

No doubt, there are good reasons why modern legislation cannot include Platonic legal "preludes"; but all the more is it the case that our legislation needs to become more self-conscious about its educative purpose and potential function. And it is arguable that democracy, precisely because or to the extent that it places genuine political power in the hands of the people, requires—more than does any other form of government—that the people give to themselves, in and through the law, some minimal civic education. This of course is the great theme of the democratic theorizing of Montesquieu as well as of Rousseau—a theme brought directly into an enriched liberalism by John Stuart Mill, and, most recently, John Rawls.[8]

A key theme in this theorizing is the insistence on the fact that in a democracy, citizens must not only obey the laws; they must also contribute to making the laws, and enforcing the laws, and judging offenders of the laws. Insofar as citizens thus enter into the activity of self-government, they must join in forming and expressing what Montesquieu and Rousseau term a "general will." The particular will of each individual, conceiving of him- or herself as a separate and competing private person, must be regulated by, subordinated to, and even in some measure transfigured into the will of the citizen, who conceives of him- or herself as responsible to and for other fellow-members of the community. Such a responsible community is animated by some measure of "fraternity," or a sympathy and concern for the welfare, for the dignity, for the liberty and the equality, of fellow-citizens.

It is true, that, in the past, ruling classes in republics have often exploited the concern for civic virtue as a pretext to exclude unjustifiably large portions of the populace. But the exclusion we are now talking about is not necessarily a relic of such. It can be understood to stand on an altogether different footing from such rightly abolished criteria as gender, race, wealth, and so forth. Felons and inmates are not disqualified because of who or what they are by birth or by socioeconomic status; they are disqualified, not for unchosen attributes, but rather because of what they have voluntarily done, and what their own actions say about their personal aims and capacities and character. And we can spell out, more precisely, the three major respects in which proven felons have manifested a failure to meet minimal standards for the capacity to participate with good faith in the electoral process.

In the first place, such felons have been proven to have acted toward their fellow citizens in such a way as to manifest flagrant disrespect for the lives, property, liberty, or dignity of their fellow citizens; they have thus been shown to be no longer minimally reliable in making important choices concerning the common good, and in particular the choice involved in voting, which requires that voters limit the pursuit of their selfish interests by a minimal respect for the most basic dignity of fellow citizens—at the least, a respect for fellow-citizens' right to be free from being arbitrarily abused.

In addition, felons have been shown to manifest flagrant disrespect for the laws, which in a democracy have a uniquely intimate link to participation in the electoral process: for in a democracy, the laws are the outcome and the purpose of electoral voting (which is the choice of representatives who make and administer the laws). In breaking seriously the law, felons have therefore been proven to have manifested a bad faith contempt for the electoral process, which, if it is to function and have the authority it is supposed to have, must presume, on the part of voters, a good faith commitment to abide by the laws that are the ultimate outcome and meaning of their participation in voting together with their fellows.

Moreover, in the light of the modern, liberal-democratic theory of the social compact as the basis for legitimate government and law, the inmates in question have been proven to manifest yet a third form of failure to live up to the minimal responsibility reasonably demanded of voting citizens (and here the argument for disqualification moves from a more classical republican matrix to incorporate a major argument from a more modern, liberal theoretical perspective). Felons' serious violation of the law manifests, in addition to the two preceding grounds for disqualification, a serious breach-of-promise violation of the fundamental social compact; for it is a basic and essential presupposition of the social contract that citizens, in becoming citizens—i.e., in becoming parties to the contract—are held responsible for keeping their implicit promise to abide by the legal determinations arrived at by due process, based on majority vote.

So in sum: the electoral laws disqualifying felons rightly exclude from voting that small number of adult citizens who have deliberately failed: first, to meet the minimal level of concern for the common good; second, to show the minimal respect for the law-making process, at the heart of which is voting; and third, to exhibit a minimal fidelity to the promise implicit in the social contract. By enacting this exclusion, the electoral law lays down and recalls to everyone these minimal standards of civic responsibility below which voting citizens in a free and democratic society ought not to fall.

What is more, this concern for using electoral qualifications to instill in the citizenry some keener awareness of its civic responsibilities is far from being outmoded, or merely an antique leftover of earlier and more demanding forms of republican societies. On the contrary. In today's mass representative democracy, in contrast to the small, more direct and participatory democracies of the past, the use of disqualification of inmates convicted for serious offenses as a means of civic education, for the citizenry as a whole, is more important and more significant than it was in any of those traditional democracies. For in modern democracy, the election process is perhaps the sole civic endeavor, apart from war, which truly involves the collective concern and effort of the entire community, acting as a whole; elections and the qualifications for voters accordingly afford a rare, perhaps unique, and therefore precious occasion for the promulgation of minimal standards of responsibility.

Now the proponents of disqualification of felons concede that it is indeed troubling that the disqualification falls disproportionately, in the United States, on groups who represent sectors of the populace historically exploited or marginalized. But this is not, or need not, and certainly should not, be the purpose of the legislation. And that this is the case can be driven home by a rigorous commitment to overturn any state disqualifying or disenfranchising legislation which does have a history of being used for purposes of invalid discrimination. We can point with approval, for example, to the 1985 Supreme Court case *Hunter v. Underwood* (471 U. S. 222), also written by Rehnquist, where an Alabama law passed in 1901 that denied the right to vote to persons of "moral turpitude," including preeminently convicted felons, was declared unconstitutional on the grounds that its enactment and implementation showed a history of discriminatory intent. And we can stress that the valid intent and effect of the disenfranchisement of felons is to promote the good of all members of the community; it is as much in the interests of Hispanic and African-American citizens as it is in any other citizens' interests to thus promote civic education in the responsibilities of voting.

In addition to this most important civic educational purpose, the disenfranchisement of felons, if properly designed, may also be defended, secondarily, on penal grounds, as a legitimate form of punishment. This is especially so if the disenfranchisement is not permanent, but the voting right is restored, either after time served or after probation or parole has been completed. In that case, the disqualification can be understood as a reasonable part of rehabilitative punishment. For the chief purpose of the disqualification, to wit civic education, is then aimed at least as much at the inmates themselves as at any other portion of the adult voting population. The temporary loss of the voting right can be understood then as a sharp medicinal or corrective reminder to the prisoner of those basic responsibilities that attend participation in the democratic electoral process. If or when the serious offenders complete their terms of penalty, it is not unreasonable to suppose that they may return to society with a substantially heightened appreciation for the importance and the responsibilities of voting in a free and democratic society.

Here, then, are some of the strongest arguments of the two sides to this controversy. Let me close by raising the question of the possibility of compromise, or a middle ground—to which I have already pointed in my last argument defending disenfranchisement. For I suggested that disenfranchisement was defensible on punitive-rehabilitative grounds only if it were considerably reformed—in comparison at least with the existing law in most states. The compromise I am pointing to is a disenfranchisement that would not be permanent or lifelong—that might best be limited to the period of incarceration—and that would be targeted at, or limited to, only those convicted of very serious crimes.

Such a policy was in fact the law in Canada, for a decade prior to the recent Canadian Supreme Court decision; disenfranchisement applied only to inmates serving sentences of at least two years in length (and this is the cutoff for truly serious crimes, or time served in maximum security penitentiaries). And variations on this sort of temporary disenfranchisement, limited to those convicted of crimes of great seriousness, are found in some European jurisdictions, and in fact in some of the states of the United States.

Yet there is a massive practical difficulty impeding such compromise at the present time. Precisely such limited disenfranchisement of felons as I have just described is under attack today in places where it exists—in Canada, for example. There the Canadian Supreme Court has now struck down—though in a split decision—precisely the law that expressed such a compromise or middle ground. And similarly in the United States, the critics of felon disenfranchisement do not tend to limit their criticism to permanent disenfranchisement; the 1981 American Bar Association's "Standards for Criminal Justice" (#23-8.4) declares that "persons convicted of any offense should not be deprived of the right to vote;" and the opponents sometimes openly write of such compromises as I have just described as mere tactical way-stations on the road to the complete elimination of any voting disabilities for inmates. Hence, of course, such a compromise position is highly suspect to those who are staunch defenders of inmate disqualification. But does this have to be another policy dispute in which the argument remains between only those who voice the extreme positions? Or is there perhaps some big room here for broadening the range of considerations through a richer reflection on the issue in light of the two great competing traditions of our tradition of republican theory?

NOTES

1. *Sauvé v. Canada* (Chief Electoral Officer), [2002] S. C. J. No. 66 (October 31, 2002).

2. See, for example, Andrew L. Shapiro, "Challenging Criminal Disenfranchisement Under The Voting Rights Act: A New Strategy," *Yale Law Journal*, November 1993; Alice E. Harvey, "Ex-Felon Disenfranchisement And Its Influence On The Black Vote: The Need For A Second Look," *University of Pennsylvania Law Review*, January 1994; Nora V. Demleitner, "Preventing Internal Exile: The Need For Restrictions On Collateral Sentencing Consequences," *Stanford Law and Policy Review*, Winter 1999, and the same author's "A New Start Calls for a Broadened Perspective," *Federal Sentencing Reporter*, September/October 1999, and "Continuing Payment On One's Debt To Society: The German Model Of Felon Disenfranchisement As An Alternative," *Minnesota Law Review*, April 2000.

3. Cited in Marc Mauer, "Felon Voting Disenfranchisement: A Growing Collateral Consequence of Mass Incarceration," *Federal Sentencing Reporter*, March/April, 2000, n. 4.

4. See, e.g., *Harper v. Virginia State Bd. of Elections*, 383 U. S. 663 (1966).

5. U.S. Constitution, Amendment 14, sec. 2: "But when the right to vote at any election for the choice of electors for President and Vice President of the United States, Representatives in Congress, the Executive and Judicial officers of a state, or the members of the Legislature thereof, is denied to any of the male inhabitants of such State, being twenty-one years of age, and citizens of the United States, or in any way abridged, *except for participation in rebellion*, OR OTHER CRIME, the basis of representation therein shall be reduced in the proportion which the number of such male citizens shall bear to the whole number of male citizens twenty-one years of age in such State." (Emphases added.)

6. Canadian Charter of Rights and Freedoms (which is Part One of the Constitution Act of 1982):

1) The Canadian Charter of Rights and Freedoms guarantees the rights and freedoms set forth in it subject only to such reasonable limits prescribed by law as can be demonstrably justified in a free and democratic society. . . .

3) Every citizen of Canada has the right to vote in an election of members of the House of Commons or of a legislative assembly and to be qualified for membership therein.

7. Hobbes, *Leviathan*, chap. 15: the "seventh law of nature"—"that in revenges (that is, retribution of evil for evil) men look not at the greatness of the evil past, but the greatness of the good to follow. Whereby we are forbidden to inflict punishment with any other design than for correction of the offender, or direction of others . . . revenge without respect to the example and profit to come is a triumph, or glorying, in the hurt of another, tending to no end (for the end is always somewhat to come); and glorying to no end is vain-glory, and contrary to reason."

8. See John Stuart Mill, "Thoughts on Parliamentary Reform," in *Collected Works*, vol. 19, *Essays on Politics and Society*, ed. John M. Robson (Toronto: University of Toronto Press, 1977), 322: "As far as the direct influence of their votes went, it would scarcely be worth while to exclude them. But, as an aid to the great object of giving a moral character to the exercise of the suffrage, it might be expedient that in case of crimes evincing a high degree of insensibility to social obligation, the deprivation of this and other civil rights should form part of the sentence"; Immanuel Kant, "Theory and Practice," in *Kant's Political Writings*, ed. Hans Reiss

(Cambridge: Cambridge University Press, 1970), 76: "Since birth is not an act on the part of the one who is born, it cannot create any inequality in his legal position and cannot make him submit to any coercive laws except insofar as he is a subject, along with all the others, of the one supreme legislative power. . . . No one who lives within the lawful state of a commonwealth can forfeit this equality other than through some crime of his own."

Part III
Civic Education and the University

8

Barbarians at the Gates: Enemies of Character

JOSIAH BUNTING III

FOR THE LAST EIGHT YEARS I have served as superintendent, or president, at the Virginia Military Institute (VMI)—a school that, as many will remember, was not a favorite of the Department of Justice. We were not successful in urging our argument before the United States Supreme Court—an argument based on our conviction that the school should be allowed to continue to enroll only young men. It was argued that changing the school's character by admitting women would put at hazard the proved efficacy of a culture that had done inestimable service to commonwealth and country for many generations.

The decision went against the school. It became law, and those charged with implementing the decision were precisely those who had opposed it as a matter of principle. Eighty years earlier, the greatest graduate of the school, George Marshall, had written a letter to a friend, responding to the friend's question: what had Marshall learned about leadership in his work as a deputy to General Pershing during World War I? And Marshall replied, among other things, that when given an order with which you disagree (the presumption is of course that the order is moral and constitutional), you must call yourself to account to execute that order with *redoubled* efficiency and enthusiasm. This is what the British call Hard Cheese. But that was our portion, and we partook.

Since 1995, the number of applications for admission to the Institute has doubled. Several years ago I began the practice of writing parents of new cadets—those young men and women who would arrive late in August. My letter is probably little different from what the president or dean of any college sends to his new freshmen parents, asking: what can you tell us about Matthew or Jennifer that will help us be useful to him as he takes up his life as a new student? What is she like? The responses to these letters always came back promptly. Most were written with such fervor and such pride—and such earnestness—that I felt myself transported to another century, the nineteenth. Who would seek admission to such a school as mine, and why, and on what grounds? The striking things about the parents' responses were these: although many of our new students were terribly bright, their folders filled with all the paraphernalia of contemporary assessment, very high SATs, APs, single-digit class ranks, and so on—almost all parents' letters were about their children's *character*, not their *brains*. And chiefly they were about certain elements of character: perseverance, tenacity of purpose, determination, longtime dedication to doing one thing well—persistence in a course of action, in an enterprise because they felt impelled to do it. They were about a certain lonely idealism that separated them from most of their contemporaries, their classmates, in some way. They were about their patriotism, about demonstrated instincts to be leaders. They were about dedication to doing something right because it was the right thing to do.

Now defining terms and words early in an essay is a great bore for a reader, so let me administer the Novocain quickly and I hope painlessly. "Character," for my purpose, is integrity through time. An important element of this "character" is what was once called, simply, a "settled resistance to the solicitation of impulse," doing what your conscience instructs you is the right thing to do, and doing it for as long as duty or responsibility demands, whether it be five minutes or a lifetime—without undue calculation of reward or risk. I do not, I hope, confound my definition of "character" with what we call "civic character," because I see them as growing as one. "We say a man with no business in the state is a man with no business at all," Pericles said to the Athenians.

Now perhaps it was because these young people proposed to enter a famously tough military school that their parents wrote what they did. (And there *were* exceptions to the norm. Every year letters arrived saying, in effect, "we can do nothing with him; you are our last hope." "He wants structure, we'll give him structure"—that was what they saw us providing.) Or perhaps it was because they were responding to a request from a military bureaucrat identified as a major general—a personage strange, perhaps even frightening to parents who had left college in 1975 or 1980 and had stayed as far from the marines, or the army, as possible. Indeed, I found that "general" was one of those archaic titles of hierarchy, like archdeacon or chief inspector, that put people on the *que vive*, that made them respond frankly, and quickly. (According to Anthony Powell, generals were to be treated exactly the way you would treat ladies no longer young—like friends of your mother's.) In any case my correspondents wrote with great conviction and pride—just as a father had written the school in 1897: "I send you my youngest and last. He is bright, full of life, and will, I believe, get on well at the Institute. . . ." The note came from Uniontown, Pennsylvania, and it was sent by the father of the only American soldier to win the Nobel Prize for Peace: George Marshall.

It was as though these letters had been written not only as testimonials but also as passionate assertions that their subjects—these 430 girls and boys in late adolescence—were bearers or representatives of qualities of which our current culture and national life had been drained. They were made to sound like children of a nineteenth century American heartland, or children rising above the hardship of the Great Depression. I thought of Abraham Lincoln's *Lyceum Address* of 1837—the year that the last signer of the Declaration of Independence died. We no longer grip hands with those who palpably embodied the spirit of the Revolution: who or what will now take their place, and how?

This is a strange, fractured, incoherent time in which we live, a time of enormous self-indulgence, of utter absorption in the self, of fantastic materialism, of sense of our neighbors' station relative to ours, of obsessive competition for place and promotion of the kind that will be used for purposes invidious to our neighbors. It is a time of manic hyper-connectedness ("phone calls were not returned" is one of its most characteristic rebukes), in which all are expected to subsist in a dense welter of emails, call waiting, pagers, and voice mails. It is a time in which all are admonished to examine the state of their health moment-by-moment, and to brook no pain, no fatigue, no HDL cholesterol, no bat wings—above all, no evidence of the erosion of the appearance of youth perpetual. And it is a time in which we are engaged in a new war, telegraphed for a year and prosecuted far out on the periphery of a new empire over the bleating objections of Hans Blix and Gerhard Schroeder—a war that competes unsuccessfully for our attention against re-threaded episodes of "Friends," but which is now all war all the time. It is a war fought by the kinds of young people who have not gained entry to Brown, Stanford, or Princeton. It is, in the words of Matthew Arnold, an "iron time of doubts, distractions, fears." It is a time when the enemies of what we call character are perched on every rooftop, every revetment, in every pillbox and bunker. They are enemies of civic and private character: ephedrine, Ritalin, Nicotrol, Grecian Formula, Botox, Dexatrim—a list nowhere near as irrelevant to our purposes as it might sound. For all of them are created or "formulated" to assist our characters in achieving what they are assumed no longer capable of doing for themselves, or to make us appear to be something different from what we are.

Now the young have little need for most of these things, but they inhabit a culture in which so many of the hurdles, difficulties, tasks, dangers, and challenges that form and strengthen character are so far as possible removed from their paths of progress. It is a culture, civic and private, in which the avoidance of risk, not to say failure, is encouraged. It is a culture in which bad conduct, either petty or serious, is routinely explained away as a consequence not of their own acts, their own will, but of *history* and *society*—of circumstances in which they have found themselves placed in the lottery of life. All of us, invited to compile a list of such things in the next ten minutes, could provide a tabulation both funny and pathetic. It might include the recruitment to a private sadness of a personage called a "grief counselor;" the hiring of a professional known as a "personal trainer," who will chart and supervise those exercises needed to make us vigorous and fit since we cannot do it ourselves. Among other things, he will ensure we never appear in circumstances of exercise without plastic labeled water bottles, so we are like infants dragging blankets around behind them.

These are what cultural historians call epiphenomena—outward signs of an inward but not invisible sickness. They are the evolved form of what David Riesman, fifty years ago, called other-directedness. That is, we have lost the habit of self-reliance, of doing and being what we think we *ought* without undue worry about what everyone thinks of us. Has anyone stopped to consider how many television hours are given over to distributing awards and small statues to actors and singers? It is a practice that begins in Little League, and continues to the grave. Americans seem to crave and need such recognition. Or consider polling. I am certain Tocqueville would notice this practice and comment. Thirty-eight percent of Americans believed that General Tommy Franks wanted two extra divisions for the invasion of Baghdad. Fifty percent said he was happy with what he was given. Twelve percent, God bless them, said they did not know. But many of the first two categories, if they were students or young teachers on the campuses of most of our universities, would be reluctant to subscribe to *any* position on the war, or on any urgent issue of civic or strategic concern.

For most inhabit academic worlds in which to assert a possibly hetero-dox or unorthodox opinion is to risk a particularly American kind of public censure, as noxious and dangerous to democracy as authoritarianism itself—the tyranny of established opinion, the very antithesis of what we mean when we talk of "liberal" education. This last enemy of character is perhaps the most dangerous of all because it is more-or-less imposed, and protected, by the adult members of aca-demic communities—appointed to their positions on the presumption that they are wise, and learned, and devoted to those they teach. De-bate is foreclosed: if you disagree you are worse than wrong, you are immoral, and beneath our contempt. It is the culture of the bumper sticker, of the political ad on TV: "here is my opinion, deal with it, I don't have to hear your response."

Now there is a tendency here to marinate in diagnosis and ignore prescription. Our full diagnosis—our identification of the enemies of character—would go far, far beyond the funny epiphenomena we men-tion, such as botox and grief counselors and devices to help us sculpt the abs of our dreams. It would comprise the whole family of activi-ties, props, prizes, rewards, luxuries, and palliatives prepared to make those things which should be hard, and challenging, easier; those deci-sions over which we should agonize, seemingly simple. In short, those things and habits designed not only to remove us from the consequences of our acts, but to explain away those acts as being the consequences of forces beyond our control.

A former military person must be allowed to fire at a target of opportunity. Here's one: those soldiers we see fighting in Iraq—how many of them are students or graduates of colleges and universities like those our country seems to admire most? According to Charles Moskos, 740 members of the Princeton class of 1954 (of a thousand graduates) entered the service. Many of these were drafted, of course. They did not become professional soldiers. Later on, when they looked back on their time in uniform, they always referred to it as "the ser-vice." As in, "I was in the service"—the predicate did not have to be stated—*the service of my country.* Unstated also are two other things, both pertinent to our notions of civic education and civic character. First, those men lived, worked, slept, and ate with Americans of every ethnicity, provenance, and place. Those lives were a daily testimony, whether they knew it or not, to the commonality of our heritage and our responsibility to our common citizenship. (No doubt a few thought of Pericles' statement in the great Funeral Oration, to which I referred earlier). And, second, they sacrificed—in the sense that they did what their country, not their own ambition, obliged them to do. According to Moskos, a recent year's equivalent at Princeton (remembering our number of 740 in 1954) was *three*. That is to say, among graduates of a representative famous liberal arts school and great university, to whose campus our brightest and best repair like lemmings, virtually none acknowledges any desire to serve or any obligation to serve in this way.

We have not had a military draft since 1972—and it was at this time, too (only a year earlier) that the twenty-sixth Amendment was ratified—the amendment which granted the franchise to eighteen-year-olds. The end of the draft and the privilege of voting both rose from a common political impulse: to remove the possibility of service in an unpopular war from those determined to avoid such service, and to answer the popular demand to give those old enough to fight for their country the right to vote for those who make the policies that send them to war.

Like Americans of a certain age I bristle when I hear the label The Sixties—used to evoke a time of mayhem, civil disorder, and sexual license. *Those* sixties lasted in fact from about 1967–68, just before the TET offensive, to 1975, with the emergence of the Alan Alda man as a new representative of the ideal type of American: the ironic, gentle, bedraggled man, self-absorbed and tolerant of everything. By then, the idealism and civic-mindedness of the early 1960s had vanished tone and tint. With it passed a vital renaissance—for the first time since 1945—of a kind of civic and national pride that would enlist the ablest members of a young generation in various civic enterprises.

There was a bumper sticker one used to see in the early 1990s. It said, *Think Globally, Act Locally*. I am afraid my own sense of prescription—however large-scale our diagnosis—must follow this admonition. The enemies of character—as I have briefly defined character and sketched the nature of some of its enemies—will always prevail over an army that is not trained both to recognize and to master them. And that "army," or rather the leaders of it, for my purposes, are the nuclear American family, the schools and a certain kind of teacher who must be prepared to labor in their behalf, the Church (if possible), groups—like scouts—and, less usefully, the residential colleges.

It is idle to imagine that liberal education can make people virtuous. Its role is both less comprehensive and more concentrated. Cardinal Newman put it famously—as well restrain boulders with strips of steel. We hear, often, the lament: "why don't we learn from history?" The question is itself idle, because it confounds knowledge with implemented wisdom (with wisdom leading to implementing what the counsels of wisdom tell us). The brief answer is that we do learn from history; but historical lessons rarely have exact applications, and human character rarely allows, supervises, or supports the decisions wisdom might suggest. Most have heard the solecism *Groupthink.* The term means the tendency of deliberative groups to skew their judgments toward some amiable center, and to cast out those who, however enlightened or original, disagree or suggest otherwise. In times of war or preparation for war, those who counsel caution are routinely castigated as craven, or lacking in "character" or strength, and shunned; or they are made pets of, and exhibits. Their own ambitions for continuing political authority or power are compromised; they hesitate to say what they think they should. Or on campuses in which there is prevailing political orthodoxy (precisely the places where there should be no such thing), those who deviate from the expected norms of opinion, however innocent or honorable their aims, are similarly shunned or castigated. It is the ultimate vitiation of what the word "liberal" once meant. "There can be no philosophy where fear of consequences is greater than love of truth," said Mill. (He could not now be a candidate for tenure anywhere famous.)

In what ways can the young be prepared for lives of virtuous actions—virtuous for our purposes defined as I have explained it? I am not sure I know, with any conviction or certainty. As I have indicated, I am devoted to what Burke famously called the "little platoons" of our community and of the state, especially the little platoons charged with educating the young—the young meaning younger than college age. It is as Hugh Curtler insists: character is formed in the years of grammar and secondary schools, wherein virtue is both educated and inspired. The principal agents in the work are adults who have answered vocations to serve these young all their days, and who embody, or teach by the evangelism of personal example, what it is to be a good man or a good woman. They teach what it is to be a selfless citizen and patriot. Such teaching rests on the old-fashioned notion of *emulation*: we are inspired, in ways that might be permanent, by the thought of trying to measure up to the best standards others have embodied, and that we may yet embody.

If we do not know with certainty how character and courage—virtues—can be formed and trained, we can recognize such things when we see them, and perhaps our own alertness to their power to irradiate our own lives and inspire us should be a staple of the way we continue to educate ourselves. For whether the process of emulation is conscious or not, seeing such things in others can remind us, at least, of our own capacities and duties. Thucydides famously wrote, "Of all manifestations of power, restraint impresses me most." Perhaps a lonely, principled persistence in an unpopular course of action not only impresses, but *inspires:* remembering that it is one thing to learn and to know, and quite another to believe so thoroughly that one is inspired and motivated to act. In a great essay written forty years ago on American leadership in the eighteenth century, Henry Steele Commager makes the argument simply: "the problem is not to define our values, it is to realize them." He might have been remembering one of the apothegms of Marcus Aurelius (a philosopher known well by American leaders of that generation): "Do not argue about what it means to be a good man: be one." War and adversity are the school of character, just as necessity is the mother of improvisation, for both entail suffering, and it is in mastering our suffering, in persisting in right action simply because it is right, because it is a duty—however harsh our sufferings, however large the risks and dangers—that we realize our virtues. Coincidentally, men and women in the arena might actually think this in such times; they may serve to inspire others to realize their virtues.

The Commager essay seriously engages a question that is a chestnut of conversation among people interested in politics: "Where did we get such men as these?" That is, how did the tiny American polity, at its beginning and during its formation with a population about the same as St. Paul, Minnesota—how did it attract, inspire, and sustain a cohort of political genius and leadership that has not had its equal in the history of the West? (Consider just for a moment the first American administration, sworn in in New York in 1789: Washington, Adams, Jefferson, Hamilton. Perhaps the leading figure in the House was James Madison, and for counsel and sage, disinterested advice, there was Benjamin Franklin, still living, in Philadelphia.) Not to particularize too finely—how did three colonies, the commonwealths of Pennsylvania, Virginia, and Massachusetts—how did they—shall we say, "produce" such a galaxy of talent, of genius? Commager's essay *begins* where most conversations about this question *end*. We all know the clichés about the great crisis bringing forth great leaders, and about how there were few other posts of honor and compelling missions to lure and reward the ablest. The essay looks hard at how such men were educated—how, in a word no longer heard, they were "raised." And of course it is here that we may locate those elements of our training, education and "upbringing" (to use another old-fashioned word) that are directly pertinent to our crisis in civic character and civic participation today.

This generation—those born, say, between 1700 and 1760—was trained and bred to self-reliance and duty; it was schooled (but not the way we "school" people today) to a sense of the best of what human beings might be capable. And again, to remember Pericles, the members of this generation were schooled to be ashamed to fall short of what they knew to be their best, and their duty. They were soaked in the Bible, in history, in the political philosophy of seventeenth- and eighteenth-century England and Europe. They particularly knew the histories of Attic Greece and its Hellenistic culture, and of Rome. And for the Roman politics of the late Republic they had a particular reverence: the stern old Roman virtues of selfless, uncompensated service to state, and moral and physical bravery. They appear not to have had a concept of what our generation calls "stress." They did their work and then retired for the evening—without complaining very much. They tended to be men of broad talents broadly cultivated: they saw no reason why men of action could not also be men of culture. They wielded fluent pens as they directed accurate artillery fire. Their parents were very hard on them—by today's standards. In political discourse and speech making, most wrote their own material, laboriously for many hours of solitary application, with quill pens, candles, and frigid nights for company. They were educated—and here is a notion that has fled from today's education culture—according to the idea of emulation. Just as Churchill said that, at Harrow, he got into his bones the elements of a simple British sentence, these men got into their bones the elements of virtuous political conduct and private integrity by watching their elders. And they learned about the best of their ancestors and those who had gone before them in work not so different from their own—in creating, building, and sustaining a new country. And they had a keen consciousness that what they were building must not be allowed to fail—it was, as it were, to be a prototype, and a prototype in which providence had a direct, unremitting, unforgiving interest.

So any modern scheme of education that aims at cultivation of a generation of great civic characters, would, it seems certain, at least try to create the same kinds of conditions in which young people might be "brought up" and educated as this greatest generation was. It would be a gigantic undertaking, and those to lead and teach these young, in the schools and colleges, would themselves have to embody the matured virtues that they profess went before them. They are virtues of temperament, and character, and mind.

You may call such notions reactionary, or conservative, or traditional, or hopelessly out-of-date. But "conservative" to my way of thinking, in matters of education and culture, is very close to what we call class, or classical: that is to say, that which has proved itself over countless generations, so that it is as fresh, as pure, as exalted—as necessary—to the successful workings of a democratic republic as it was in the century of our founding.

For the generation that made a Revolution, republican Rome was a school of character, instruction, and emulation. Our own later history is full of such sources of inspiration. I think of such disparate figures of the middle of the nineteenth century as Thaddeus Stevens, Robert E. Lee, Ulysses Grant, and Charles Sumner—all of whom persisted in courses of action that excited the scorn and censure of friends and enemies, simply because their consciences, and their habituation to duty, insisted that they do no other. And it would be difficult to conceive of four men whose convictions and missions were less similar.

And for a contemporary example, think of Tony Blair: five years ago we could not have imagined this man could fill the shoes of the leader we admire so ardently today. To persist in a course of action whatever the political risks—simply because it is right. He seems now to embody, for all with eyes to see, this principle. And mark how much more searching, how much more demanding, is the path of a prime minister, in such broils, than that of a president. There is no distance between leader and angry critic, no buttressing of retainers and pomp of majesty. There is just Mr. Blair, facing down angry critics in the House of Commons—many of them at that, of both parties, but mainly from his own—with eloquence, resource, passion, and good will. He has taken the supreme political risk—no different in kind from those of Pericles or Churchill, Lincoln or Woodrow Wilson: leading a great nation into war as a matter of necessity and principle, unwilling to deviate from the path of conviction or duty. His was necessary action impelled by conscience and understanding, sustained by duty—without calculation of personal reward or risk. "I heard a voice calling, 'whom shall I send, and who will go for us?' Then I said, 'here I am, send me.'"

And I hope I will be forgiven if I suggest a re-reading of the Book of Acts of the Apostles, as the most powerful and moving testimonial in Western history, to this quality of sustained virtue, now made impregnable by faith, in the life of one man, Paul of Tarsus—Roman citizen, builder and sustainer of the Church, and Saint.

9

Liberal Education
and Civic Education for Our Time
STEPHEN H. BALCH

"WHERE AM I?" "What am I?" These are the twin questions that lie at liberal education's core. Trapped in Plato's cave, liberal education is charged with leading us out of the shadows and into the sunlit uplands of truth—discovering our real natures thereby.

Civic education is generally thought of as being part of liberal education—"liberal education," after all, having originally denoted that type of education most suitable for free citizenship. But at first glance civic education might seem to offer something rather humdrum compared to liberal education's lofty ascension toward perfect forms. Civic education, as often conceived, comprises little more than a recitation of essential facts—how a bill becomes a law, how the electoral college operates—or a list of dates, places, and names, that provide the basic roadmap of our country's political history. Thus imagined, civic education can claim some utility but little grandeur.

Yet civic education can have grandeur when rightly understood. If liberal education in its broadest sense involves rumination on everything from the nature of the soul up to and through the nature of the cosmos, civic education might be conceived as that part of it preoccupied with the middle range—with an understanding of the collective life of mankind and our place within it. As such, it too can be an ennobling enterprise, allowing us to see the world through new eyes. Indeed, at its best, it should be able to motivate us, as nothing else could, to take up the great purposes that citizenship in its highest sense involves. But it will only do this when it is allowed to paint on a broad canvas, when it is designed to afford us a glimpse of the larger human project of which each of us is a part.

The design of the civic component of liberal education must thus be grounded in an assessment of what is genuinely most important about mankind's collective experience. The curriculum must reflect that estimate, rather than becoming—as it now generally does—a mere function of market economics, intellectual fads, or the lowest common denominator of departmental horse-trades.

Where then might we arrive if we seriously attempted such an assessment today? Perhaps—given the blinkers that the last several decades of cultural evolution have placed on us—not where we should be. Years of bad education do not equip one capably to educate others. And, in fact, many contemporary educators would flatly deny that the notion of "importance" has any objective meaning when applied to human affairs. In preparing ourselves for this task we are thus not likely to profit much from any recent examples academe might provide. As it turns out, however, an interesting example of such an assessment can be drawn from the world of popular journalism.

Just before the turn of the century a briefly revived *Life Magazine* devoted a double issue to the task of identifying the hundred most important events and people of the millennium.

Exercises of this type, of course, are always more interesting for what they say about those undertaking them than the questions addressed. This is why the results of *Life*'s exercise were so surprising. They reveal an outlook more characteristic of American intellectual elites at mid-century than that which prevails among them today.

Take, for example, the editor's unabashed materialism and rationalism. Almost half of their "greatest events" involved mechanical inventions (printing taking first place), scientific discoveries, or the introduction of new foodstuffs like tea, potatoes, even Coca Cola. And, *mirabile dictu*, none other than Thomas Edison, handyman extraordinaire, got *Life*'s nod as the millennium's most influential human being. Rather than viewing technological civilization as something problematic, or searching for ways to diminish its human significance, *Life* celebrated it as the defining quality of modernity and looked forward to its ever-fuller realization.

Or take the Eurocentric pride contained in *Life*'s acknowledgement, albeit as "a paradoxical embarrassment," that the millennium's most influential individuals were disproportionately Western males, representing a singularly Western achievement. (All but seventeen were from Europe or the Americas, and all but ten were men.) To be sure, the editors hastened to predict—no doubt correctly—that this pattern is unlikely to hold.

On the other hand, *Life*'s editors did show a blind spot about historical causality. They failed to show an adequate awareness of the extent to which economic, technological, and scientific achievement—the whole world of wealth and power they extolled—is itself the product of deeper transformations. Thus, while their concept of a "great event" was generous enough to encompass the Reformation, unionism, feminism, and environmentalism, but the Enlightenment, political liberalism's and philosophic rationalism's great watershed, was strangely absent from their list. Moreover, neither the English Civil War nor the Glorious Revolution scored hits, despite their long-acknowledged status as landmarks in the development of representative institutions.

The Whig view of history, which *Life*'s editors apparently did not share, had as its central theme the struggle for liberty, pitting rights against power. Once the intellectual mother's milk of English speaking peoples, Whig history can be uncomfortably tendentious, present-minded, and selective. But it did convey a sense that changes in formative principles and institutional frameworks had immense consequence for everyday life. Since Whigs understood liberty as anchored in the security of property, freedom and prosperity were inextricably linked as well.

Although not Whig historians, *Life*'s editors at least had a coherent perspective, which allowed them to give order to the human experience. Moreover, their perspective was a triumphal one. They rejoiced in modernity, fostering no illusions about its Western origins, and looked forward to the wonders of a third millennium, demonstrating thereby a refreshing belief in human progress. Truth to tell, by simply accepting the possibility and propriety of "greatness" they bid a healthy defiance to the self-denigration so fashionable in highbrow circles.

For all their imperfections the editors of *Life* were better custodians of civilized consciousness than those now professionally charged with the task. Our current educators are sadly ill-equipped for it. Clear perspective has nearly vanished from their precincts, the best unconvinced of larger meaning, the worst passionate for its misinterpretation. As a result, the academy is adrift, with civic education shriveled, drained, and frequently perverted in purpose.

What forces now drive curriculum policy?

The first is faculty and institutional self-interest. In an era of aggressive specialization professors desire to teach the narrow subjects they research much more than the broad-gauged ones that provide a rounded undergraduate education. And, in an era of mass education, institutions find that this latitudinarian approach to requirements also helps them recruit and retain more students. The result is disintegration, leading to curricula without thematic cohesion, intellectual continuity, or serious rigor. Such an approach is incapable, except by accident, of preparing anyone for either citizenship or a self-aware life.

The second driving force is the adversarial mentality that has come to dominate the American university, alternatively relativistic and egalitarian, given to slighting or disparaging the West, doubting or denying rationality, and generally downplaying the study of high achievement. Most evident in the humanities, and some of the social sciences, it is inclined to celebrate civilization's vanquished far more than its victories, persistently jiggering the moral accounts to accentuate the debits. It can be counted on to sour such content as remains within the curriculum's shredded core, systematically distorting a student's sense of civic and cultural identity.

This unhappy state of affairs has been a long time developing. Its history is worth a brief glance.

However eternal its verities, the academy's forms have always been time-bound, geared to servicing the needs of the ambient culture. In most societies well-established leadership groups, the vested interests of their times, defined what those needs were. The secular and religious hierarchies of medieval and early modern Europe, for instance, expected their universities to train clergy, lawyers, and physicians, each making very specific contributions to state and society. Likewise, the denominational elders and local notables who founded innumerable American colleges during the nineteenth century sought to provide ministers, attorneys, doctors, as well as educated civic leaders, for recently settled communities. While these institutions certainly entertained disagreements, and even harbored heretics, opposition to the communities supporting them was not part of their job description. There was nothing problematic about their civic purpose.

This decisively changed with the advent of the scientifically oriented research university toward the end of the nineteenth century. Admitting of no truth other than what could be empirically verified, it could never accept the role of servitor. Bereft of dogma, indeed fascinated by the heterodox, it understood itself less as an agent of stability than of progress, with progress applying equally to the material and human domains.

Yet the research university did not regard itself as civically subversive. Its captains confidently supposed that critical inquiry would prove a greater boon to society than the hidebound defense of tradition, especially if that society was the liberal kind they prized—ever bent on self-improvement. In fact, an education fostering a healthy open-mindedness, and unafraid to question authority, might be essential if progress and democracy were to survive. For optimistic progressives the university could both destabilize and preserve.

This uneasy resolution of cross-purposes disintegrated as the twentieth century waned. The result has been an acute institutional bifurcation in which antithetical academic projects have sprung up side by side.

On one side appeared a massive growth of business and professional education, powerfully buttressing the university's service role. By late century a baccalaureate degree was seen by many as the *sine qua non* of upward mobility, even an entitlement. This led to a change in the prevalent outlook of students with many more seeking degrees solely for their pecuniary value. Institutions hustling for enrollments were therefore compelled to relocate vocational training at mission central, while easing up on the traditional academics that lacked professional utility.

Instead of resisting this trend, numerous professors, including many in the humanities, expressed delight, throwing their weight behind it. With specialized research overshadowing teaching as the principal index of academic success, many regarded general education responsibilities as a bothersome distraction, if not a major peril to their careers. Others, drawn tightly into the tunnels of their expertise, lost sight of the big human picture entirely and could no longer articulate why it was worth grasping. Though they might support the civic and civilizing purposes of liberal education in principle, they couldn't argue persuasively on their behalf.

On the other side arose an aggressive disposition—centered in the humanities—to question the possibility of truth in any form, even the provisional one claimed by the natural sciences. Suspicious of standards, and fueled by egalitarian passion, it inclined to debunking high achievement as the pretense of power, while favoring the popular, the everyday and, most particularly, the sexual, as these were refracted through the prism of an increasingly esoteric and nihilistic body of theory.

This represented a huge break with the past. During most of the twentieth century, to say nothing of earlier, teaching about high civilization and free institutions had usually been conducted with a certain sympathy for their content. This rarely descended to outright adoration, because that content was too vast and heterogeneous to be indiscriminately admired. But even its strongest critics generally acknowledged civilization's formidable achievements, regarding themselves as its inheritors.

By contrast, the proponents of the new scholarship show little affection or loyalty toward high civilization or the civic culture. Taking up radicalism's old torch, they carry it much further. Uninterested in a mere reordering of civilization's economic and political institutions, their goal is a deeper revolution of mind and passion. Their attack centers on civilization's intellectual foundations, seeking to problematize its assumptions and undermine its traditions, most especially including its political ones. Viewing themselves as emancipators, they turn the civilizing function of liberal education on its head. Instead of sustaining the great tradition of inquiry they seek to loose its shackles, symbolized less by wage slavery than the tyranny of the inherited culture, and even of reason itself.

This sensibility has become the ground for a range of positions, each understanding knowledge about human customs and behavior to be inherently politicized and socially contingent. At a minimum one finds a deep skepticism that Western ideals and "bourgeois democracy" embody the good, the true, or the beautiful in any all-encompassing sense. Further along appear assertions that all ideals are merely social constructs, void of essential validity and meaningful only in relation to the standards of discrete communities. Finally come arguments, rife in new fields like "science studies," that propositions of every type, even physical and mathematical ones, are also socially constructed and hence relative to context.

By denying necessity, relativism encourages utopianism. This appears odd since the possibility of transcendence that utopianism seems to require is also denied. Yet emancipators are anything but the cool cynics their nihilism implies. In practice, their egalitarian ethos triumphs over their egalitarian epistemology, generating a gush of leveling enthusiasm that "celebrates diversity" instead of simply acknowledging it, and transforms "the affirmation of difference" into the kind of absolute it purports to overthrow. But however paradoxical the emancipator's passion, it is also his great political advantage, providing immense activist energy. Multiculturalism is his promised land and "race, gender and class" his ever-repeated mantra.

The idea of "greatness" has been one conspicuous casualty of this movement. Though still taken for granted by *Life*'s editors and the general public, within the academy it now suggests stratification, bigotry, and absolute value, provoking unease among many. Often dismissed as a social invention, or an oppressive fraud, the concept's use as adjectival modifier more readily qualifies as a lapse than an expression of good taste. Indeed, not long ago, the members of the English department of the Milwaukee campus of the University of Wisconsin felt compelled to vet their course descriptions scrupulously with an eye to expunging all references to the "greatness" of works, books, or authors. From their perspective, searching for greatness through the dreary tedium of a thousand years ranked as a fool's errand, or worse.

Yet we live in a great time, quite possibly the greatest of all times, and its signal qualities cry out for explanation. But less and less of our teaching and scholarship tries, preferring the mundane and lowly over sweeping deeds and decisive events. In history this has produced "history from below," specializing in the powerless, the despised, or—to use the trendy neologism—"the other," groups given short shrift in traditional narratives because of their small role in politics, diplomacy, high culture, and the more organized sectors of commerce and industry. Literary scholarship has also been intensely affected by this trend, a leading symptom being the shift in critical jargon from "work" to "text" as the word signifying what professors of literature study. "Text," a less elitist and purposeful term, diminishes suggestions of achievement or authorial intent which might otherwise control what readers, observers, auditors, and critics perceive.

Any serious revival of liberal and civic education will involve a process of prioritization as challenging as undertaken by *Life*'s editors. This is because the heart of curriculum design is the ordering of knowledge by relative importance and logical sequence, which cannot be attempted without provoking controversy, especially in an intellectual situation such as ours has become.

Yet even in the face of more than four decades of continuing curriculum change, almost always in the direction of disintegration and trivialization, there is little controversy of this sort today, at least at the highest executive echelons of the academy's leadership. Where once the nature of liberal education sparked ringing debates between giants like Harvard's Charles Elliot against Princeton's James McCosh, silence now reigns, reflecting a consensus both strange and barren. On the one hand it is a consensus that cheerfully accepts intellectual fragmentation, believing there to be just too much "new knowledge" to cram into the old standard survey courses, and too many diverse students to be satisfied by them. On the other hand it is a consensus that aggressively preaches moral unification, taking the emancipatory norms of multiculturalism and the new scholarship as its reference points. As a result, these norms color such remnants of the core as survive, as well as many of the electives that have replaced the greater part of its shattered bulk.

There are, of course, academic liberals—derisively labeled "conservatives" by their foes—who deplore this barren consensus. But though their dissent sits well with the public, and occasionally scares the university's brass, they fight a rearguard action that rarely alters institutional policy.

What unites academic liberals is not a political program—there is hardly a point on (or off) the political map where at least a few may be found. Rather, it is a generalized affection for their civilization, a sensibility that puts them at loggerheads with the emancipatory crusade, but deprives them of clear-cut academic goals of their own. This leaves them at an immense conceptual and rhetorical disadvantage when competing with those who know precisely what they're about.

Absent a defining project, liberal education becomes at best an introduction to the sensibility of science—critical thought without much in particular to think about. Taken to an extreme this can yield a raft of half-truths now beloved of educators. Facts, some tell us, become obsolete almost as soon as they are reported, knowledge grows too rapidly for anyone really to master, and established fields of study are everywhere breaking down. The conclusion reached is that liberal education must eschew a preoccupation with content in order to avoid obsolescence, concentrating instead on the thinking skills and habits of mind needed to survive future knowledge revolutions.

Besides being weak on its merits, this line of thought has a grievous practical side-effect. Multiculturalism has a set of uplifting and compelling goals—involving the purported eradication of myriad oppressions—which liberal education, in its purely procedural articulation, notably lacks. Unfortunately, within the academy, as in the world at large, desired process rarely gets defended with the same zeal as desired results. Multiculturalism's repeated victories to a very large degree stem from this imbalance of passion.

But liberal education need not surrender the field. It did not in its original formulations, and does not now, require the embrace of only the most transcending purposes or, even less, of pure process. It too can have goals of substance, force, and clarity capable of instilling an active ardor in its champions. Indeed, it is difficult to imagine a liberal education worthy of the name that did not have such goals in abundance. Recognizing this fact, defining these goals, and getting out the word, are essential steps if its dispirited friends are to be rallied.

•

There are many perspectives that could shape a fine liberal education. And many that could inspire one with exciting purpose. Since there is nothing the academy needs more than a dose of honest pluralism, a single size needn't fit all. But there is one approach that seems especially compelling to me because it addresses what is perhaps the central civic question of our age: can the spectacularly free and bountiful dispensation we enjoy be sustained?

The question has force because modern civilization is far too anomalous, and—for most—far too desirable, to be taken entirely for granted. Have we crossed a threshold over which there is no return, or could we one day lapse back into a grimmer normality? Because its fate hangs in the balance, the younger generation should be most interested in finding the answer. And because any serious attempt to do so requires precisely what a liberal education best affords—the creative integration of many fields of learning, harnessed to the civic purpose of preparing students wisely to make the choices free citizenship demands—it might be possible to generate some real excitement among young people for the project. It might even spark a bit of passion among their elders.

Why is this question academically fruitful? And why is it so centrally related to the highest tasks of free citizenship? Primarily, because it requires a recognition and assessment of modern civilization's most extraordinary traits, a subject diminished, brushed aside, or inadequately treated by relativist curricula. It also entails asking why this civilization emerged in the West, only spreading elsewhere afterward. This, in turn, demands a serious exploration of world history, politics, philosophy, culture, economics, technology and science. Instead of downplaying intellectual content, the cultivation of many areas of knowledge thus becomes inescapable. Furthermore, in sharp contrast to the reality of multiculturalism, it impels genuine cross-cultural study, promoting an awareness of a wide spectrum of civilized and pre-civilized experience. Finally, though a great deal is known and can be usefully said in answer to this question and its subsidiaries, they are anything but closed or pat. Many are the debates to be opened and enjoyed. And these debates will all draw us back to a recognition of our highest responsibility as free men and women, reflecting on how our personal and collective choices sustain, enrich, or diminish the heritage we pass along to the future.

I offer this idea convinced that modern civilization, at least in its liberal incarnation, has been remarkably advantageous. No doubt most of those wishing to pursue it would think so too. Yet grasping the pedagogical potential requires only acknowledging the crucial difference modern civilization has made, not its basic goodness. In their assiduous efforts to reshape existing attitudes, multiculturalist educators concede this point by implication. What they don't allow is an honest argument about modern civilization's worth, which would demand exposing students to its substance.

We live under a dispensation extraordinarily different from that of our forebears. Imagine them, for example, only five hundreds ago, conducting the same thought experiment that engaged *Life*'s editors. Their retrospective, reaching back a thousand years to antiquity's sunset—from the Year 1500 to the Year 500—would have opened much as it closed. At both ends humanity's masses work the soil—with a village for their world, a few decades for their lives, and servitude for their habit. Distances are, for most practical purposes, equally immense, with armies moving on foot or horse, and navies by wind and oar, to try conclusions at close quarters. Rulers are by God and blood anointed, their politics dynastic feuds. But it is nature's raw reality that is truly sovereign, governing the rounds of daily labor, the divisions of sexual labor, the seasons for campaigning, and those of famine and pestilence. Its processes, however, remain cloaked in mystery, making struggle a constant and untimely death a familiar.

Of course early modern scholars would have hardly noticed these things, so striking to us. They would have consigned them to the givens of life. Nor would they have detected "progress," a concept not yet hatched. Though we might see the fifteenth century's possession of gunpowder, printing, clocks, compasses, and spectacles as representing major advances over the ancients, the consequences of these inventions—gunpowder excepted—were not yet sufficient for their importance to be adequately assessed. Even the significance of Columbus's discoveries would not have quite sunk in. While Christianity's thousand-year spread across Europe would have cast a hopeful ray of light, it would have only partly pierced the pall caused by the loss of antiquity's learning and art. These the early moderns were exuberantly working to recover, an enterprise later dubbed the Renaissance. If anything, the intervening centuries would have probably seemed a cultural trough.

There have been three great dispensations in mankind's history and we live in the glory of the third. During the immemorial reaches of the first we were hunter-gatherers, a calling that shaped our evolution. About twelve thousand years ago came husbandry, allowing surplus production, and hence civilization, to become a possibility. But the civilization achieved was one of persistent scarcity, hierarchy, and immobility, in which affluence and learning were available to only a few.

All this changed in the twentieth century when the gathering forces of technology and science finally became strong enough to remake radically ordinary life. Indeed, the defining quality of the third dispensation is that everyman is in most respects better off than the grand seigniors of old. As far as necessities are concerned the perennial problem of scarcity has been solved. Liberation from brute labor, safety in childbirth, immunity from virulent diseases, and freedom from famine are the common lot, as are expanses of leisure, variety in diet, cleanliness and comfort independent of the weather, instantaneous communication, nearly instantaneous travel, and a dazzling range of diversions—from the Goldberg Variations to Eminem.

This revolution in human affairs was made in Europe and North America, where its full impact is still concentrated. But it gives every indication of becoming the basis for the world's first truly global civilization. If so, the West's achievement provides that civilization's foundation, a precious gift for others to enlarge and enrich. To make the best preparation for our global future we must thus understand that achievement, becoming knowledgeable citizens not only of our country, but of a better future world. The search for such an understanding would be a grand and glorious goal around which liberal education might at last be reorganized and revived. It would embody the best realization of liberal education's civic mission.

10

Restoring the Essential Experience of Liberal Learning: Transcendence and the Study of Politics in the University
Timothy Fuller

THE PREMISE OF THIS ESSAY is that classrooms have been politicized, obscuring the encounter with transcendence, intruding a corrupting element into the engagement of teaching and learning. A crucial task before us is to think about what it means to restore or recover the academic virtues. It is necessary, in order to proceed, to reflect on what "politicizing" means and what "restoring" as a kind of transcending of the existing situation means. Restoring involves transcending the moment but ultimately recognizes even more the encounter with the transcendent, implied in transcending the moment, as integral to liberal learning. In what follows, I hope to make clearer what I mean in saying these things.

Politicizing is the attempt of proponents of particular ideological fashions to dominate others. In short, it is the advocacy of political correctness, the intermixing of explanation and advocacy or, as Max Weber put it famously, the substitution of speeches for lectures. But the issue cannot be merely one of ideology. Ideologies come and go. That they come and go is rather obvious. We reasonably therefore may wonder why the passion for them persists in the face of their evanescence. Has not the university historically defined itself as the place where standards other than mere fashion and volatile opinion prevail? However problematic to define, is it not essential to universities to maintain their commitment to the search for truth? If universities today invite fashion to matriculate, is this a loss of nerve? If so, might it have a deeper explanation that eludes us in typical contemporary discussions? Or, when we notice the fickleness of fashion, why, we might wonder, is retreat to relativism often seized upon as the only convenient retreat?

The struggles of politics can be an object of research and reflection in university study, but the university must remain disengaged in taking up that task. Freedom to teach and to explore, the essence of academic freedom, imposes upon us the responsibility to distinguish between partisanship and academic study. The search for truth is difficult and its pursuit is long, an arduous quest of too great importance to be reduced to the repetition of passionate convictions; the latter is a parody of academic freedom. The distinction between practical action and dispassionate reflection is symbolized in the fact that, for twenty-five centuries in the West we have allowed to be set aside places of learning, providing for this distinction to be evident and available to us, reminding us when we cross the threshold from one mode of activity into another. This provision is not intended to signify indifference to the practical issues but rather to take them especially seriously in a way that will otherwise be lost from sight. How often we speak of dialogue and yet how often do we fail to observe the discipline which dialogue requires, and the fact that dialogue assists us to transcend mere concern for our personal feelings and opinions.

Politicizing also manifests aggression against received patterns or customary practices, as if they are nothing more than arbitrary power relations to be dissolved and reconstructed, in favor of reforms, which are asserted to be irrefutably desirable or necessary.

The fact of politicizing forces us to ask ourselves, can we maintain or restore traditional understanding after it has been questioned? Is defending a traditional engagement compatible with being self-aware and self-critical? Is there a persistent experience of liberal learning? A persistent meaning for the place of learning? We cannot avoid these questions given the intense pressure to reexamine our practices and traditions, even if we believe that we are in danger of losing something that should be preserved or restored. Loss of nerve would show itself either in refusing to accept the challenge or in easy capitulation as if we could conceive no cogent response. We shall welcome a challenge we cannot avoid in any case, and try to think through its implications.

We are challenged to accept as stark alternatives that we must be either "inside" or "outside" a tradition. A tradition, it is alleged, cannot, once questioned, adequately defend itself or persist if it must become more than merely habitual conduct. Moreover, not every tradition is worth preserving. To know ourselves as "traditionalists" is already perhaps to have detached ourselves from that which we defend. The implication of this challenge is that traditions have little to say for themselves other than that they may have so far escaped intense questioning. They are simply waiting their turn to be demythologized. The endless undertaking to demythologize looms before us, beckoning us to conclude that to disbelieve is among the highest intellectual achievements, perhaps disbelief is itself the essential experience.

The commitment to disbelieve traditions is supported by the claim that traditions are fixed, rigid outlooks rather than flexible manners of responding to inevitable change; they cannot, it is alleged, evolve, expand or incorporate elements that at first seem alien. The will to disbelieve and the cult of discontinuity go together. Such attitudes pervade much current thinking, but their validity should also be open to question if legitimate responses to such questioning are available.

In speaking of the idea of the university, then, I mean to say that the university is neither a sectarian movement nor a neutral conduit through which social forces flow unimpeded. It is a place of a particular kind with distinctive standards of its own, and its members are initiated into it principally by association with, and absorption of, its practices through apprenticeship. It is the place where all voices may be heard but in which the engagement is specifically not the political aim of contestants prevailing over and extirpating their opposition. The purpose of the university is to understand the world, not to change it. The actual institutions called universities today are, of course, mixtures of many different, often conflicting, practices, purposes and aspirations. Thus what I describe here is not the empirically observable totality of our educational institutions but, rather, that defining feature which is characteristic of the university *qua* university, the idea of the university without which we would have an institution that is something else.

Politicization responds impatiently and angrily to genuine philosophic reflection, judging the quality of discussion by whether it terminates with certain conclusions. Politicizers express shock and amazement when capitulation is not forthcoming. In doing so, they deny the point of academic freedom, which is, first, to foster inquiry as an end in itself, and, second, to recognize such inquiry as an essential ingredient in the quest to explore the furthest reaches of human self-realization. It is also likely that, at the furthest reaches of self-realization, we shall encounter the possibility of something even greater, pointing to an encounter with what transcends us and deflates our passions for the immediate and temporal. Thus university study, while properly understood as learning for its own sake, does not end there but opens the way to the possibility of something higher than learning itself. The prospect of such an experience can never be ruled out because it has never failed to appear and it is understood, implicitly or explicitly, by those who resist or oppose it as a threat to their aim to reduce every-thing to the political or the ideological. It is thus that I speak of the "essential experience" of learning which goes beyond the otherwise important question of what the content of education should be. Dis-putes over the content of liberal learning cannot, and will not, be re-solved if we are inattentive to the question of the essential experience which animates the choice of things to study.

As associates in a joint undertaking to understand what there is to understand as profoundly as we can, our sense of being self-constituting communities of inquirers—expressed in the commitment to academic freedom—is constrained by the conversationality that distinguishes the university from other places. We are members of a common enterprise with a persistent meaning.

Let us, following these observations, identify politicizing by refer-ence to its general attributes which are not tied to any specific ideo-logical program: They include lust for change, boredom with conver-sation, a preference for activism over reflection, a taste for melodra-matic tension and "creative problem-solving," quests for the authentic life through policy formation, rejection of tradition for fear of the in-fluence of the past, demand for diversity as a function of a desire for ultimate homogeneity, the belief that there is an ideal pattern of his-torical existence of which actual historical conditions are a mere dis-tortion and caricature, either accidental because not yet directed by the correct program or contrived by a disguised, conspiratorial elite.

All human institutions are embodiments of the struggle to respond to our temporal, mortal existence. Politicizing is a way of responding to the ineluctable temporality of human existence in submission to independently premeditated programs. The political engagements of modern times often energize themselves on the illusion of fending off insecurity by the formation of policy, and console the excessively anx-ious by giving them lots of tasks to do in the absence of any final out-come. In theological terms, we might say these bespeak the effort to rationalize the delay of the practical eschaton.

Universities, too, are responses to our temporal, mortal lives. In establishing universities as special places of learning, their founders, with greater or lesser clarity, acknowledged the experience of the non-temporal encountered in the midst of time, setting aside places where this experience could become central to thinking. In pushing universi-ties to accommodate merely contemporary preoccupations, the idea of a place of learning is diminished into a response which resists the experience of transcendence.

As this is an age which pays little respect to merely habitual, unself-conscious conduct, one might think that we would find in greater openness and self-criticism also greater opportunity to think through the transcending encounter with the being that is beyond our particularity. But this is not the case. Politicizing rejects restoring or recovery and instead translates ideas of transcendence into modes of temporal and material aspiration and distribution. Insofar as the university takes its bearings as a place of preserving or restoring, it can offer its apology for liberal learning. But we find that the necessary words are hard to come by, particularly when to defend or to speak of restoring is to be accused of defensiveness and outmoded irrelevance. But defending, as the act of restoring is not defensive, it is steadfastness.

If, in a world preoccupied with change, traditionalists may seem defensive, this is in part because they experience change as loss, and are eloquent in lament. That they are less able to cope with change is not so. But because traditionalists also know that change means loss as well as gain, they are protected from the illusions of revolutionary moralism, the latter demanding that doing something is always better than not doing something, regardless of consequences.

Restoring, by contrast, means retrieving to sight or re-seeing what is permanently true of the human condition. Bringing back to sight what is permanently true of the human condition is not uplift; it is, often, a sobering experience, and a limiting one. Experiencing disillusion with illusion is still, at least preliminarily, an experience of disillusionment.

Restoring does not imply a plan for going back to what is past, nor is it easily translated into policy; it means acknowledging what persists into the present, but which carries at the same time a profound sense both of its having persisted, and of its having had to struggle to persist. It does not require sticking slavishly to a fixed vocabulary, but rather involves constrained renewal of the forms of expression. Restoring is thus at first both a philosophic and a poetic, not a political, activity. It involves the renewal of the resources of our inheritance in a manner that is not simply antiquarian. Philosophy and poetry at their best establish limits to the pretensions of politics, but they do not do so by contesting politics for power. Rather, they remind us of other expressions of the human spirit which cannot be reduced to politics or the struggle for power.

Restoring is a rediscovering that inevitably involves reformulating, but it is not an antiquarian reassembling or a rationalist reengineering. The engagement to restore can be resisted, but it cannot be eradicated because the past is necessarily present to us; to be aware of its influence is inescapable. Yet "going back" is at most a metaphorical engagement. When we study the great books of our civilization, it is not to go back to an earlier time; it is, rather, to make vivid to ourselves the presentness of thought about, and response to, the human condition, eliciting our own thought and response. These works evoke dialogue, both inviting and constraining our subjectivity, rescuing us from easy opinions, imposing upon us the hard distinction between opinion and knowledge, between advocacy and explanation.

Tradition is the elongation of dialogue through time. It does not permit us to forget the presence of past thought upon the human predicament. Tradition's promise is not to rescue us from change, but to assist in realizing our capacity to keep our bearings as we maneuver through inevitable alteration. To invoke tradition is not to abandon the drama of life, but to find drama in dialectical engagement within the inescapable polarities of past and present that are our conscious existence. Much of the lust for novelty in our time stems from the fear of finding nothing important to say. To believe that to speak of what has always been true is to say nothing important is our great misfortune.

The question, then, is not whether we ought to observe connections to our past. We cannot escape such connections, even though we can understand them superficially and also misunderstand them. If we think we can live apart from all that we have been, we deceive ourselves. The reality of this condition emerges either in resistance or in affirmation. Neither resistance nor affirmation alone could constitute what it is to be human. This means that we must suffer through periods of deep uncertainty and disagreement—as we do today—about how best to understand and express our connectedness. We may think this either a curse or a blessing. In conversation, however, as Michael Oakeshott proposed, we might hope to turn the curse of Babel into a blessing:

> In a conversation the participants are not engaged in an inquiry or a debate. . . . Thoughts of different species take wing and play round one another, responding to each other's movements and provoking one another to fresh exertions. . . . There is no symposiarch or arbiter. . . . Conversation . . . is an unrehearsed intellectual adventure . . . it is impossible in the absence of a diversity of voices: in it different universes of discourse meet, acknowledge each other and enjoy an oblique relationship which neither requires nor forecasts their being assimilated to one another.[1]

Conversation, so understood, acknowledges novelty's inevitable intrusion without exalting it; in the university it is the academic form of the virtue of moderation. Claims of novelty can, in any case, be misleading. Every moment carries potential for the unanticipated. What we call new is often a re-encountering. Aristotle, for instance, saw that conflict between equality and merit in debates over justice would be interminable since the claims on one side cannot be perfectly reconciled to those on the other side. There are reasons to treat citizens the same, and reasons not to treat them the same, and every human circumstance is a complex mixture of same and not same. This is no less true for us, despite the enormous efforts of contemporary moral philosophers to formulate plans to distribute everything fairly once and for all. Aristotle's analysis illustrates also the categorical distinction between reflecting on politics philosophically, identifying the permanent features of politics, and politicizing philosophy, which seeks a remedy for the irremediable.

Restoring combines tradition and conversation in interpreting and responding to the vicissitudes of change. If we cannot avoid connection to the past, we are also not permitted an uncritical connection. Even in receptivity to the past, we have to make it our own, somehow appropriating it. Honesty compels the admission that all human achievements are hostage to change—to ineluctable temporality and thus mortality. What we think must be currently overcome in saving what we do not want to lose affects the ways of salvage we devise.

In seeing what is permanently present for us, we must use, and cannot extricate ourselves from, the resources of our time and place. We can only experience transcendence in our historical situatedness, our radically temporal, crumbling dust. There is an element of poetic invention in restoring, where restoring is neither merely old nor merely new. Restoring is thus not a project—another, competing novelty. It is the interminable engagement to see ourselves rightly in the midst of a never fully disclosed, mysterious whole.

To restore what we are in danger of losing is not to define or demand an assured benchmark, a state of affairs requiring no interpretation or appropriation. To search for a set of conditions to which we can attach ourselves, hoping thereby to rescue ourselves from the ravages of time and circumstance, is to exhibit faithlessness no less than to grovel before the passing shadows of the *dance macabre* of wants and satisfactions.

To understand this faithlessness, consider the alternative ideas of the relation of skepticism and faith. St. Augustine's skepticism toward the world, for example, signified a faith, engendered in encounter with the divine, that looked beyond the world, establishing withdrawal from dependence on worldly success and historical achievements. Faith in worldly monuments to him was actually faithlessness. For a long time now, we have gone the other way: We have learned to be skeptical both about achievements that are not visible and material, and about commitments to the "useless studies" that formulate no policies and enhance no techniques of social engineering.

The skepticism of Socrates or St. Augustine toward worldliness is the awareness that honest examination of ourselves and of the world's affairs—the "examined" life—forces us to confess intellectual arrogance, pretense, sin. As the Platonic Socrates seems to show to his Comrade in the dialogue *Hipparchus*, we cannot properly accuse others of the vulgarity of loving gain if we have not considered that it is impossible to be a human being without loving gain.

To the Socratics and the Augustinians, the world was full of contingency and uncertainty; it is a world of complex mystery that will not fully disclose itself, a world in which human beings, having insufficient power, need grace; a world in which maddeningly, the wicked prosper and the innocent suffer. They acknowledged the offensive and incomprehensible bondage of time and space at the center of their experience.

The choice, then, can only be of alternative responses to our temporality and mortality. In restoring, one pays attention to the presence of the non-temporal, the eternal, finding in the resulting tension what it is to be human. The perpetuity of this tension—our capacity to become aware of it even in this era—directs us to the task of restoring as re-seeing what it is to be human. Resistance to identifying the centrality of this tension is manifest in education, and yet the university remains the site of restoring or recovering as understood here.

The pervading attribute attending all teaching and learning is both philosophical and poetic. Institutions of liberal learning incorporate diverse teachers and students with diverse motivations, including vocational and professional preferences expressed in anti-philosophic and unpoetic idioms. Reflective thinking is nevertheless required throughout.

Teachers define themselves and their professional vocations in diverse ways, but each teacher lives and moves in an atmosphere animated by the idea of the university, not hiding the extremities of which human thought is capable, but teaching due measure of response through conversationality. The university is the place that provides a modest existence with no other calling but to think; and the peace, which this requires.

> The idea of the university lives essentially in the individual students and professors, and only secondarily in the forms of the institution. Once that life fades out, the institution cannot save it. Yet the essential life can be awakened only from man to man. . . . The student looks for the idea, is ready for it, and is really baffled when it does not come to him from the professors. Then it is he himself who must make it come true.[2]

Speaking from the standpoint of the vocation to philosophy, Karl Jaspers recounts how, by contrast to those who enjoy the support of vast scholarly apparatus and professional techniques, the philosopher has

> [n]othing behind him but a philosophical history that is singularly grandiose in spirit but sociologically non-existent. . . . For all our clarity and conviction, are we philosophers not engaged in something which our impotence renders illusory and absurd? Self-confidence in this situation is *restored*, first by a sober *recollection* of the principles of philosophy, and secondly, by bringing *back to mind* the university as the institution of independent philosophical truth.[3]

In the passage from his *Philosophical Memoir*, Jaspers gathers together in reflection his situatedness, the task of recollection and the way of restoring.

> The sense of being en route, of achieving each success in our temporal existence only in the imperfect form of a new "onward," brought me—by the good fortune of a professorial career assuring unlimited freedom of work—to many years of studying the great departed. Systematically I absorbed what has come down to us, whatever I believed I understood. I have been told as a child about Antiquity and the Bible, but it was only now that I consciously took them seriously as the foundations of our Western historic life, not as authorities but as challenges, to be heard and translated into the present.[4]

Philosophizing

should also result in the modest recognition that no man is everything, not even the greatest, and that when I definitely realize myself and know where I stand, I am the more definitely in need of others. . . . At an early age, however, I came up against the limits which will not let us believe that there is harmony in reality . . . to be sure, I also search for the point where all conflicts cease. But since I am here and not there, these ideas of mine must become apparent in the consequences for my life and actions in the world . . . the world as a whole cannot be understood as rational, but I, within it, can resolve to side with reason. . . . The rational will to reason, which must still be upheld all the time by something else, by Existenz; the awareness of the origins, which are unfathomable; the basic will to be permeated in action by the manifest present through which eternity speaks. . . . This kind of reason embodies itself in the existence of a historic reality, and in the thinking of its orders.

It would be idle to want to know our era for the purpose of learning what to take up. . . . We cannot figure out what the times require, what is timely, and then plan to satisfy this requirement. Everyone, by his original life, is a factor in his time . . . the point of philosophizing remains beyond each era and all time.[5]

The task of the university is then to resist, indeed to refuse, the centrality of political activity in the pursuit of its own categorically distinctive engagement. This will not cause the demotion of politics in the eyes of most in the world. The university will never "rule" over politics. Such pretensions will only be laughable in the world of getting and spending. The university presents as its necessary service what can only be performed by abstaining from, while studying, politics. The point for academics is not to win a contest for priority, but to maintain the categorical difference between political and academic engagements.

One may mention once more poetry and philosophy. These provide revitalization by continual use of the intellectual, moral and artistic resources of a society. Politics seeks to dominate and to displace conversation with debate, to replace pursuing the intimations of life with victories and defeats. Politics is hard pressed to see that its driving force is the constant pursuit of ought-to-be's that are not yet come to pass. Its hope of perfection contradicts its reliance on the perpetual enjoyment of unfinished business. This incoherency is its charm and attraction. Yet politics is liable to be indifferent to its own self-delusions or to define its success by transitory achievements, appearing in sharp relief for what it is only against the emotional and intellectual integrity of poets, philosophers, the lovers of learning.

Yet those who hope to amalgamate poetry and philosophy to politics will reenact the ancient tragedy of the opposition between politics and philosophy. The modern disposition is to deny this tragedy, but it has signally failed to find the means to supersede it and this failure shows us that there is a disjointedness at the heart of our condition which cannot be mended by one sort of human activity seeking to control all the others. To deny this is to do no service to the practical wants and needs of social life. Politics' forgetfulness of careful distinctions will not be remedied by academics succumbing to the same forgetfulness to themselves.

The search for truth is not and cannot be in itself practical, but it need not foolishly oppose practical life which is as real as any other aspect of our lives, and must not define itself merely as that which contradicts the practical. To remember this and to bring it to attention is the task of the university, and to incarnate the university we must heed our calling. This is our part and thus our duty. In raising this sort of question in the midst of all that would drown it out, we acknowledge the task of restoring what we have almost lost in that now we see it dimly, but we have not been permitted to lose sight of it altogether.

NOTES

1. Michael Oakeshott, "The Voice of Poetry in the Conversation of Mankind," in *Rationalism in Politics, New Expanded Edition*, edited by Timothy Fuller (Indianapolis: Liberty Press, 1991), 489–90.

2. Karl Jaspers, "Philosophical Memoir" in *Philosophy and the World*, (Washington, DC: Regnery Gateway, 1963), 252–53.

3. Jaspers, *Philosophy and the World*, 291; italics added

4. Jaspers, *Philosophy and the World*, 300–301.

5. Jaspers, *Philosophy and the World*, 302–4.

ABOUT THE CONTRIBUTORS

STEPHEN H. BALCH is the President of the National Association of Scholars, a director of the American Council of Trustees and Alumni, and a founding vice president of the American Academy for Liberal Education. His articles have appeared in *The Journal of Social and Biological Structures, Commentary, Politics and the Life Sciences*, and *Presidential Studies Quarterly*.

LT. GEN. JOSIAH BUNTING III recently retired from the Virginia Military Institute, where he served as Superintendent. He has written several novels including *All Loves Excelling, An Education for Our Time*, and *The Lionheads*, which was selected one of the Ten Best Novels of 1973 by *Time Magazine*. General Bunting has also edited new editions of Thomas Babington Macaulay's *Lays of Ancient Rome* and John Henry Cardinal Newman's *The Idea of a University*. He currently serves as Chairman of the National Civic Literacy Board at the Intercollegiate Studies Institute.

WILLIAM DESMOND is a Professor of Philosophy at the Institute of Philosophy at the Katholieke Universiteit Leuven (Louvain). Dr. Desmond has written numerous books including *Hegel's God—a Counterfeit Double?, Art, Origins, Otherness*, and *Ethics and the Between*, the second book of a trilogy of which *Being and the Between* is the first volume. His many articles cover aesthetics, Hegel, ethics, and the philosophy of religion.

JOHN FONTE is the Director of the Center for American Common Culture and Senior Fellow of the Hudson Institute. Dr. Fonte is the coeditor of *Education for America's Role in World Affairs.* His articles and essays have appeared in *The Chronicle of Higher Education, Commentary, Journal of Education, National Review, San Diego Union-Tribune, Transaction: Social Science and Modern Society,* and other publications. He has appeared on Voice of America, NewsTalk TV, Channel One, and National Empowerment Television as well as numerous radio programs.

TIMOTHY FULLER is the Lloyd E. Worner Distinguished Service Professor at Colorado College. Dr. Fuller has published many essays and has edited numerous books, including *Reassessing the Liberal State, Leading and Leadership, The Voice of Liberal Learning: Michael Oakeshott on Education,* and *Michael Oakeshott on Religion, Politics, and the Moral Life.* In March 2002 he was appointed by President Bush to the President's Advisory Council on the Arts.

ROGER KIMBALL is Managing Editor of *The New Criterion* and an art critic for the London *Spectator* and *National Review.* Mr. Kimball's most recent publications include *Lives of the Mind: The Use and Abuse of Intelligence from Hegel to Wodehouse, Art's Prospect: The Challenge of Tradition in an Age of Celebrity, Experiments Against Reality: The Fate of Culture in the Postmodern Era,* and *The Long March: How the Cultural Revolution of the 1960s Changed America.* He serves on the Board of Advisors of the Gilder-Lehrman Institute of American History and the Board of Visitors and Governors of Saint John's College.

THOMAS PANGLE holds the Joe R. Long Chair in Democratic Studies at the University of Texas at Austin. He was formerly University Professor of Political Science at the University of Toronto and Fellow at Saint Michael's College. Dr. Pangle is the author of many books including *Justice Among Nations: On the Moral Basis of Power and Peace,* and *The Learning of Liberty: The Educational Ideas of the American Founders.* He has also written numerous journal articles and book chapters.

ABIGAIL THERNSTROM is a Senior Fellow at the Manhattan Institute, a member of the Massachusetts State Board of Education, and a commissioner on the United States Commission on Civil Rights. Dr. Thernstrom has coauthored many books with her husband, Stephan, including *America in Black and White: One Nation, Indivisible,* and

Closing the Gap: Race and Academic Achievement. Her 1987 work, *Whose Votes Count? Affirmative Action and Minority Voting Rights,* won four prestigious awards. She frequently appears on "Fox News Sunday," "Good Morning America," and "This Week with George Stephanopoulos."

COLLEEN A. SHEEHAN is Professor of Political Science at Villanova University, where she specializes in American political thought and politics and literature. She has been a visiting professor and research scholar in the James Madison Program at Princeton University and has authored numerous articles and essays. She is coeditor, with Gary L. McDowell, of *Friends of the Constitution: Writings of the "Other" Federalists, 1787–1788.*

BRUCE THORNTON is Professor of Classics and Humanities at California State University in Fresno. Dr. Thornton is the author of numerous books including *Searching for Joaquin: Myth and History in California, Greek Ways: How the Greeks Created Western Civilization, Humanities Handbook,* and *Plagues of the Mind: The New Epidemic of False Knowledge.* He is a frequent guest on talk-radio shows, has lectured for the Air Force Academy and the Smithsonian Institute, and has appeared on "Politically Incorrect with Bill Maher" and "Uncommon Knowledge." Dr. Thornton currently writes a column for the online magazine FrontPageMag.

BRADLEY C. S. WATSON holds the Philip M. McKenna Chair in American and Western Political Thought and is Fellow in Politics and Culture at the Center for Political and Economic Thought, Saint Vincent College. He directs several of the center's educational initiatives, including its biennial Culture and Policy Conference on which this volume is based. He is also Research Associate at the Intercollegiate Studies Institute's Center for the Study of American Civic Literacy. His books include *Civil Rights and the Paradox of Liberal Democracy* and *Courts and the Culture Wars.* He is a Fellow of the Claremont Institute for the Study of Statesmanship and Political Philosophy and of the John M. Ashbrook Center for Public Affairs at Ashland University.

INDEX